Back to the Family

Back to the Family

How to Encourage Traditional Values in Complicated Times

Dr. Ray Guarendi

Villard Books New York/1990

Library of Congress Cataloging-in-Publication Data
Guarendi, Raymond.
Back to the family / by Ray Guarendi

p.   cm.   ISBN 0-394-58576-3
1. Child rearing—United States. 2. Parenting—United States.
I. Eich, David Paul II. Title.
HQ769.G87   1990   649'.1—dc20   90-30036

9 8 7 6 5 4 3 2
First Edition

Book design by J.K. Lambert

To the families, who shared their lives
To children, who forever benefit from a loving family
To Him, who makes it all possible

Preface

In January 1987 I was invited by a very special teacher to interview a very special family. The purpose of that first interview was to determine why these parents and their children were role models for other families. During the next eighteen months, one hundred families from all fifty states would share their stories of family life: their values and concerns, the good times and bad. *Back to the Family* is the result.

This book is a message of hope and confirmation for all of you parents, regardless of your suburban environment, big-city address, or rural post-office box. It does not matter that you may have only two little ones or a house of ten or more, or that this might be your second marriage or that you might be a single parent. Nor will it matter if you are a New York professional, a Cuban refugee, or of Jewish descent and living in the Blue Ridge Mountains. If you or your children are in less than perfect health, you will still fit in. And finally, whatever your own childhood was like, whether Pollyana or boot camp, you will be able to identify with the families in our story.

For you see, what you are about to experience will reinforce your own beliefs about strong family life. In the end, I believe you will realize what we did: that fostering traditional values is not reserved for only the best of families, but, rather, for those families who can say they did their best.

David Paul Eich
Executive Director
In The Company of Kids^(sm)

Foreword

I am a clinical psychologist with a special interest in family life. When Children's Hospital of Akron asked me to author a book about excellent families, my first question was, "How did you determine excellence?" As this project's designers explained their rationale for asking Teachers of the Year to search for outstanding families, I saw the merit in their approach. Still, I was determined to study the interviews firsthand and judge for myself if these families are as good as others say. Within the first several interviews, I had my answer. These mothers and fathers showed a real understanding of what makes family life work. What's more, so did the kids. Many were teenagers, as a group notorious for not seeing eye-to-eye with anything remotely resembling a parent, yet they were showing maturity far beyond their years. Repeatedly I thought, "These kids could teach us grown-ups a thing or two about childrearing." As a psychologist and a parent, I understood what these families were doing. It made sense, but studying their philosophies and life-styles was enlightening. They were putting the best theories of mental health professionals into elegantly simple practice, with enviable results.

This project has been far more than an opportunity to study strong families. It's also changed my personal life. I've always thought myself a good father to my son and daughter. In writing this book I've come to realize how much better a father I could be. I've learned much from these families. I believe you can, too.

Dr. Ray Guarendi
April 1990

Acknowledgments

This book reflects the efforts and support of many people. It owes its existence to those who for nearly three years have involved themselves in its purpose: to make a difference in the lives of families.

Thank you to Bill Considine, president of Children's Hospital Medical Center of Akron, for believing in this concept from its origin with a "What if?" question. Thank you to David Eich, for posing that question, for visiting families, and for guiding this project from its start to its tomorrow. To Harry Stitzlein, Duane Isham, and Charlie Horn, members of the hospital's Board of Trustees, who saw the value of focusing on the strength of the American family. To Patty Jo Freeder, Ohio's 1986 Teacher of the Year, who nominated the book's first family and who encouraged her fellow Teachers of the Year to nominate families from every state. Thank you to the members of the National-State Teachers of the Year organization for enthusiastically searching through their careers to find the best families they had ever encountered. To Pat O'Desky, for her thoughtful interviewing style and recollections. To Linda Emore, a tireless researcher, whose warmth and good humor made comfortable every family she contacted. And thank you to Kathy Schleicher for typing, revising, and re-revising revisions without so much as one sigh.

Special gratitude goes to Diane Reverand, my editor at Villard Books, for her guidance and insights as an editor and as a mother.

Writing a book is so much easier when it's a group collaboration. To all my colleagues and friends at Children's Hospital, for your helpful comments, encouragement, even stingingly accurate criticisms, thank you.

Contents

Back to the Family

The Quiet Experts

*M*ore and more experts are telling parents how to be parents. Everywhere you look and listen there's a childrearing specialist giving advice on how best to raise an emotionally fit child in an emotionally fit family. *Back to the Family* asks a very different group of experts to speak out—those trained by experience and skilled by years of trial, error, and success: excellent families themselves.

A parenting expert's advice on how your family should be living may or may not be useful to you. The ultimate value of that advice lies years away in how your children mature. But the success of exceptional families is visible for all to see. They are doing and have done what most of us are hoping to accomplish for our children and families.

This book began when Children's Hospital Medical Center of Akron designed a project to study family life at its best. For several years, we have visited, interviewed, and maintained ongoing contact with the most exceptional families we could locate throughout the country. We sought to identify the factors underlying their success. What were the childhoods of excellent parents like? How do strong families juggle careers and children? What phases and stages do these families endure? What are their most effective forms of discipline? How do parents reach unreachable adolescents? How are family decisions made and house rules established? We heard about the insecurities, fears, and guilts of even the most competent mothers and fathers. We interviewed the children for their perspective on what makes a good parent and family. In effect, we studied three generations within each family.

One question sums up the guiding aim of this project: What can families everywhere learn from these highly successful families? Put another way, how can others benefit from their wisdom as well as imperfections? What we uncovered was a wealth of parenting ideas and practices for a strong family life. Some of these findings most likely will affirm your own beliefs. Others may surprise you.

Certainly not everything that these families say and do will relate to your own family. What is helpful to you will depend upon your family's values and life-style. Excellent families will tell you what works for them. You select what will work for you.

TO DEFINE EXCELLENCE

Excellence is a slippery concept, especially when applied to families. Is it measured by the number and scope of the children's accomplishments? Does it reflect the stability of the home life? Does it tap into a child's character or the family's cohesiveness? Or is it some combination of all of these?

It is not possible to measure the quality of a family precisely, as there are no objective gauges of excellence. If there were, excellence would be a much less slippery concept. One thing is certain, though: *Excellence,* as defined in this book, does not mean material success or status. We weren't interested in talking with famous families. We didn't seek heads of households who were also heads of companies. We didn't look for the most prodigious of child prodigies. We searched specifically for those families who embodied the highest commitment to family life and whose children collectively showed strength of character.

Since no standard criteria for family excellence exist, and most likely never will, we turned to the next best thing. We looked for the best judges of excellence available. And our search brought us to the National-State Teachers of the Year organization.

The rationale for using teachers to identify excellent families is that no one spends more time day in and day out getting to know children and their families than does a teacher—not a psychologist, counselor, social worker, or pastor. No one sees a broader picture of healthy and unhealthy families. And no one sees a more long-term picture. Not only do teachers watch a child develop through the course of a year, but often they've taught more than one child from the same family. In most cases, the teachers who selected these one hundred families had had contact over many years with two, three, sometimes four or more of their children. After observing the same high level of maturity and emotional adjustment, child after child, they felt confident that exceptional parents were behind it all. The best indication of a family's excellence is the consistent quality of its younger members.

Just as no profession is more closely involved with children and families than teachers, few teachers are more involved than those selected each year to represent the best of their profession—State Teachers of the Year. The title Teacher of the Year is not an easy one to earn, but is the result of a long and exacting test. Every year students, teachers, and administrators make their nominations for State Teacher of the Year. These nominees begin the process of demonstrating to their respective state departments of education that teaching for them is more than a career; it is a commitment, one by which they continuously strive to reach well above the accepted standards of their profession. For example, the Teacher of the Year from Ohio, as part of her screening process, compiled a seventy-five-page scrapbook covering her experiences in teaching starting with her first days in the classroom. Competing with more than one hundred other outstanding educators from around the state, she was judged one of four finalists. At that point, she traveled to the state capital for a series of extensive personal interviews before being awarded the title Ohio State Teacher of the Year. With the winners of each state or territory, she subsequently joined the competition for National-State Teacher of the Year. Here the selection procedure becomes even more rigorous. Representatives from top educational organizations throughout the country closely study the candidates and select finalists based upon their contributions to students, schools, and communities. Each of these teachers is once again visited in person. Videotaped sessions and reports are given to the judges, who make the final selection.

Our judges of excellence, then, were teachers who themselves had been judged excellent by demanding standards. In short, we asked the very best of teachers to help identify the very best of families.

As expected, the teachers responded with irrepressible enthusiasm. From all fifty states came nominations of families who, said the teachers, when compared to all the families they'd known in their careers, clearly stood out in terms of the overall quality of their family life. Typically, the teachers confirmed their individual judgments by asking colleagues and administrators, "What one family that has come through this school over the years has most impressed you with its commitment to family life?" Frequently, the same name, almost like a reflex, came up.

When asked specifically why these particular families, the teachers responded with comments like:

- "This family is, without a doubt, the most loving, most unselfish, and most extraordinary family I have met during my thirty-year teaching career. Dennis and Barbara give of themselves constantly, and the result is a family of children eager to learn more and who excel in everything they do. These parents *have* made a difference."
- "Of all the families I've had contact with in my eighteen years of teaching, I selected the B.'s. While they did not seem truly outstanding, that is, newsworthy, I realized that this search is for ordinary families who manage in an unobtrusive way to love and nurture each member. They do it by being totally committed to parenthood and involved in the lives of their children."
- "All members of this family are unique in their zest for living and in their ability to all talk to each other, sharing experiences and wonderful conversations. They are a blended family and have learned to accept each other's differences, failures, and successes. They are a delight to know."
- "It would be difficult for me to find parents with as much love and dedication to their children as Jim and Melinda. They have one biological daughter and have adopted four handicapped children. They face difficult decisions daily and have major responsibilities, financially and emotionally. But in all the time I have known them, I have never heard them complain. They have given a home to children who otherwise might not have been adopted, not merely a house, but a true home where they are loved, respected, and nurtured. They also exhibit the sense of humor necessary to survive the daily hills and valleys of parenting."
- "What distinguishes them, I believe, is their closeness, not only with their

immediate family, but with their extended family, and the enjoyment they all derive from each other. No other family in my acquaintance shares such a special relationship in this regard. . . . The other thing is the support which they give each other. In good times as well as in times of trouble, they rally around each other like nothing I've ever seen. Difficult times that pull some families apart pull these folks together."

- "The L.'s are as enthusiastic about family life as anyone could hope parents would be. They exude feelings of love, excitement, and success in what they're doing. In short, I've never encountered another family who demonstrates the mutual respect and love for all family members that this family daily shows. In this environment everyone excels, parents and children."

Judging from such descriptions, the teachers feel very confident that they succeeded in what they were asked to do—to capture that slippery concept, excellence.

The philosophy underlying this book can be captured by the phrase: To learn from the best. The Teachers of the Year identified for us the strongest families they had ever known. We will introduce them in WHO ARE THE EXCELLENT FAMILIES?

Chapter 2

Who Are the Excellent Families?

*T*he one hundred families who speak throughout this book live in all fifty states. They make their homes in big cities, on small farms, in medium-sized suburbs, and in towns so little that, as one father quipped, "Both city-limit signs are on the same stick." They are farmers and pharmacists, secretaries and social workers, teachers and tellers, surgeons and salesmen, homemakers and managers—"two closely related careers," said one mother of several youngsters. They own small businesses, work in factories, program computers, drive buses, and teach college-level geology. In some families, one parent works outside the home. In some, both do. And a few have seen neither parent employed for a time.

White, Black, Spanish-American, Asian—the families represent several races and colors. Catholic, Baptist, Lutheran, Presbyterian, Jewish, Methodist, Mormon, Episcopalian, Christian Scientist, Buddhist—a range of religions appear in this sample of successful families.

Parents' educations range from seventh grade to M.D.'s and Ph.D.'s. Most are either high school or college graduates. Some left college to raise their family and never returned. Others enrolled in college while raising their family. And a few said they were forced to return to college to be able to help with their kids' seventh-grade science projects.

Some families call themselves poor, but quickly add, "only in a material sense." Others earn incomes near the upper economic levels. The majority began in somewhat tight monetary straits and grew more economically comfortable over the years, even after taking into account their teens' tastes for a back-pocket label.

The typical family makeup is two parents, married once to each other, raising two to four natural children. There are also families headed by a single parent and families with step-parents, half-siblings, adopted children, foster children, and every combination of the above. In addition to five biological children, one family in New Jersey has opened its door to more than fifty foster children and infants, including several youngsters with severe developmental handicaps. The median number of children is three, but the range is from two to eighteen—and all eighteen in that family are biological children. You can bet this family will later hand us a few creative strategies for quelling sibling battles, including calling out the national guard! A few of the larger households tell of the recurrent side comments and side looks they attract from others. A veteran mom of eleven from South Dakota observes, "I think people around us were more apprehensive and anxious about our big family than we were. I remember someone saying to me, 'Lucille, when are you going to quit having babies?' Feeling it was no concern of theirs, I said, 'To tell the truth, I haven't figured out what's causing them yet.'" Last we heard, Lucille had figured it out. She said she saw a film about it.

The youngest child in these families is seven months old. The oldest is forty-four years. Most children are in their middle to late teens, with many in college or having recently left home to begin their independence. Some parents did confide their worry that the kids would sneak back in a few years. The slant toward families with older children is related to the screening process used to find these families. The National-State Teachers of the Year looked for households with at least a decade of family life under their belts. As one teacher put it, "I know families who I think are outstanding, but their kids are too young for anybody to really predict with confidence how they'll turn out. The pie just isn't cooked yet." Older children are more reliable "proof" of a time-tested quality family life.

Though generally in good physical health, these families know handicaps and chronic illnesses. Several have children with learning disabilities. In one family, both dad and son are learning-disabled. A single-parent mother is raising a son and a daughter with Tourette's syndrome (an epilepticlike condition marked by involuntary bouts of tics, animallike sounds, even cursing). A California family is caring for a profoundly handicapped daughter who, at age fifteen, is just now learning to walk. Death has also touched these homes. Some have lost spouses, others children. A few live with the daily reminder of their mortality. A family in New York has a four-year-old daughter with a chronic, likely terminal blood disorder. Cerebral palsy, diabetes, epilepsy, pituitary growth disorder—conditions some families are living and loving with every day. Perhaps the most besieged family is one from Wagoner, Oklahoma, who experienced the near death of a six-year-old son in an explosion, an operation on their nine-year-old daughter for a life-threatening tumor, and a debilitating stroke affecting a third child at age twenty-two. Happily, all are now recovered and well. Through their lives these families will show that excellence doesn't necessarily follow a smooth road. Sometimes it emerges from the no-choice need for emotional durability.

A CROSS-COUNTRY ALBUM

Any composite picture of these families would not do justice to the rich variety of life-styles present. A sharper look at their personalities can be gained through a series of "snapshots" focusing on a unique aspect of a family's life.

Let's begin in New England. New Hampshire is the home of a family named, appropriately enough, Love. Their seven musically talented children are naturals to play the von Trapp family in *The Sound of Music* and, in fact, have performed for Maria von Trapp herself.

In Vermont, we can eat bean sprouts with the most "natural" family in this book. All of them are vegetarians. All wear clothes of natural fibers. All use no household appliances. And all are evidence that you don't need technology to raise a great family.

Rhode Island is the home of a family formerly from New York City and now living in Providence. Father, blind since his mid-twenties and prior to marriage, was chosen as a 1969 National Handicapped Person of the Year. He and his wife have shared a common vision in raising their eight children, including a son who plays professional basketball. This father is living testament that excellent parenthood emanates from the mind and heart.

In Florida we can visit another large family—eight children, aged ten to twenty-three. If it's early evening during study time, dad will be making sure that any child who has no homework chooses a letter of the encyclopedia from which to write a report on a subject of choice. His philosophy is that children can never learn too much about the world they live in.

In Fort Knox, Kentucky, resides a military family that has lived in many places throughout the country. Wherever they've dwelled, they've taken the gold in their family life with them. According to mom, that gold is having two children who, at ages sixteen and nineteen, know right from wrong and who live what they know.

We can learn a lesson in strength through adversity from a Wisconsin family who weathered a tornado that completely destroyed their home, put both parents in the hospital, and permanently disabled the father. Nevertheless, in every member's opinion, the whole family emerged stronger after the storm.

In South Dakota a family reunion softball game is in progress, pitting a family's nine daughters against its nine sons. Just your basic eighteen-child family. At last tally the girls were leading the series, three games to two.

Lincoln, Nebraska, is home to a single mom and her two teenage girls. Working full-time as a teacher, mother still makes time to instill the singular values that helped her younger daughter be selected as most caring girl in her senior class, and her older daughter achieve honor-society status and academic scholarships.

In downtown Dallas, Texas, live a mother and father extremely appreciative of their life in the United States. Separately, they fled Castro's Cuba and are firmly convinced that only here could they be blessed with the family they now enjoy.

The family at one Houston address could be a real-life *My Three Sons*. All in their twenties and living on their own, the boys flew back to be with their parents during the family interview. Probably to make sure they wouldn't say anything incriminating.

In Tucson, Arizona, a mother and father are watching their two adopted children head in separate, but equal, directions. Son is a National Eagle Scout with a chestful of awards. Daughter has a learning disability and has used it to fuel her drive to place herself on her high school's honor role.

At the base of Mount Shasta, near the border of California and Oregon, a family shares its home with a pet pig, a dog the size of a horse, and a mouthy bird. Everybody, even the animals, enjoys listening to Merritt, aged ten, play piano with the skill that earned her fourth place in her age group at an international competition.

In Montana, we can knock on the door of a family who probably isn't home. They're most likely en route on one of their ten-hour round-trip drives to support their high-school-aged son's athletic career. Montana is a big state.

Alaska is home to a mother and father whose more successful marriages came with their second spouse. Beginning their new family twelve years ago with three children, one of whom was "his" and two "hers," they now enjoy five children who are "ours." Their example shows that family cohesiveness derives from love and commitment, not genetics.

These cross-country snapshots offer us a glimpse at the individuality of these families. For a closer look at who they are and why they live the way they do, we need to visit a few of their homes, observing and talking to them firsthand, as our interviewers did.

EXCELLENT FAMILIES CLOSE-UP

The Love family, Jerry (aged forty-one) and Rita (also forty-one) and their seven children, aged six through nineteen, live in Tilton, New Hampshire. Jerry owns and operates a hardware store. Rita considers her most fulfilling calling to be "wife and mother." She says, "If someone were to ask me what I've done with my life, I would say 'Family.'"

Two words used by the interviewer to capture the personality of the Loves were "unassuming" and "spiritual." Rita, a petite woman, quickly shared her nervousness and doubts that she could put her thoughts into meaningful words. Over the next several hours she then offered moving and eloquent insights on successful family life. Prior to the interview Jerry and Rita asked the interviewer to join hands with them praying to God for wisdom and guidance in their answers.

Looking back on her most vivid memories of childhood, Rita said, "My mom used to take all the kids in the neighborhood on hikes. Sometimes there were as many as twenty of us." Rita continues this practice with her own children, considering it a source of family cohesiveness and a prime time to talk about anything and everything.

While Rita described her upbringing as "not made of real up's and down's. It was more an even-keeled, repetitive sort of thing," Jerry recalled a childhood marked by hardships, even trauma. "I had to leave home and live with some friends when I was a teenager because of the difficulties my parents were having. While I was away, our home caught on fire. Everyone else in the family got out, but my father was still inside. He lived for several days until he died. At that time, as much as I thought I didn't like my father, I still knew I loved him. That was the paradox for me. Today, I know I love him even more than I could imagine then. This is much of what brought me to my own feelings about my children and fatherhood today."

Rita and Jerry always pictured a large family but didn't plan it out child-by-child. Says Rita, "I think *we* got pregnant on our honeymoon, and although we wanted six kids, they were coming so quick that we calculated, at the pace we were going, we'd have about forty." That thought alone must have scared them because they stopped at seven.

We asked them, "What were the best of times in your parenting?" "We are still in the midst of the best of times," said Jerry. "Talking to my children like adults and watching them begin college are the best of times. My daughter called the other night from college and said, 'Dad, you talk to me like a parent, but you write letters like a friend.' What a feeling! I am experiencing adulthood with my children."

Rita likewise took a wide-open view of the best of times with her children. "The best of times as a parent is parenting. I tell people who don't have children, 'You can't know what you are giving up when you say you don't want to be a parent. There is no way you can sense what you would be missing unless you are a parent.' I am so glad this is what we've given our life to—raising our children and to each other."

When have they failed as parents? Rita: "The times I fail most are when I get angry. When I get angry, I cease to function. Feeling what the kids are feeling is the most important thing to me. When I'm angry, I don't listen. Then I am totally ineffective. All the things that make someone a good parent are gone when they are angry. At my angriest times, I try to go off privately, sometimes cry, then come back and talk to everyone like I should have in the first place."

Jerry also sees his biggest parental failure as anger, not toward the children, but toward Rita. "If I am angry at Rita around the children, I feel I have not been in control as father of the household. I don't know how the kids see it, but I see it as a parental failure."

What lessons about discipline have they learned from their children? Rita has learned to be flexible in her firmness. "If a child is being grounded for a week, there is a need to stick to the punishment. But once in a while, a child has really learned his lesson. I think it is then okay to call off the discipline. We try to be in tune to those special times when the kids will gain more by our cutting short the discipline than by letting it drag on. Rather than being resentful of the continuing punishment, the kids appreciate the unexpected freedom and their parents' sense of judgment." Jerry thinks it is wise to "sometimes give the children a say in how they are disciplined. There are times when I give them several choices."

If Jerry and Rita were going to write a book on parenting, we asked, what would they include in it? Unconditional love heads Jerry's how-to's of child-rearing. "Praise and encourage your children constantly, whenever and however you can. Don't tell them they're good. They are better than good. They are great." Rita, too, focused on the positives. "Make the love relationship with your children the most important, and the other parts of family will follow. It isn't work or play that makes life happy or not happy, it is your relationships. If you are together as a family, you can be out all day working and at the end of the day, you will have a wonderful feeling. Also, instead of giving to children material gifts that wear out or are outgrown, give gifts that last—traditions, music lessons, education, travel, hobbies. It is amazing how perceptive children are. They recognize and value the gift of our time."

One question made the Loves pause an extra while before responding: "What have your children accomplished?" Jerry and Rita could have cited their oldest son's acceptance to MIT and their second son's recent acceptance to Princeton, along with numerous citizenship and scholastic awards for all the children. They didn't focus on any of these. Instead, Jerry said quietly, "My children are sensitive human beings, sensitive to others' feelings, sensitive to where they fit in society, sensitive to where they are going, and how that affects not only them, but this family." Rita added, "I think they seek after good instead of bad. The quality of a person is what he seeks, and the kids are sensible here."

An integral part of every family interview was separate interviews with the children. When fourteen-year-old Nolan was asked, "What are your family responsibilities?" he surprised the interviewer with his perspective. "Aside from the normal chores, my responsibilities are, as a brother, to support and set an example to my siblings. As a son, I am responsible for respecting and obeying my parents. As a family member, I am responsible to remain honest and to keep up the family reputation outside the home."

When asked, "Why do you think other people think your family is special?" six-year-old Echo replied, "Because we can get along so good, because we love each other, and because we are one of the people who are getting written about in a book."

Ten-year-old Aubrey said his best times with his parents are "when we get good grades and when we are with them. I like to have them around."

Seventeen-year-old son, Fayvor, said his best family times were "when my parents spent time with me that I needed and at the time I needed it. I felt happiest also when doing something useful for my parents without being asked." Of course, at age seventeen, Fayvor is not always pleased with his folks. "My parents handle arguments by exercising supremacy. They—mom usually agrees with dad—like to think they are right. They will end an argument when they think it is getting out of hand. Lately, since teenagers also like to think they know everything, we older children have made it increasingly difficult for my parents to just cut off an argument. If they do, they can rest assured the same argument will turn up in one form or another later on." In case you can't tell, Fayvor is the feisty one of the bunch.

Perhaps the best picture of Ginger and Garrett, aged eighteen and nineteen, can be found in portions of an essay Ginger wrote for herself a few days after her brother left for college. Her recollections during the trip to school create a touching portrait of siblings and their bond.

- "My memories brought me back to when we had been small. I smiled at the thought of his appointed protection over me that had bordered on tyranny all throughout grade school. That same protection had molded and merged with genuine care and concern as we grew. My heart ached at his tears when the boys at school labeled him 'bookworm' and 'four-eyes' when he wanted so much to be star of the Little-League baseball team. I had to laugh at the ridiculous arguments we had gotten into, and recontemplate the more serious debates we had engaged in of late. I remembered the countless times that he had worked mathematical solutions into my very frustrated brain, and the times I had asked for an honest opinion on an outfit, or given an unasked opinion of his.

  "I relived seventeen years with my big brother. I felt the good times and the bad, the love and the frustrated anger. I don't believe I had ever before realized or valued more the bonds of love and understanding that we have.

  "I did not cry as he gave me a final hug and a 'See ya, Sis.' I did not trust myself with words, but gave him a brave smile. There was much perhaps that I could have said. But now when I look back, I realize that words were unnecessary. Those memories and feelings that I cherished would not disappear from his mind any sooner than they would disappear from mine. I realized that he was in truth entering a new life, a new phase of his life, but he was not entirely leaving, and never would entirely leave, the old one behind."

The Loves—their name tells their story.

————

Jay and Mary Willett live in Phoenix, Arizona. They have two children, Jason, aged nineteen, who is in prelaw at the University of Arizona, and Meisha, aged twenty-one, honor student, college sophomore class president, and "very wholesome," according to her dad. The Willetts feel a special gratitude for their children, as each nearly died in their young lives. At age eighteen months, Jason needed an emergency tracheostomy to breathe, and at age ten, Meisha survived open-heart surgery.

Jay briefly played professional football, but is now an artist and high-school teacher. Mary works part-time outside the home as a substitute teacher. The Willett's interview was marked by tears and intense emotion. Some minutes into it Jay's voice began to tremble, and soon he was sobbing. Mary, too, began to cry. After regaining his composure, Jay said, "Forgive me, for as you see, I am a very emotional person. When you asked me what are my fond memories of my children, it suddenly hit me that I could no longer hold and protect my son and daughter in my strong arms. The days of childhood are gone." The scene was powerfully moving. Here was a six-one, 230-pound man—an imposing image of the word *macho*—filled with such sensitivity and warmth for his family, and sadness because his childrearing experience was nearly complete.

Taking us back to his own childhood, Jay revealed the roots of his emotional nature. "I remember a home, but I don't remember being in it very often. Whenever my father was home, there was always pain because he was always drunk. He was a strong, powerful guy and he was dangerous. He abused me until I got too big to push around. The more my dad was around, the worse times were. The poverty wasn't so tough. Having to deal with my father was what made it tough. He was the epitome of exaggeration in every sense. If I knocked a glass of water over, he would knock me over. For years I walked around with a giant chip on my shoulder. I held up a facade of toughness. But I never really was a tough person; I was just tough for the sake of it. I wasn't a bully. I wasn't even a fighter. My father would sometimes show up on the holidays just in time to be totally obnoxious and destroy whatever joy existed at the time. My mother tried very hard to do what she could to hold things together, but she just wasn't strong enough."

How did Jay emotionally survive his abusive childhood? "Athletics meant everything to me. I was recognized that way. High school and college were the height of my self-esteem. I think I got most of my values from my football coach, the YMCA director, and my uncles. My mother remarried when I was in high school, and we moved out of a slum apartment into a home. That made an unbelievable difference in the way I saw things and the way I felt." The interviewer later commented that Jay's story was one of the most inspiring he had heard. Not only did Jay emerge intact from a background seemingly designed to create future maladjustment, but he has worked to become a model father, determined to show and give his children the very opposite of everything he knew as a child.

Mary's childhood by comparison was near idyllic. "Our home was very solid, with high values and standards. My parents provided my sister and me with a loving environment and lots of traditions. I can only remember a couple of times when my parents argued. When I married Jay and we had our first argument, I thought we were ready for divorce. My upbringing was really a bit unrealistic in that sense."

When asked how he overcame his own upbringing to become the parent he is, Jay responded, "The first thing I did was to work hard. Whenever I could, I tried to make a little extra money painting or doing carpentry work. I wanted to first provide a house that was far superior to anything that I had. That was one part of being a good parent. I also tried to play with the kids whenever I could. When I wasn't working, I was home. I remember the song "Cats in the Cradle." After that song came out, I used to think back and try to figure out what I had done *with* my kids that would keep them coming back. Have I given them the time they needed? I worked hard at not being a person who never had time for his kids, and who then would never have time for him."

When asked, "Your family has been nominated by others who perceive your relationship as something special. What do you think that something is?" Mary replied, "I think there is a lot of love here. There is a lot of touching, hugging, crying. There is some misunderstanding, too. But we always try to come back, rehash it, and talk it out. If there needs to be an apology, we make it. We can't let things go by. Some things may be uncomfortable, but they are talked about." Jay feels their specialness derives largely from support. "We give a lot of support to our kids, openly and among the family. People can see this."

What was Jay's one wish for his children? "I would want my kids to always stand up and face the wind. I think that is a reflection of the strength that is often required of people to maintain themselves in our society today. I hope we've taught the kids to stand up and face things as they come, always being accountable for their own actions."

Mary hesitated little in considering their most important contribution in raising their children. "I think it is example. We are not perfect and we certainly make mistakes, but Jay and I have had a mutual goal—raising these two kids—and we have dedicated our lives to it. It will be difficult when Jason leaves next year, because we have really surrounded ourselves with them and their activities."

The Willett children both do well academically. What kinds of things did Mary and Jay do when the kids were younger to help foster their sense of achievement? Mary: "First of all, we had extreme TV limits. Then, there was reading, every day before naps, and at night there were book readings. I would say Jay was more the recreation person with them, and I was more the reader and the one who got out the flashcards." How about athletics? Jay: "I would never push my kids athletically. As a matter of fact, I wouldn't let Jason play football until he was a freshman in high school. I have never even coached my son except on occasions when he's asked for it." Athletics are something Jay and Mary support one hundred percent, but remain determined not to relive any of their own athletic dreams through their children.

The Willett family—born of the resiliency of the human spirit.

———

Retha Kilpatrick is a single mother living in Sweet Water, Texas. Her two sons are Cole, aged eight, and Clay, aged eleven, making Retha the head of one of the younger families in this study. Retha supports her family on her bookkeeper's salary, which she calls "lower income." A single mom for the past six years, Retha considers herself poor economically, but fabulously wealthy in family life. When asked, "Why do you think others see you as such a good parent?" Retha gave the credit to her sons. "I don't think others would see me as a good parent if I didn't have good boys. They make parenting a joy." Retha downplayed her own role in the success of her family, but as the interview progressed, it became obvious that Retha's style of parenting is so lovingly natural that she seldom gives conscious thought to her parenting abilities.

The interview began by seeking the one experience Retha most remembers with her father and mother, and how her upbringing affected her own parenting. "My dad was a farmer. So many times when he was farming near the house I'd get on the tractor with him. It was hot, dirty, and noisy, but that was okay because it was just him and me. It was too noisy to talk, but we were together and we both liked that. . . .

"When I was six years old, my horse threw me into a barbed wire fence, nearly cutting my ear off and cutting my leg badly. We lived twenty-five miles from town, and I remember the strength mom had, to get me to town so the doctor could sew me together. She was so strong through the whole thing. . . .

"Because my parents involved us kids in their lives and outings, I have done the same with mine. I kiss, hug, and tell my kids often how much I love them because physical affection was and is important to me, too."

Retha shared her main anxieties as each son came along. "I never thought about them being unhealthy. I felt God would take care of them. My main apprehension came when I was pregnant with my second child, Cole. I loved Clay so much it seemed impossible to be able to love another child that much. Of course, I realize now how silly that was, as there is more than enough love for each of them."

Thinking about the best times in her parenting, Retha said, "My sons are eleven and eight, so I feel I'm just getting a start on parenting. But I'll never forget when I delivered them, that immediate love that is complete, unexplainable, and so strong. Now, it is when I'm walking along the river with Cole, not even talking, and have him just put his hand in mine and squeeze. Or when Clay says, 'Mom, I need a hug!' These are just the beginnings of the best times."

Retha was not ashamed to speak of her parental failures. "When I've behaved badly or scolded them unfairly because I'm down or tired. The way I deal with this is to call them to me, hold them, and tell them, 'Mom behaved badly, I was wrong. Please forgive me.' This makes me feel better, plus it shows them it's okay to say, 'I blew it. I was wrong. I'm sorry.' "

As a single parent, Retha knows that no matter how much love she shows for her sons, when it's time to discipline, she has to act fast and firm. Otherwise, two energetic boys could quickly overwhelm one thirty-four-year-old, working, housekeeping, childrearing mother. "A couple of years ago, the boys and I were going to a carnival with my brother, his wife, and three boys. Being on a very limited income, I explained to the boys before we left that we only had so much money to spend, so they could each have only two rides and a hot dog for supper. If they didn't want that, we would have to stay home. If the other boys got more, my boys were not to complain. They agreed that two rides and a hot dog was enough. Everything went smooth until supper. Clay decided he wanted fried chicken. When I reminded him about our agreement, he started to throw a fit in the restaurant. I immediately took him outside and explained that because of his actions, he would have to sit in the car quietly, while the rest of us ate supper. I could see him from where we were. That made an impression on him, his brother, and three cousins. My sister-in-law thought I was cruel, that I should have given in. Was I cruel? I think not, because he knew the consequences of his actions, and he chose to disobey. Now I don't have that problem with him, or his brother or cousins. I try to make sure the boys know beforehand what is expected of them, so there is no confusion."

Retha also makes sure to find time for herself. "To save my sanity as a single parent, and so I wasn't feeling like a martyr, I started setting aside one night a week for myself. On that night I don't have to do anything—cook, clean, play with the kids, unless I choose. It works nicely. The boys fix themselves peanut butter and jelly sandwiches. Mom reads, stitches, or maybe even gets a baby-sitter and a date."

When we asked Retha what advice she would give her children when they had children of their own, she summed up her whole childrearing philosophy in one sentence: "Treat your kids as you like being treated."

The Kilpatricks—a single mother and a complete family.

———

The Loves, the Willetts, the Kilpatricks—families who felt flattered to be profiled up close. Throughout the remaining chapters of this book, these families will speak again, as will ninety-seven other families, who all share a common bond: They are fully committed to making family life succeed.

THE DIVERSITY OF EXCELLENCE

The word that best captures the makeup of these one hundred families is *diverse.* Since nearly every demographic combination is present, families that closely resemble your own in their structure are likely present. By their very diversity, these families are sending an identical message to all families: There are no social, geographic, or educational barriers to excellence. Excellence doesn't depend upon your hourly wage, address, or the number of degrees after your name. You don't have to be a biological parent with only natural children to develop a strong family life. You can be an adoptive parent, a single parent, a parent of healthy or handicapped children. A lifelong spouse or a particular set of religious beliefs are not requirements for excellence. And you certainly don't need to be a psychologist or counselor to raise an emotionally fit child. Indeed, there are no psychologists among our families. And I'll admit, I'm a shade nervous about how that reflects on my career choice.

Excellence lies within you. Your drive to make your family the best that it can be need not be blocked by your particular life circumstances. To be sure, your path may be more winding and littered than some, but as each chapter of this book will show, excellence is an internal quality, not easily squashed by external conditions. It is a desire to make the most of yourself and your family, whatever your talents or situation.

While diverse in their life-styles and composition, these families still reveal far more similarities than differences. The primary similarity is the high quality of their family life, which we will look at next in EVIDENCE OF EXCELLENCE.

Chapter 3

Evidence
of Excellence

*"If 'special' means exclusive, or precludes someone
else from being special, then we're not. Everyone has
something special to offer as a family."*

Mother, Las Vegas, Nevada

The credibility of every insight or bit of advice in this book depends
upon your being satisfied that these families are indeed special and worth
hearing. The nominating teachers fully believe this, as they based their
selections upon years of association with these parents and children. What
is it that the teachers saw to convince them of these families' quality? This
is the question we will now answer.

CONSISTENCY: A MARK OF EXCELLENCE

There are 387 children in our sample of families. To our knowledge, none
have ever been in serious trouble with the law. None have been suspended
from school. None have an alcohol or a drug problem. This is an amazing
testament to the power of a healthy home life, especially given the tricky and
seductive nature of the world in which kids grow up today. This unblemished

record is even more impressive considering the reality that some kids by their nature are just hell-bent on learning about life the hard way, no matter how good their parents are. As Lucy, the seasoned mother of eighteen, reminisced, "No one is perfect, but with seventeen married, no forced marriages, no wrecked cars, and never having to go to Police Court, in spite of all our mistakes, we have to look at the end results." There was more than a hint of pride in her voice. There was downright relief.

Quality is more than just the absence of negatives. It is also the presence of positives. When describing the children in these families, the teachers consistently spoke to their moral character, their social sensitivity, and their overall maturity:

- "These are two very well-adjusted children who excel both academically and socially."
- "All the W. children are givers, and by giving, they are receivers."
- "In the many years that span their first to last child these parents have nurtured polite, well-rounded young men and women."
- "Each son has a solid sense of self-esteem and, in turn, accepts the differences in his family members, friends, and human beings in general."

Attributes such as *well-adjusted, well-rounded,* and *solid self-esteem* are as hard to measure as excellence. As personality traits, they are broad, general descriptions. However, the social and academic accomplishments which follow naturally from these traits are measurable. Certainly an exceptional child can come from an emotionally struggling family. An excellent family, through no fault of its own, can turn out an emotionally struggling child. But where there is consistency in character in all the children, achievements tend to be consistent as well. Here are some examples:

- A family in Nevada has seen each of its seven children inducted into the National Honor Society. Among them are one class valedictorian and two salutatorians. (It wasn't uncommon for all the children in a particular family to be honor students, as diligence in academics was both encouraged and expected.)
- Two of three children in a Delaware family are listed in *Who's Who Among American High School Students.* The third child is diagnosed dyslexic but has received several academic achievement awards.
- Good citizenship awards were given thirteen times to three of four children

in a family from Alabama. The fourth child was voted "class favorite" in his middle school.

- All six children in an Arkansas family have been recognized in *Who's Who in FBLA* (Future Business Leaders of America).
- Parents from Georgia have watched all seven of their children enter and complete college. Last word was that mom and dad will make their final home refinance payment in September 2078.

In any family, the children are not equally gifted intellectually, physically, motivationally, or otherwise. When all strive to reach their potential, the denominator common to all of them is their parents. It is mom and/or dad who must encourage and nurture whatever abilities the children are blessed with. Barbara, a New York mother to four girls, aged four to eighteen, put it this way, "I see my children's accomplishments as falling into two categories: the kind you list on a résumé and the kind that really matters in life," for example, character, maturity, self-discipline. So often, the résumé listings evolve from those kinds of qualities that "really matter." When both types of accomplishments are present in each child in a family, something very positive is taking place in that family.

FROM THE MOUTHS OF BABES

Perhaps more revealing than the judgments of teachers or a psychologist are the judgments of children. Kids, especially adolescents, can be the toughest graders we parents face. Children aren't content just to live with us; they also scrutinize us, spotting weaknesses and probing for inconsistencies. How else can they stay several steps ahead of us?

The children of these parents, like all children, feel they know their folks better than anyone does. A few below-average grades were given, but on the overwhelming whole, the kids were convinced that their parents are as good as others say, sometimes more so. When asked, "If 10 is perfect, how would you rate your parents on a 1-to-10-point scale?" the kids offered some thoughtful observations, not only about their parents, but about parenting in general:

- "I would have to give mom and dad an 8 if 10 were perfect. They are not perfect. A lot of times when the perfect thing to do would have been to say, 'No, we can't afford it,' they would say, 'We'll see if there isn't some way we can work it out.' There were times when I probably needed my bottom spanked and they gave me a break. There were times when they really had work to do and they took time to play with me. They are not perfect, but then perfect people do not need love. It is their imperfections that make them special, that make them my parents. They are close enough to perfect for me."

- "My parents are now at a 9+. As our family matured, they also matured, acquiring more wisdom about parenting. I rate them at a 9+ because they seem more human now, with all of the frailties and imperfections that go along with being human. It is so much easier to relate to people who are less than perfect and, because of their imperfections, they are more perfect parents."

- "A 9. Nobody's perfect, and they have particular faults, but each in their own way shines. I had to learn from *other adults* that one does not automatically become mature at twenty-one."

- "I think I would rate my parents a 9. I'm too logical to go for the full 10 even though they come pretty close. I would never say my parents were without fault or that they didn't make mistakes. They admitted they were wrong on more than one occasion, but I loved them all the more for not being perfect. They allowed us to exceed some of the goals they had reached. They let us know that making mistakes was just evidence that we had actually tried to do something."

- "My parents would rate an 8. The primary reason they don't achieve a 10 is because they taught me too well, too quickly, and too thoroughly. I am only seventeen, yet I feel as though I have gained all that I can from my parents and I must gain the rest from experiencing life."

- "When growing up, I felt that my parents were so different. Now I realize that it is everyone else who is different. Things that seemed important to our society—materialism, greed, social competition—seemed silly to them. Since entering college, I've realized how in touch with reality my parents truly are."

A few of the kids refused to be bound by a 10-point scale. Said twelve-year-old Jamie from Utah, "I would put my parents at a 12. They are understanding, have a sense of humor, are *very* fun to be with, and they love us so much. For instance, when all my friends stay out, my parents say no because they don't want us to risk ourselves getting hurt." Now either Jamie hasn't hit adolescence yet, or he's softening up the folks for his request for a Porsche.

Other children judge parents solely on effort. Nineteen-year-old Christy and twenty-one-year-old Sean said, "We would give them a 10 for effort. They have made mistakes, but they have really tried." Christy and Sean both recognize that great parenting begins with the willingness to really try.

Then there are those assessments that cut right to the quick with insights that only kids can produce. Ten-year-old Molly carefully weighed her feelings before being too complimentary: "8. I like them sometimes." Ten-year-old Tom from Illinois had a specific reason for his less-than-perfect rating of 8.5. "They send me to my room." On the other hand, twelve-year-old Brian from Kansas gave his folks a perfect 10 because, "They are nice, but mean when we do something wrong." In simple words, Brian captured the essence of parenthood: unconditional love coupled with the will to discipline. Travis, a junk-food-loving twelve-year-old from Montana, linked his performance rating to his mother's willingness to indulge his sweet tooth. "A 9. She doesn't buy enough ice cream." Ah, if only it were so simple to raise our status in our kids' eyes just by buying a few more quarts of chocolate-chip ice cream.

The older children can get pretty particular when judging our strengths and weaknesses. Said sixteen-year-old Cindy, "At first I was going to give them a 9. Then I thought, no, their curfews are a little tight: 8." And admitted twenty-one-year-old David, "They're pretty good, probably the best I've seen, but they still have a couple of rough spots. Overall a 9.00. I've been watching the Olympics."

Then, too, some kids aren't afraid to judge parents on the basis of our results. "I think that how good parents are really depends upon how good their kids turn out to be kids. They did pretty well here, I think," seventeen-year-old Craig asserted. Mike, aged nineteen, couldn't resist taking a little credit for his parents' success, "No doubt, they're a 10. I couldn't have asked for better ones. I trained them pretty well, didn't I?" The last word on quality comes from twenty-one-year-old Alex, the youngest of six children, three natural and three adopted. "An 8. They did a pretty good job. I can't complain, but no parents are perfect. If they were, we would never move out of the house." Judging by how long some kids hang around, their parents must be pushing 9.999.

One conclusion was clear from the kids' ratings: They were their folks' number-one supporters. Even though all the youngsters weren't as eloquent or witty as those above, they generally expressed similar respect and warmth. In addition to giving a testimonial to their parents, these youngsters are saying several things to the rest of us:

First, our kids like and appreciate us more than we think they do. Consistently, the parents predicted their children would rate them lower than they actually did. Ernest, a father of seven from Colorado, said, "The kids would rate me a 2.5. They won't understand until they are parents. We didn't appreciate our parents as much as we should until later in life." In fact, five of his children gave him a 9 or above. It's easy to underestimate our kids' goodwill toward us because more frequently we hear only the ill will and nasty comments aimed at us in the heat of a disagreement: "How come you never make Chastity stand in the corner? She's your pet, that's why. I'm the slave around here. How'd you run the house before I was born? I wish grandma were my mom. She loves me. I wish dad were my mom. He only comes home at night." The most reliable time to assess Buster's perceptions of us is when both he and we are calm. Of course, this may be an occurrence about as frequent as Halley's comet!

Second, a child's opinions of his parents are not static. They change constantly, rising and falling with the years (with the minutes?), typically taking their steepest plunge during the onslaught of adolescence. One twelve-year-old arranged her perceptions this way. "From birth to fourth grade, my parents were a 9.5. I never had any problems. Well, maybe a few, but nobody's perfect. From fifth to seventh grade—8.0. Mom gets angry at me for not making decisions, but when I do, she sometimes gets angry because I didn't make the one she wanted."

Teens grade on the curve, often ranking every other parent in the state above us. Sometimes we have little choice other than to weather our temporary unpopularity. There is consolation, though. After the dust of the "teen age" clears, the kids' final rating almost always rebounds to levels above and beyond that which they held in their early teen years. Virtually all youngsters in these families noted that as they outgrew adolescence, they once again viewed mom and dad as actually being in touch with the real world and knowing something about how it operates. Summing up her maturing appreciation of her folks as she herself matured, Kathy, now in her early twenties, said, "I would rate my parents a 10, and it keeps going up every day." This is one of the delayed benefits of raising great kids. The older they get, the more they understand us and our parental motives. To paraphrase Mark Twain, who must have plowed through adolescence himself: When I was fifteen my father was the dumbest man in the world. Amazing how much he learned by the time I was twenty-one.

A few parents didn't want to chance even the slightest dip in their popularity. A New Jersey father, surrounded by his four teens, when asked what he thought his children would give his parenting on a 1-to-10-point scale, wasn't above bribery, "They'd better give us a 10 or there is no dessert."

Finally, the kids are telling us that sometimes it just takes a neutral third party to pull out what they genuinely think about us. Since the interviewers were not related to the kids, they heard more willingness to "brag up" the folks. Youngsters are sometimes reluctant to tell us personally how much they actually admire, even respect, us. For teens especially, this can be an embarrassing, even "uncool," display of emotion. Mainly, I think they just worry that we'll get too cocky and assume they'll now be willing to go along with our rules.

EXCELLENT? WHO US?

The one group hesitant to talk of quality or excellence were the parents themselves. Typically their attitude was one of "Why did you pick us? Sure we think we have a nice family, but so do lots of others." In fact, several parents were so embarrassed by their nomination, they were unsure about going ahead with the interview. A mother and father in Florida settled their doubts by putting the decision to a family vote. Not only did the kids vote in a solid yea block, but they made it very clear to mom and dad that they should feel honored, not self-conscious.

Comments from a few of the parents when asked to assess themselves will give you a flavor of their rather unassuming style:

• "I'm not sure exactly [why their family had been nominated], and at some later date I'd like to discuss this with the individual who suggested our name. She has known and observed us for the past fourteen years in school, church, and community activities. . . . We have been told by others that they view our family as special. Although our problems haven't seemed as drastic as some, it doesn't mean we don't have situations that are, or were, troubling. My hope is that we remain humble and do not feel better than others."

• "We think we are average. Through the years we have had problems with our children. It has been nothing major, but we make wrong decisions and sometimes we don't understand the kids, and sometimes they don't understand us, but we try."

- "On the whole, I would probably rate myself a 6 or 7. There are days when I'm a 10 and other days when I struggle even to make a 1."

Of course, sometimes the kids wouldn't just sit idly by while mom and dad downplayed their own abilities as parents. One young daughter, upon hearing her parents rate themselves a 5 or 6, immediately spoke up, "Mom and Dad, you think this guy flew this far just to talk to a 5 or 6?"

The parents did not display a false sense of modesty, but a genuine belief that they were only doing what was right and to be expected. When posed this question, "If you had one wish for your children, what would it be?," Norman, father to Kim, eighteen, and Chip, sixteen, said without hesitation, "that they would be blessed with the kind of children that we have." Many parents will recognize this as the rare flip side of the standard parenting curse, "I hope you have three kids just like you!"

Candy, a mother from Arkansas, said that any specialness in their family comes from their children. "The kids have learned that it is not what happens to you, but how you handle what happens to you, that is important. They are truly responsible and loving people. They are so much smarter than we are. They continue to make right choices daily, and I'm sure many [choices] that we are sheltered from." Can you tell this is coming from a mother of two teenagers?

Ed from Oregon, a father of two boys and two girls, aged four to fourteen, asked rhetorically, "Are we good parents because we have good kids, or are they good kids because we are good parents?"

Obviously, behind every good kid lives a good parent or two, or maybe three. These parents seem to be understating their own continued role in developing their youngsters' character. They are quick to believe they've had a hefty share of good luck, been blessed with wonderful children, or have had positive results despite all their faults. Nonetheless, they can't deny that the consistently high opinions of others—teachers, a psychologist, their own children, along with tangible evidence of their children's character and maturity—together compile a convincing package that very special things are happening in their families.

Many of these families have already been where many of us want to go. Often they've learned the hard way how to pull forth the best in themselves. Barbara, from Mobile, Alabama, is fond of telling her four children, "A wise man learns by his own mistakes, but a wiser man learns by the mistakes of others." If these excellent parents are willing to talk freely of their mistakes and their corrections, the rest of us can profit and perhaps steer around a few bumps and potholes we would have otherwise hit.

ELEVEN THOUSAND YEARS OF PARENTHOOD

Eleven thousand years. This is how much parenting experience, give or take a few hundred years, is represented by the families throughout this book. The figure was reached by taking the number of parents in each family (usually two) and multiplying that by the number of kids and by their respective ages. For any child aged eighteen or older, the parents received "credit" for only eighteen parenting years. Although, as any mom and dad of older children would be quick to point out, this is an artificially low cutoff age for two reasons. First, you never really stop being a parent. As they become adults, legally anyway, the kids may fire off lines like, "I'm eighteen now, so don't tell me . . ." but we can always counter with, "As long as you live in my house, young lady . . ." Long after our kids have become seasoned parents themselves, we may still be consulting, lending guidance, or giving an unasked-for opinion or two. Second, in bygone generations kids regularly pulled up the home stakes at age eighteen or nineteen. Now, after twenty-five or twenty-six years, they're still hanging around. They might leave for a couple of years, just to tease us, but soon they're sliding in the back door again.

Even if our sample were made up of troubled parents and kids, in eleven thousand years they most surely would have learned a few things about family life, if mainly from harsh experience. Add the element of quality that typifies these families and you have the lessons of almost eleven millennia of parenting trials, errors, and solutions to draw from.

Some of us may feel as if we alone have been on the parenting scene for upwards of a few hundred years. One mom lamented, "I was a parent for thirteen years until he hit fourteen last year. Since then, it seems like I've been at this the past sixty years." No matter how long we feel like we've been raising kids, we still don't have the variety of experiences offered by so many successful families. So feel free to listen in and pick your favorite ten or twelve years of advice. If you have any kids between ages twelve and eighteen, maybe you'd better sift through about one hundred fifty years' worth.

This book seeks to define excellence by studying one hundred families who represent the word. If we accept that these parents are exceptional, the next logical question is: "How did they get that way?" or more specifically, "What were *their* parents like?" Some surprising answers can be found in THE MAKING OF AN EXCELLENT PARENT.

Chapter 4

The Making of an Excellent Parent

"There was no communication in my family, no display of affection with any of us. I grew up with a poor self-concept. My mother was never pleased with me. I came into parenting with the attitude that I wanted to be a different, and better, parent than my own."

Mother, Ranchester, Wyoming

Does excellence have its roots in childhood? Put another way, were excellent parents themselves raised by excellent parents? Many child-development specialists say so. They assert that to reach the peak of your parenting potential you must have grown up with at least one positive role model. Indeed, most people believe you reflect how you were raised. If you were blessed with quality parents, you will likely become a quality parent. If not, you may be destined to repeat the mistakes of your own upbringing.

The parents we interviewed agree with neither the experts nor with common belief. To be sure, some of them had model childhoods, a "Ward and June Cleaver existence," as one dad dubbed it. The majority had what could best be called solid or unremarkable childhoods, which they used as a base for developing their own parenting style. A surprising number of these model parents recalled childhoods that were anything but model.

Those parents who talked of enjoyable childhoods used adjectives like *religious, stable, carefree, simple, traditional, secure, close-knit, slow-paced.* These positive childhoods revealed great variety:

- "We were taught absolute standards of good and bad, right and wrong. Total honesty was expected at all times."
- "Mom's responsibilities were the house and children. Dad's were to make money. The two *never* crossed paths."
- "You couldn't get into too much trouble because the neighbors would watch over you."
- "Usually a look or a few words of displeasure were all it took to keep us in line."
- "We were not trapped by old traditions. We had opportunities to develop our own traditions."
- "I don't think I've ever seen anybody as hard-working as my mother."
- "We had a very soft-spoken household."
- "Everything my parents taught me was by example."

Perhaps the warmest of the warm memories was this: "I grew up in an earthy environment. I can smell my childhood—the ground, the apple orchard, my friends. I can feel it—crusty mittens and gloves in the winter, old broken buckles on my shoes."

Such recollections speak of content childhoods, filled with emotionally durable memories. The most moving childhood experiences for these parents persisted into their parenting, helping to create for them a personal definition of *parent.*

- "I was serving as an altar boy in church. I had to light the candles. I was obviously having trouble with this one candle and was starting to panic. Dad came walking right up the middle aisle. On one hand, it was very embarrassing. On the other hand, he knew I needed help. He came up and lit the candle for me."
- "My mother took four of us children on a long bus trip to visit our grandfather when we were young. To stay together we all occupied the backseat of the bus. One night as mother dozed, her head hung at an uncomfortable angle, so I braced her head with my hand until the next morning. When she realized what I had done, without a word, she gave

me a look that expressed everything. Later in my life when I had eye trouble which couldn't be remedied at the time, she offered to donate one of her eyes to me."

- "My father had a silent way of being there for me. He would say only a few words, but he always hit the nail on the head. I knew if he approved of what I did or not, even if he didn't always say so. He was quiet and a great listener."

- "I was about ten years old. I wanted to get my mother something for her birthday so badly, but I didn't have the money. I kept telling her, 'I want to buy you a present, but I don't have the money.' She really didn't have the money either, but she gave me some anyway. I went to a store near our house and looked for the longest time and bought a set of glasses. She didn't even need the glasses, but she knew how important they were to me. They were not a present for her, they were a present for me, and she understood that."

- "The extent of my father's formal education was the seventh grade. Yet he enrolled in a correspondence school and learned enough about algebra and math to help me with my high-school homework."

Good parents take advantage of the experiences they valued as children. They benefit from their parents' wisest philosophies and practices, carrying them virtually unchanged from childhood to parenthood.

- "Some of the jobs and chores we thought were awful as kids, such as weeding the garden or picking up stones from the field, have turned out to be the most memorable. So, when our children complain about spending a lot of time working, we laugh and tell them we're making memories."

- "The best times for me growing up were summers. Mom was a quiet, constant presence. As I went through my teen years, I preferred time to be alone. She let me have it. I read books, pondered questions. I defined the person I wanted to become. My husband and I try very hard to provide our children with the same unhurried summers filled with opportunities for just being."

- "When I was about nine or ten, my parents started to give me an allowance to cover all my personal expenses, clothing, and spending money. Some of it would come in cash each week. The rest would be tabulated in an account book to be used whenever and for whatever I decided. If I wanted something special, I had to save for it, and if I spent too much on one thing, I had to give up other things.

"We used the same system with our children. It totally eliminated conflicts about money and what they could and couldn't have. They knew their choices along with the consequences. It taught them to manage their personal affairs well."

- "My dad always took time to discuss and explain things to me—why he felt something was important, why he had certain values, why he had certain rules. He treated me with respect and as a mature person. He made me feel equal to anyone, never that I couldn't achieve something because of my gender. Consequently, I felt independent and responsible and grew up believing I could do whatever I was willing to work hard enough to achieve."

Even in good childhoods, some of the most durable childrearing lessons arise from negative experiences. Many parents learned from their parents' shortcomings.

- "The worst times as a child for me were during adolescence when I was being talked at and made to feel very guilty. I resented the way my dad saw every misbehavior so seriously. I was sensitive and he always spoke in extremes. For example, the day I got caught for skipping school he said, 'I can *never* trust you again.'

  "The impact of all that on me has been to realize that life is too short to be taken so seriously all the time. It is so valuable to see the humorous side of things. Self-esteem is fragile, and children need it built by parental encouragement, which forgives a wrong in the present and looks toward a right in the future."

- "I remember every night how my parents would tuck us in bed and kiss us good-night. All of a sudden they told us it was time for us to tell them good-night downstairs and go to bed by ourselves. I was about a second-grader then, and that just crushed me. I wasn't ready for that at all."

- "My father was arbitrary and dictatorial much of the time. I've reacted to that by trying to give our children sets of options to choose from, even when they were small. I wanted them to participate in most decisions.

  "Sometimes my mother and sisters—really, all of us—played one person against another. Mom would get in the middle of our arguments, taking sides, or would discuss one daughter's business with another. I have worked hard to remain impartial regarding the children's arguments and not to pit one against another."

• "My dad once told my little sister his propane truck [his business] was more important than she was. I realized where he was coming from. In effect, he was telling my little sister that without a propane truck we couldn't have the material things. But my sister really didn't understand this. She could only take it personally.

"I learned at that time that my dad had no idea where we kids were at. His way of loving us was to provide us with material things, and we had every material possession, but we didn't have him. As a result, I've tried to be aware of my kids' point of view instead of perceiving their needs through my circumstances. I also learned that material possessions can never take the place of the time a child wants to spend with his parents."

Barbara from New York recognizes that parents sometimes overcompensate for experiences that adversely affected them as children. "I remember the day I bought myself a book, a one-dollar-twenty-five-cent hardcover copy of *Lad: A Dog*, and my parents and I had a terrible fight because they said we couldn't afford it. I've probably reacted to that by showering my children with books that they can't possibly appreciate."

The best childhoods have dark spots that contain lessons for the future. Adverse experiences, even in the extreme, may have ultimately positive effects, as we will see shortly.

WHAT WOULD MOM OR DAD DO?

Many parents viewed their upbringing as a prime source of childrearing information. Some considered their own parents the true childrearing experts for them. "Going into fatherhood, the only experts I knew were my parents and grandparents," said a Nevada father. Carl and Joanna, parents of four sons, agreed. "We basically wanted to raise our children the way we were raised." In essence, these parents used their solid past, whenever possible, to create a solid present for their children.

Taking lessons from your own parents has several advantages. First, your childhood was on-the-job training for your own parenthood. You lived with the effects, good and bad, of what your parents did, good and bad. You once wore the same shoes your children now wear. By trying to recapture how you felt, say, when your father lectured you about how he had to walk sixteen miles to and from school, carrying all six of his brothers on his back, you can better sense the impact of any similar lectures on your youngster. (You had it easier. You only walked ten miles, carrying three brothers.) The more you can recall what it was like to be on the receiving end of discipline, the more sensitive a disciplinarian you will be. "I do things for better or for worse, relying much on my own instincts and past experience. Our parents weren't perfect, and we've tried to learn from that. We aren't perfect, and hopefully we can learn from that, too," shared Jan, mother to Sean and Christy. So listen to your memories. They'll give you some valuable, childlike guidance.

Going one step further, even though you saw parenting through a child's eyes at the time, now that you're a parent, you can reassess your childhood through a parent's eyes. Your experience was that of a child, but your evaluation is now that of a parent. Many of the parents we interviewed actively looked for parallels in their own childhoods to help handle current parenting problems. Pat from Connecticut said, "I reflect a great deal on my own upbringing—what I now feel worked and what didn't." Rita, the mother of seven we first met in chapter 1, concurred, "Much of parenting for me is just little flashbacks of growing up and how I felt about things. A lot of it is mirroring my mother in the good sense and trying to be the good parent she was." Of course, these parents didn't rely on memories only. Sometimes they asked mom or dad directly. "As far as outside advice, I probably took the most from my mother. She was a tremendous help without taking over. She showed me how to handle things, but then she would go home and let me care for my child without interference." Okay, where is this grandmother, and does she consult to any other families?

Finally, copying one's own parents can occur quite naturally. Carrying the experiences of your childhood into your childrearing can happen without thought, without effort. Lois, a Minnesota mother of two, said, "Dan and I were very definitely influenced in our parenting by our own childhoods. Those growing-up patterns became almost instinctual. The fact that my mother hugged and kissed us a lot meant that I did it without even thinking. The fact that Dan experienced a very positive relationship with his dad through outdoor activities meant he just assumed he would do the same with his children. So for us, the parenting modeled by our own parents was the strongest influence on our parenting."

These former children are advising: Choose the best your parents had to offer. Make your childhood help you understand your children. Actively reminisce about your childhood reactions to your mother's or father's decisions. Your own upbringing is a well of parenting guidance, probably covered over a bit by the years, but with some mental effort it can be retapped for everybody's benefit.

SELF-MADE PARENTS

While approximately seventy-five percent of parents recalled positive upbringings, about a fourth were raised on the negative side of the childhood spectrum, some down near the worst end. They remembered their pasts with much different words and language: *depressing, volatile, unsettled, violent, abusive, traumatic.*

- "If I played you a videotape of every time I saw my parents together, it would either bore you or terrify you."
- "We were very mobile. When I entered high school, it was my thirteenth school."
- "One time my parents didn't speak to each other for eighteen months. I had to pay all the bills and take on all the responsibility."
- "I remember having to go and get both my parents out of the bars and the fears of them driving home."
- "I remember playing slot machines in a bar while my dad played poker in the next room. I won a jackpot at age five."
- "Mother would lock dad out of the house. They threw knives, hammers, skillets, dishes at each other."

A few parents had no consistent role models at all, good or bad, but grew up bouncing from parent to grandparent to aunt to uncle. One father feels his upbringing came from priests. "I cannot hold my family up as an example. There were too many loose ends in my family. I still look back to the Jesuits and the religious education as what did the trick for me [in his role as a parent]. That is my measuring stick."

Another father was grateful he had older sisters. "I was physically and verbally disciplined by my sisters. They would spank me and ground me. My younger sister was the physical one. She was a drill sergeant. I can remember her coming to me one time when I was in junior high, and she said to me very simply, 'You will bathe regularly or I will bathe you.' Of course, I knew she would."

It's no surprise that many of the parents with whom we spoke considered their childhoods good. Essentially, they have copied and improved on the way they were raised. The real surprise, and the real message of hope for all parents, is provided by those moms and dads who were given little or nothing to build on. Somehow they still managed to pull the best from themselves and become the kinds of parents they could only dream of having when they were children. An unexpected lesson in excellence will come from those parents who rose above their pasts to become not just adequate moms and dads, but moms and dads whom others see as worthy of imitation.

ABUSED CHILDREN, ABUSING ADULTS?

Many parents nowadays will never, under any condition, spank their children, not because they disagree with spanking in itself or see it as necessarily unhealthy, but because they were physically abused as children. Consequently, they parent beneath a shadow that says, "If you were abused as a child, you have more potential to abuse your own children." They fear that one day their past will return to haunt them, and even a single episode of spanking could lead to uncontrollable fury. Further, these parents live with the notion that they are relegated to be substandard parents and disciplinarians because much of what they knew years ago was substandard. While in the overall picture there is some truth to these perceptions, on a parent-to-parent basis they are nonsense.

A number of well-above-standard parents talked openly of abuse-ridden childhoods. Their stories will help calm the fears of any parent who knew abuse as a child.

- "My father physically beat us, and I think when you have that overwhelming physical fear of someone who is so big and so frightening, it just dominates your life. There was always a threat that we were going to be beaten. I remember one time when my father was beating me and my mother stopped him. It was the only time she did it. He held up his hand as if to hit her too, and she told him not to even think of doing it. Then she moved aside, and he continued to beat me."
- "I was always being punished. My mother and dad didn't communicate with each other, and when they didn't get along, they didn't speak at all. I think because I was there, they took it out on me. Everything I did I got punished for. If I left something on the cupboard, I would be grounded

for a week. I did dishes from the time I was five years old. My dad made me a stool so I could reach. If they found a dirty fork or spoon, I would have to wash all the dishes over. I had to wear a pot on a string around my neck one time when I was about twelve years old because my father found a couple of dirty dishes in the cupboard. He sent me to the neighborhood store like that.

"My own children do get disciplined, but they don't get grounded for weeks. The punishment fits the crime. It might be only one day and then they get a chance to do better. My children do not get beat, but they do get a smack on the bottom. I try not to holler because my mother and dad screamed constantly."

• "Often my stepfather would come home drunk. He would threaten our lives and my mother's. At one point, he attacked us with a knife, and my brother beat him off with a baseball bat. The most difficult part of it all, aside from the sheer terror of the home situation, was having to face kids in the neighborhood and schoolmates who would see the police responding to our house quite frequently."

How have such violent childhoods affected these parents? First, without exception, all have resolved never to put their families in any situation remotely like what they knew years ago. Second, not a one is a child abuser, in either the physical or emotional sense. They have not assimilated their own parents' styles, but have excised any brutal methods from their own childrearing style. Third, many of these parents do spank or have spanked. They recognize that spanking and abuse are not parts of the same continuum. One can be an effective form of discipline for younger children. The other is nothing more than cruelty, which teaches no lessons and only puts distance between parents and kids. Finally, and most critically, these parents have learned: If you were abused—verbally, physically, or sexually—as a youngster, you are not predestined as a parent to abuse your own youngsters. What you are now and what you want to be has far more impact on your parenting than what you were or what you knew. A thirteen-year-old son understood this as he described his mother. "My mother was abused as a child, so she had to teach herself affection. Out of that she became a better person. Out of anybody in the whole family she is the most affectionate."

There are many ways to react to hardship and trauma. Imitation is one of them. But resilience and resolve never to commit similar abuses is another.

As we shall see shortly, reverse resolve is an option open to anyone and can be a powerful force for excellence.

ADULT CHILDREN OF ALCOHOLICS

Nobody will argue the destructive effects of an alcoholic parent on family life. And nobody will deny that the effects can reverberate for the next generation or two. Among our parents, by far the most recurrent traumatic themes wove around a childhood distorted by alcohol. With emotions that are still fresh, these parents share parts of their early lives.

- "The worst experience [of childhood] was seeing my father put on a train, so drunk he didn't know where he was, when I was eight. I never saw him again until I was twenty-five, when I went to bury him. I spent a great deal of my life trying to find the father I never had."
- "It is almost impossible to think of a good experience with my father. When he was sober, he was tense, so he was not any good to be around. The few times I did see my father [sober], he would want to wrestle, but the wrestling matches always turned out to be painful because he would hurt me. If he would throw the ball, he would throw it too hard and hurt me. He liked to fish. He and his brothers or his drinking buddies would go fishing and he would take me. It would start out fine, but in an hour or two they would all be drunk, and all of a sudden I was a piece of baggage. I can remember sitting behind a bar in the car for hours on end because if I would get out of the car he would kill me."
- "The example my father showed me in his life-style—alcoholism, affairs— left me with little respect for him, and I pretty much did as I pleased. We had no family traditions. The holiday season was an unhappy time for my family. My mother handled all the discipline since my father was gone a lot. When I was younger, because my mother was so frustrated with my dad, she was pretty abusive. From my junior high through high school years, my parents were both alcoholics and spent most of these years in the bars. From that period on, we [kids] were basically left on our own. A lot of decisions and life-styles changed in accordance with my parents' new set of values and perspectives on life. My parents never came home, and when they did, they were always fighting. I remember the terrible fights and waiting in bed at night for mom and dad to come home. I always had mixed

emotions because I was relieved they made it home, but I hated to have to listen to the fighting. It seemed as though we suddenly ceased to be a family, and I was bitter and angry at my parents for making that choice. The impact on me now is a decision to abstain from alcohol. I am no longer bitter toward my parents for the choices they made at that time. However, my priorities are now being the wife and mother that I know the Lord wants me to be and to work faithfully at communicating with my husband and children."

The parent above overcame growing up under the influence of two alcoholic parents, but her success as a mother is all the more remarkable given what her husband says about his own childhood:

- "The worst times for me were when my dad was out drinking and never came home. When he did come home, my parents fought all the time. My father moved out several different times, and once my mother took us with her and left. This went on all through my childhood. I've made a choice not to use alcohol. I do not want my family subject to that type of life-style. I am involved in drug and alcohol prevention programs with our school system."

So, out of a total of four parenting models for these two parents, three were affected by alcohol. However, this mom and dad not only reached beyond their own harsh upbringings, but merged to provide true parenting models for their own children.

Some experts theorize that the offspring of alcoholic parents are limited in their parenting potential. These "adult children of alcoholics" may someday painfully inch their way beyond the influence of their own parents, but only after much hard work and sometimes therapy. Apparently, excellent parents are not aware of such ideas. Their lives disagree with the experts' theories. Like former abuse victims, they too make a clear statement to all grown-ups who missed much of childhood because of one or more shaky parents: The potential for excellence lies in the present, not in the past. Although you may have seen and experienced much turbulence, you are not indelibly marked with bitterness and the inability to leave everything behind. You may be bound to remember the past, but you are not bound to live by it.

REVERSE RESOLVE

We've listened to many parents tell of childhoods loaded with emotional baggage, and yet somehow along the way to adulthood, they left that baggage behind. Why haven't they mirrored the parenthood they saw years ago? How have they become responsible parents after watching only irresponsible models of parenting?

Almost without fail, those parents with chaotic pasts spoke, in different words, of the same phenomenon. One father tagged it succinctly, reverse resolve. Here is how some parents explain it:

- "In our house, children were seen and not heard, so I have been careful to listen to my own children. . . . I knew when I had children I wanted to play and vacation with them because I had always wanted to do that as I was growing up. . . . My worst times with my parents were listening to them quarrel early in the morning. I hated to hear anyone raising their voice or insulting another person; so, I try to be very careful to not call names and to try to criticize in such a way that no one loses face."
- "The worst time of my life was the death of my little brother. He was two and I was four. I was his little mother and even at such a young age, I felt a great void in my life. Also, the knowledge that, according to my parents, the wrong child died affected my life in many ways. The unloved feelings that I experienced, however, helped me in that I grew up determined that any children I had would *never* experience that feeling."
- "I was the last of seven, of which four survived. My father was forty-three when I was born. By the time I got interested in sports at the ten/eleven-year-old age, he didn't have time for me. I wanted to do things, but he didn't have time. I said to myself then that if I ever had children of my own, I would give them a great deal of support—spiritual or whatever they needed—and I would be with them. I can vividly remember the day my dad died. I came home from the hospital and there was a picture of both my parents on the bureau. I went up to the picture, and I looked up at my dad and said, 'Dad, it is a shame, but I never knew you.' I made a vow to myself that this would never occur in my family, and I do spend time with the kids."
- "My father was raised in an environment where sons were considered an asset and daughters a liability. Sons were a measure of a man's virility,

daughters a weakness in his manhood. My worst times [as a child] were a result of the beliefs he had. I remember a family reunion where the men had gathered and were teasing one of the men for having his fourth daughter and no sons. My dad spoke up and bragged that he had three sons. He never mentioned he had a daughter.

"The impact of those attitudes affected my determination to be better and amount to more. It made me my own person. It also affected the way our children were raised. Their sex did not enter into any decision. The only thing that mattered was that, if it was a chore, it needed attention, and if it was an activity, it only mattered whether he or she wanted to try it—that's all."

Reverse resolve is that reaction by which parents refuse to remain victims of their own childhoods and resolve instead to rise above them. It is more than a desire to avoid repeating their parents' mistakes. It is the determination to use painful memories to fuel the drive to become genuinely good parents despite a lack of childhood training. As these parents left the direct influence of their parents, they were able to reinterpret past events, no longer being controlled by them, but turning them into vivid guidelines for what not to do at all costs with their own families. In essence, they made past pain work to their families' present benefit.

Emotions are powerful motivators. They can drive an individual to do the exact opposite of whatever happened to him to create the emotion. For example, if loneliness was the dominant childhood emotion fostered by a neglectful parent, that feeling can evolve into the underlying self-will never to be even slightly neglectful if and when one becomes a parent. Again and again, the stories of these parents' pasts illustrate this theme.

To be sure, much of the strength in all one hundred of these families arose directly from the parents' own positive childhoods and role models. Many parents had the chance to learn from and build upon the upbringings their parents gave to them. But not all parents are so fortunate. And if you are one of those parents, then a primary message of this chapter is for you. It bears repeating once more, for it is critical to your success as a parent. By example of their successful family life, these parents are living proof that no matter how you were raised, no matter what abuse or cruelty you witnessed or experienced, the seeds for achieving a quality parenthood still live within you. They cannot be destroyed. Your past does not place a ceiling upon the heights of parenting you can reach. You are not destined to become what your parents were, or even a small part of what your parents were. You have the capability to stretch yourself far beyond the adequate to raise a family the likes of which you never knew. Believing in your potential for excellence is a necessary first step to a quality family life. It primes you to watch, listen, and learn from others how to build upon your own strengths.

In these first chapters, we have set out to identify family excellence. We have looked at what excellent parents and families are. For a complete understanding of the word *excellent*, we must know WHAT EXCELLENT PARENTS (and families) ARE NOT.

Chapter 5

What Excellent Parents Are Not

*"At times you just act on emotions because you are
frustrated and don't know what else to do as a parent
to work out a bad situation. You finally just throw up
your hands and start yelling. When things cool off,
then you try to figure out what needs to be done and
go from there."*

Father, Caldwell, Idaho

Excellence can be an intimidating word. It can conjure up all manner
of lofty, even unattainable, attributes. When applied to parents or families,
it can make them seem unreal, possessing rare qualities that most of us don't
have, either through our genes or our life circumstances.

A range of adjectives has been used at one time or another to describe the
individual parents in this book: *involved, model, child-oriented, loving, excellent,* even *outstanding.* The one description that fits all of them is *real.* These
parents are like all parents. They know triumphs and happy endings, but they
also know failure and sadness. They struggle with questions, insecurities, guilt.
They overreact, firing off hot words and threats they neither mean nor plan
to carry out. They misjudge and miscalculate, at times becoming as childish,
or even more so, as the kids they're raising. Their youngsters exasperate them
just as kids everywhere exasperate parents. Scott, father to Sean and Christy,
now both in college, confessed, "There was a period of time with both kids

when we'd rather have just packed them up and shipped them off to somebody, if we could have found somebody stupid enough to take them."

Excellent parents don't necessarily live low-stress lives or raise low-stress kids. Their children are not all docile, eager-to-please creatures who greet them each day with, "Good morning, Mother. I was wondering, do you want me to first mow the lawn by hand to save gas, work ahead three weeks on my homework, or take that punishment you forgot about last week?" If even one kid like this exists in these families, I missed him, or maybe his parents are hiding him somewhere to keep the rest of us from making a parenting pilgrimage to their house.

The children in these families are as real as their parents. They display fits of rebellion, childish shortsightedness, and tolerance for siblings that can vacillate between slight and zero. The teens here, like their peers, are capable of intense anger aimed directly at their parents. "I think the worst times are arguments with my parents. I must admit that much of the time I am the cause of them, but when we are in the middle of a dispute, I could just punch my parents or scream my head off at them," says a fifteen-year-old daughter, who in between arguments calls her parents "the two people I care for most in the whole world."

The remainder of this book will present a variety of ideas and techniques to help you get the most out of your parenting and family life. It will allow you to pick and choose from the best that others have to offer. But to understand what excellent parents are, you must know what they are not.

Excellent parents are not all born to be parents. They are not paragons of patience. They don't have all the answers. They are not living stress-free lives. And they certainly aren't the parents of perfect kids. If they were any of these things, then the quality of their family lives would be nothing special. It would be a common outcome of some uncommon gifts, and we mere mortal parents couldn't relate to these super-parents. Fortunately for us, and for them, these mothers and fathers are quite human.

EXCELLENT PARENTS ARE NOT ALL BORN TO BE PARENTS

Every mother and father we interviewed loved being a parent—not every minute of every day—but overall. Not every parent, though, considered parenthood his or her calling from the beginning. A good number of the children were unplanned and unexpected. A few were born out of wedlock. Some parents had to work hard at accepting the reality of impending parenthood. The prospect wasn't always initially embraced eagerly. Upon learning she was expecting her first child, one mother said, "It wasn't exactly the best news. I think I was more upset than he was." A father recalled, "I couldn't accept my handicapped daughter's condition when she was first diagnosed at birth. I couldn't face up to it and all its ramifications. I felt disappointed in myself." And a mother of two, upon finding out she would soon be a mother of three, admitted, "Our second child was born profoundly mentally retarded. Exhaustive tests found no known cause for the retardation. Therefore, we were reluctant to have another child. My husband and I were older, thirty-six and thirty-four, and had become quite comfortable with our foursome. We were frightened for our baby's health and had mixed feelings about another baby at this point in our lives."

Even when a child was enthusiastically conceived, the feeling of anxiety was sometimes gut-wrenching. "I remember having nightmares about having our first baby and the idea that I wouldn't be able to remember that I had it and to keep track of it. I was unable to imagine what it would be like to have that kind of responsibility," said Sharon from Omaha. Perhaps Tom, looking back at his oldest son Patrick's birth seventeen years ago, best captured many first-time parents' feelings with his simple confession, "I was scared witless."

The range of emotions upon finding out that a first child, or maybe a second, third, post-forty fourth—even an eighteenth—child was on the horizon covered a spectrum from thrill to shock, from acceptance to panic. As the happier emotions are normal, so too are the more unsettling ones. Having at first wrestled with confusion, misgivings, or downright depression at the thought of a baby in no way means you will be less a parent for the experience. Every parent who spoke of early emotional upheaval, during pregnancy or as new parents, grew comfortably into the name *dad* or *mom,* and the children grew comfortably as a result. It isn't so much the emotions you struggle with when they're babies or in the womb that can distort the joy of parenthood. It's the emotions that rock you from toddlerhood through teenhood. These can sidetrack your best intentions, but we'll get to that later.

Sometimes a parent may worry that a second child will detract from the attention, even the love, given to a first child. A number of these parents, too, had these feelings, but they found out almost immediately after the birth of their second that their fears had been totally unfounded. Lois from Minnesota said, "The moment our second child was born I knew that parental love is not a limited quantity. If we would have had five children, we would have loved them all with the same intensity. Certainly in this case, supply meets demand." Barbara, a mother of both natural and adopted children in New York, concurred, "I was concerned how the advent of each new child would take away from the 'quality of life' of the previous children. I didn't realize how much it would add."

There is no need, indeed no reason, for your childrearing to be plagued by guilt left over from years ago because you weren't immediately one hundred percent enthusiastic or accepting of this major life change. Even the best of parents often begin by wrestling with such feelings, and it doesn't stop them from becoming the best.

EXCELLENT PARENTS DON'T LIVE STRESS-FREE LIVES

Some of these parents said they couldn't feel grateful enough for what they considered smooth lives. They acknowledged day-to-day pulls and strains on their family, but on the whole they saw themselves as blessed far beyond their fair share. Others were similarly grateful for their lives, but spoke of stressors that unexpectedly invaded their quiet existence. Chapter 1 gave a brief glimpse of the health handicaps that some families are growing up with. Several families also have lived through the death of a member.

- "We were on our way home from visiting our second child in Los Angeles when we'd gotten word that our daughter, Beth [aged twenty-one], was very sick. She had been sick for about a year, but worked in the hospital [as a nurse] until two weeks before she died. She swore her doctor to secrecy so no one would know that she had leukemia until less than a week before her death, which was a week before Christmas."
- "Our son, Joshua [born with Down's syndrome], was so dear to us. When he died [at age nine months], a part of us died, too. There was an empty spot in our hearts that will always be there. Having him in our lives taught us to really live each day."
- "The worst time in our family was when our oldest brother drowned. It was in the summer before I went into eighth grade. I knew my parents were suffering a lot of grief and stress, but it did not really hit me until I took my home-economics teacher home to meet mama. When mom opened the door to welcome us, I realized in less than three months she had turned gray. It scared me."

Death is the most uncompromising event to affect these families. But they've weathered many other kinds of hardships. John from Atlanta, Georgia, recalls his most self-doubting moment as a father of four:

- "I was unemployed for a long period when the kids were young. The mental pain was great because I had always been taught to provide for my family as best I knew how. It got to a point where my best was my worst. I would just break down and cry, or I would go out in the yard and turn my back to the window and just look up in the sky and cry and wonder. I knew the kids needed things, but they would just make out with what they had. They never complained about what was on the table for dinner."

A few families were stretched nearly to the point of snapping before they rebounded and regained their former stability. Connie, mother to Jenny and Andy, recalls the weeks after the birth of her younger son:

- "I was suffering from postpartum depression, and we were in the middle of a job transfer from Vermont to Delaware. I had to be hospitalized to alleviate all of the outside stresses, and that meant separating the family. This was such a difficult time because my husband and I could not communicate in *any* positive ways. The marriage was strained as far as it could have been, and only the time apart, hospital/professional intervention, and family support for our two young children gave us what we needed to return to health."

A mother of five natural children—and of more than fifty foster children—described this most challenging time in her family's life and what both she and her family gained from it.

- "There was a period when we cared for four severely handicapped children. The task was, at times, overwhelming. One child was a quadriplegic and in an electric wheelchair. Another was a paraplegic in a regular wheelchair and braces, another was a twelve-year-old girl in a twenty-four-hour brace due to fibrous dysplasia, another an eighteen-year-old retarded girl. One of the children had spina bifida and was psychotic and self-destructive. Therefore, we had to keep her with us at all times so we could keep an eye on her. After struggling with these kinds of problems for a period of three years, I took a year off [from foster motherhood] and worked in a preschool handicapped program.

"This whole experience has taught our children compassion and a willingness to share not only their material possessions, but more importantly, their time. They were called upon to share their rooms, toys, space in the car, and time with their parents. We do not believe this has hurt them."

Stress can either make cracks in a family's bond or strengthen it. In the above family, it strengthened it. Michael, now grown, recalls this emotionally trying, yet rewarding period during his young childhood.

- "I remember how devastated my mother was when her own mother died unexpectedly. My mother was so emotionally depleted that she did not have anything leftover to give the family for what seemed like a long time. Being a child, I thought that the world revolved around me, and I did not understand when my mother withdrew from all of us to try and heal herself. It was the first indication I had that there were no guarantees and that death was something that could happen to my brothers, my parents, and even myself. I had to come to terms with one of the basic truths, and I had to do it by myself because my mother could not help me at the time. My father spent a lot of time with me, trying to explain how my mother was feeling and giving me the support I needed. He put the situation into an eight-year-old perspective for me, and eventually I came to terms with the fact that death was natural and not to be feared and worried about. I also came to understand that Mom was human and fallible. It gave her a new dimension. It made me understand and appreciate her more than I had before."

Jacob, a sixteen-year-old from Hot Springs, Arkansas, also believes that hard times can create closer ties.

- "My parents and I have been closest in my most trying times. These were the first days of my junior high school career. Every morning I would wake up with stomach pains and not be relieved of them until three-fifteen in the afternoon. For a solid month, I couldn't stomach any breakfast and would cry before going to school. It wasn't uncommon for me to—how do I put this pleasantly?—'toss my cookies.' As it turned out, these were some of the best times of my life, but I couldn't have made it without my parents."

The same theme surfaces from each family who has withstood life's unpredictable, often random blows. If your family is reasonably sturdy as it enters into a time of trouble, it will emerge even sturdier afterward. Strong families are like steel. When they are softened by fire and then cool themselves, they become emotionally tempered, toughened by the circumstances they were forced to endure. A father in Hawaii summed up this idea: "Children can sometimes learn more from suffering through adversities and setbacks than from successes."

If your family has been faced with more than its share of unavoidable strains, these families are telling you not to despair, for one defining characteristic of a healthy family is resilience, the ability to bounce back to levels even higher than before a slide. In many instances, after all the smoke cleared, these parents were grateful for the chance to learn from their tests.

- "A few years ago I was stricken with a ruptured disc and was confined to bed for three months during the holidays. I was in unbearable pain and worried about how everything would get done for Thanksgiving and Christmas. My son had just turned sixteen and had begun to drive. He took charge, and with his sister kept things organized. They did grocery and Christmas shopping, laundry, housecleaning, cooking, and gardening. Never a word of complaint. They know how much I love Christmas and how unhappy I was not to be able to be up and out of bed during that time. They decorated the whole house and went out on their own and purchased a six-foot tree, which they set up in my bedroom. That was probably the best Christmas of my whole life."

Sometimes life has to put us parents on our backs to make us see how tall our family stands. Most of these parents watched an inner strength surface in their children in the face of hardship. Contrary to many psychological theories which characterize children as fragile little beings capable of being easily shattered if bumped or dropped too hard, the reality these families have experienced indicates that if your children are surrounded by a supportive home life, they are capable of walking through some very unsteady periods and emerging a few inches taller for it. A parent from Columbus, Ohio, summarized it well: "Some of the best of times I have experienced as a parent had to do with difficulties our family has gone through and prayed about—sickness, injury, loss, financial problems—and which have had a happy resolution." Stress is not an antagonist of excellence. It often breeds it.

EXCELLENT PARENTS ARE NOT PARAGONS OF PATIENCE

To be a good—even great—parent you don't need to be a paragon of patience. Your emotional fuse doesn't have to be fifty-feet long—about the length of the average house, with you at one end and the kids at the other. Certainly a long fuse would be desirable, but it's not necessary. Regardless of how long your fuse is, kids can sometimes still burn it all up. Every parent we spoke to talked of losing patience, of overreacting, of feeling nonparental. As long as mothers and fathers are built human, and as long as kids are built human—no matter how competent we get at our calling, no matter how rational we strive to remain—we will have moments (hours?) of irrationality. This does not render us poor parents. While the boiling points of some of these mothers and fathers may be a few degrees above 212 degrees, this seems more the result of years of working at maintaining their cool during hot times. It is not because they were born with the enviable ability to barely even flinch when most of us would get fully riled; rather, calm is a parental state that almost always needs years and a few kids to develop. Furthermore, complete calm is seldom achieved until about four years after the last child leaves.

Here is a sampling of some not-so-fine times experienced by some fine parents, times to which many of us can personally relate:

- "My oldest son had colic the first three months and a cry that made your head vibrate. At the time we were living in a thirty- by eight-foot trailer, so there was no getting away from him. I can remember feeling I would do anything to get him to stop crying. It's a thin line we all walk, and I was thankful for a helpful husband and grandmothers during that time."
- "I can remember putting our five-year-old daughter out of the car and driving up the road, leaving her behind. I had warned her many times to behave or I would stop and put her out. She didn't listen, thinking I wouldn't go through with my threat, but I opened the door and put her out. When I stopped to pick her up, she just got in the car and sat down the rest of the trip. She didn't even cry, but I did. I probably ran out of patience, but that's no excuse. There were many other, better ways to handle it."

- "The worst of times for me as a parent, I suppose, would be those frustrating times when things go wrong and I've heard, 'Why can't I do that?' or 'What should I do?' You just want to tear your hair out of your head and say, 'I could be doing many other things besides staying at home with you children.' It's a frustration that comes with being a parent."
- "I think I may have handled the situation with Kimberly's boyfriend poorly. I think I am a pretty levelheaded, even-tempered person, but I had a difficult time being rational about that turkey. But as I told her and I told the boy she was dating, 'I didn't treat her like I did for eighteen years for you to mistreat her!' I felt strongly about that, and I would never give him my blessing."

The parents agreed: Calmer is better. But they likewise agreed: When parents and kids live together, all cannot be calm. Patience is an ideal to strive for. It is not a day-to-day reality. If you accept that fact, you will be less demanding of yourself and your kids. Emotions are deeply wired into human beings, and most deeply wired into parents. The most laid-back of us can be pushed to rise up angrily. That is the nature of parenthood. More than that, it's the nature of excellent parenthood. Excellent parents care with intensity, so they feel with intensity, and can react with intensity. Every parent here is saying: Allow yourself the reality of your nature. Don't punish yourself because you don't always respond with unflappable patience. With effort and experience, anyone can lengthen his or her emotional fuse, but the fuse will always be there. And that's not all bad.

EXCELLENT PARENTS DON'T HAVE ALL THE ANSWERS

It would be no real feat to stand heads above the parenting crowd if you were gifted with the ability to solve all childrearing dilemmas and difficulties instantly—in other words, if you knew all the answers. When it comes to our kids, I'm sure most of us would be ecstatic to know fifty percent of the answers, or even just to be able to make a good guess.

The parents in this survey have a lot of answers; otherwise, we wouldn't be listening to them. Of the answers they do have, many were learned through experimentation, by a process of elimination. Every mother and father knows the humility inherited from one's children. The most confident, knowledgeable physicist, doctor, or teacher can be reduced to a mumbling mass of uncertainty when forced to deal daily with a five-year-old. Not a single one of these parents claims to have a secret, God-given talent for sizing up children and immediately finding the psychological "cure" for a troubling situation. These parents have learned from experience, the best and most demanding teacher, and they all agree that smart parenthood does not lie in knowing all the answers, but in knowing that you can't know all the answers. Knowing how much you don't know is an indispensable ingredient in being a wise parent.

- "After the twins were born, I had a lot of problems. My husband was working long hours. I had these two babies, and I didn't know a lot about babies. I can remember thinking my whole life has been totally changed and I will never get out of this. I felt I would never again have control of my life."

- "We sought professional counseling for our son when he was seven. He chased his older brother with a metal table, fought, even shoplifted. There was total family disruption due to his name-calling, temper tantrums, intimidation."

- "I see inconsistency as my biggest failure with the children, which breeds self-doubt, which breeds new approaches, and thus further inconsistency. It is a vicious cycle, which is a trap I can fall into easily. The only way I can deal with this is to open myself up for critique by my husband and trust that he can view the situation from outside my cycle of self-doubt. Many a morning cup of coffee has accompanied our discussion of a parenting technique or issue."

- "My husband Stephen has said that I was a great parent when the girls were young. Now I am just a good parent. Dealing with preteen and teenage girls is a mind-boggling, psychologically damaging experience for parents. Now I know why my parents became gray haired. . . . I can't pinpoint a specific time. Things started to change around grades five to seven when hormones, changing bodies, surroundings, and pressures changed the children."

- "For me, early adolescence and teenage years were the most challenging. I remembered my own times of frustration, confusion, and struggle trying to learn who I was and where I was going. I was empathetic with my children and their problems but, because the times were so different from my teenage years, I often felt lost in how to direct them into productive, happy adulthood. I read books, went to discussion groups, and talked with other parents, looking for answers. It was difficult to find clear direction or answers, and this uncertainty caused anxiety. The values and moral attitudes I accepted when growing up are constantly being tested and challenged today."

- "Todd is going through the adolescent period of trying to identify himself. I can't find any way to help him and I find that very frustrating. I don't think there is any way for anybody to help him, he has to do it himself. As Nancy went through adolescence, I didn't even know what she was feeling at all. . . . I can see Todd is struggling with girlfriends. . . . He hasn't learned that when you play real hard in a sport and your team loses, the participation in the game and working as hard as you can is really the fun. He hasn't learned that yet and he doesn't listen, so he'll have to learn on his own. As a father, those kinds of things I can feel, but I haven't the foggiest idea what it feels like to put on your bra for the first time."

For most parents, uncertainty peaks somewhere in the teen years, no matter how smoothly the preceding ten to fifteen years have passed. Indeed, these parents stressed that during adolescence you are sometimes forced to plead ignorance and hope the kids have mercy. Never, but never, though, give up your status as parent, as the one who expects certain behavior, as the one who makes the rules. It is one thing not to know what to do. It is quite another to do nothing. Good parents may be ignorant now and then. They are not apathetic.

There's a bright side to teen turbulence, say these parents. As exasperating as these years can be, the rewards of watching your youngster gradually put into real-life practice the values you've been instilling for over a decade will far outweigh any temporary sense of uncertainty. Ross and Julie, parents of four from Utah, marveled, "The best times of parenting are when we see the values and character traits we've tried to teach being developed and used by our children. The two oldest are now becoming independent enough, free-thinking enough, and free spirited enough to involve these principles in their lives without us being there. It is frightening because our influence is decreasing. But it is gratifying to see that they can incorporate these values and ideas on their own now."

EXCELLENT PARENTS DO NOT HAVE PERFECT KIDS

All children are not created equal. From day one, each child comes into this world with a temperament all his or her own. Some children are born with natures on the mild side. They don't relish pushing parents to the limit, and they have an admirable ability to take the world in stride. Others are born with natures on the wild side. Their will versus your will is their favorite mode of operating.

No doubt about it, some children just make their parents look good. They almost cooperate in their own upbringing. A few of the parents here claim to be raising at least one child of this kind. On the whole, though, the full range of temperaments is present, from the quiet to the rowdy, from the passive to the active.

At times, these kids could be as impulsive and rebellious as all kids can be. They didn't necessarily make their folks' lives a breeze simply because they appreciated their efforts. The family ties were not without some frayed ends.

- One family purchased a large gate to place across their two-year-old's bedroom door to prevent him from wandering the house during the night, opening doors, and turning on appliances.
- One four-year-old cried daily at having to attend preschool and refused to eat anything there for nearly two months. No source of the separation problems could be identified. They disappeared almost as mysteriously as they arose.
- From a son in Nebraska—"How many families have boys who would try to see what five gallons of gunpowder would do to a country bridge, or make homemade guns from matches and bike spokes, or try to hang a brother? We gave him a fair trial."
- A daughter in Wisconsin took a "vow of silence" in the eighth grade in anger at her parents. Every morning before school she refused to speak. This went on for most of the year.
- A seventeen-year-old girl moved out of her family's home for several weeks because of friction over the family's foreign exchange student. She returned home on the advice of a psychologist.
- The second oldest daughter of a very religious family became pregnant out of wedlock—"The hardest time in my life was when I had to tell my parents I was pregnant and not married. I will never forget the pain in their eyes. It would have been easier for me had they yelled and screamed and hated me. But instead, my dad held me on his lap and cried with me and let me know that he loved me."
- From a daughter ready to leave for college—"I think they sort of resent the time I spend with my boyfriend. When I'm not with him, I'm usually

with my friends. As a result I'm not at home as much as my parents would like. They give me early curfews now and that's where the hardships begin. I usually end up coming home later than they tell me just because it aggravates me to think, as an eighteen-year-old, I need my parents to say, 'Be home early so you can get a good night's sleep.' "

As the kids make plain, sometimes they not only don't cooperate in their own upbringing, they downright fight it. And that's standard kidhood. If kids saw parenthood through a parent's eyes, they wouldn't need us to discipline them—they could discipline themselves. On the first day of first grade, we could gently advise Newton, "It's very important to learn your arithmetic, Newton, because you don't know what you'll want to do with your life twelve years from now," and he would respond with immediate gratitude, "Thank you, Father, I see what you're saying." And we'd never have to bring up the matter again. Right!

One final point. Even the best of parents sometimes feel helpless to guide a youngster away from dead-end temptations and toward mature choices. That is one of the scarier realities of childrearing. If this happens to you, it doesn't necessarily mean you fell short somewhere as a parent. It may be that the power of your youngster's temperament is asserting itself over and above your best parenting efforts. There is good news, though. When you've woven a solid value system throughout a child's feisty temperament, even if temporarily she turns slightly away from what she's been taught, eventually your lessons will win out. In the end, her high values will combine with her high spirit to produce an admirable young adult.

To be an excellent parent, you do not need endless patience, all the answers, or easy kids. If this were the case, none of us could be even adequate parents. What we do need is a willingness to learn from our mistakes, from our humanness. This willingness must stay with us always as we mature through CHILDREARING: THE ULTIMATE LEARNING EXPERIENCE.

Chapter 6

Childrearing: The Ultimate Learning Experience

"I do listen to people. I listen very carefully when they talk about their kids, and any good idea, I devour it. If you are smart enough to look around and see what people are doing well, and are able to discriminate, that is what's important."

Mother, Califon, New Jersey

The ancient Greeks gave two basic instructions to their students: One, sit at the feet of the masters. And two, listen. In modern language, hang around those who know something and soak up everything you can. The parents of this book favor learning by the same method. They observe, listen to, study what other parents do. They draw upon their experience, not their advice necessarily, but their actions, positive or negative.

In the healthiest sense, the better parents are users. They use the best of other parents, other families, other children for their own family's benefit. "What worked?"; "What didn't?"; How did everything turn out?"—questions asked either aloud or silently by parents, in the words of a Nebraska mother, "to learn from the victories and failures of others."

- "We had children later than the other members of our families, and we became great observers. Much of what we did or didn't do in our children's earlier lives was influenced by the experiences of others. For example, one brother's children wandered their home all hours of the night, but never had an established bedtime. Our children had a set bedtime, and one we seldom deviated from. We never encountered the problem this brother experienced."

- "Take the opportunity to listen and learn from others. All parents come to the job with fewer tools and skills than will be needed. It is important to continue to learn. I would suggest joining or making up a support or interest group. If you have preschoolers, get to know other preschoolers' parents. The same goes for teenage years or groups that focus on other health or social conditions. If you like to sew, cook, play cards, athletics, etc., join an interest group."

- "Group sessions with similarly besieged parent neighbor-friends—over coffee and donuts, of course—are very helpful. Having had two dogs before we had children was good insight into sibling rivalry, but not good enough!"

- "We had my husband's sister, who was only a phone call away, and you would not believe the calls we made. She was our consultant. She laughed at some of our calls. I feel we learned a great deal visiting with and observing other parents. Exchanging ideas and seeing how they related with their children was invaluable."

A critical distinction must be made here between active listening and passive listening. There is no shortage of people ready to give you unsought advice or comment about your childrearing. They will regularly back up their opinion with the article they read in *Discipline Today Monthly* or the latest talk-show trend. "The toilet trainer they interviewed on *The Thirty-Minute Mother* said that the kinds of school problems your son has are caused by your not spending enough time toilet training him when he was two." A standard hazard of parenthood these days is being the focal point at which several streams of advice—often conflicting and nearly always confusing—converge. Passive listening, or taking to heart what everybody says, is not good for your parental mental health. There is too much information to digest, and struggling to consider it all will only paralyze your ability to decide what's helpful for you and your family. The parents we interviewed strongly warned against letting yourself become prey to unasked-for advice, no matter how well-intentioned. Sherry, mother to Brian (eighteen) and Laura (fifteen), in California, put it plainly, "While we did receive all kinds of advice from parents and friends, we listened to it and then did what we wanted."

Much more beneficial to your emotional well-being is active listening—deliberately choosing to question other parents, to watch them, or to tune in closely when they talk. Active listening is a prime way to sharpen your parenting skills, providing you are, as the mother at the beginning of this chapter said, "able to discriminate."

In so many words, learning from other parents is really the crux of this book. These successful parents, who have learned much from others, are in turn making themselves available to us. They are inviting us to listen in and take from them what we will to make our own families a little stronger.

EXPERTS, EXPERTS EVERYWHERE

Every parent in this book is an expert in his or her own right. How, then, do these moms and dads view the recognized childrearing experts and their advice? A few turned often to the experts for guidance. Jay from Arizona said, "Mary read everything that was ever published! She drove me crazy with Dr. Spock. There was a time when I could have punched him out. She was big into everything that came out—newspapers, magazines, books. She still does that today." Mary was quick to defend herself, though: "We never were the kind to read a book and go with it one hundred percent."

Nancy, mother to David (eighteen), Susan (sixteen), and Julie (thirteen), had similar respect for the experts: "I practically memorized dozens of childrearing books and pamphlets. I always loved to talk with others about the do's and don't's regarding children. I would relate these philosophies to Larry, who would often be better able to sift out ideas and practices that were unrealistic, far-out, etc."

Parents from Oklahoma valued the overall sense of competence gleaned from a wide sampling of the experts: "Jane and I both read a lot of magazines and newspapers. We have always done a lot of current reading, feeling that these are the things that help mold your thinking, not necessarily your childrearing itself, but your overall view of what is going on."

At the other end of the spectrum were those parents who looked to the experts seldom, or who had little use for their ideas:

• "Initially we read books by the experts. After our first child, we junked the books and relied on our intuition and our backgrounds to raise our children."

- "I didn't rely heavily on what the experts said. I thought some of them were full of kidney beans."
- "The more I read, the less attention I paid to what I read."

The majority of parents were neither turned off by the experts nor greatly indebted to them. Their preference was to tap the experts for some guidance, but in so doing, they voiced a number of cautions: The experts are not gospel. They give opinions and suggestions, not truth. They are potential support to good parents, not "the right way." If we as parents don't always view experts for what they are, we will become intimidated by them and doubt our own judgments. After all, we might reason, they are the experts; we are only parents. Further we can quickly fall prey to the false belief that somewhere out there in the mind or book of an expert lies the perfect solution to our particular dilemma. We just have to search until we find it.

A basic belief held by all these parents is that there is no such thing as the right way to raise a child. Said one father, "A long time ago I learned that there is no cookbook approach to raising children, or even to life in general. Childrearing is a blend of things. You learn a little bit from each cookbook. There is no one cookbook that is going to tell you how to do it all." Nancy from Wisconsin advised, "Realize that there is not one perfect way to do it. What feels comfortable for you is many times the thing that is best to do with your children. There are just so many right ways to be a parent."

PICK AND CHOOSE. Etch this phrase into your mind as a parent. It is the right way, if you will, to make the specialists work to your family's full advantage. Take what advice you think would be helpful to your family, ignore that which is contrary to your value system, and discard what isn't working for you. Childrearing specialists may know much about childrearing in general, but they don't know your particular child. Where your youngster is concerned, you are the expert. You must judge how best to practice what other experts say. A mother of four youngsters in Roy, Utah, summed up how most of these parents view the experts, "It is impossible to study childrearing for each particular child. Books represent ideas or help, but each child is so different that he has to be treated as such."

In the main, the experts are nice to have around—I should say this, I'm called one. Experts inject a healthy flow of new ideas into parenting, ideas much in need as this world becomes a more tricky and complicated place to raise kids. But experts can never take over the job of childrearing. Parenthood belongs first in the hands of parents. It always will.

COMMON SENSE: A PARENT'S PERSONAL GUIDE

Common sense, instincts, judgment—words these parents used repeatedly in describing successful childrearing. The opinion was nearly unanimous: Good parenthood is grounded on good sense. When asked what advice they would most want to give their children when they became parents, Ed and Elizabeth from Ohio shouted out simultaneously, "Use common sense!"

Listening and learning from others is invaluable to skilled parenthood, as we've stressed, but ultimately you must decide how to put all advice into action. No two parents, no two children, no two families are exactly alike. Therefore, you are forced to rely heavily on your judgments, because nothing else could ever perfectly fit the variety of situations you encounter in a week, much less in a parenting lifetime. Other people can provide great support, but a parent's closest ally is her own judgment, honed sharper by the experiences she faces daily.

When asked, "How did you prepare for parenting?" these parents consistently underscored the importance of developing self-trust in guiding one's childrearing:

- "It is important not to take advice from everyone around you. I think raising children is as much on instinct as it is on education or being advised on it. How things work for Rita and I would never work for some other people."
- "As a teenage baby-sitter, camp counselor, and nurse, I have observed many families and have sifted through my impressions for both positive and negative examples of parenting. Many of these experiences were guides for me, as well as experiences of friends whose children were older than ours. In general, however, I have relied on my gut feeling to guide me when making difficult decisions. An example: I was promoted from first to third grade and was thereafter the youngest and smallest child in the class. I did well in school, but always felt at some disadvantage socially. When we were asked, then advised, to have our daughter skipped ahead a grade, my gut feeling was to say no. We did some research among friends who had similar experiences themselves or with family members, and the common feeling was that the practice was inadvisable for social reasons. We declined, some curriculum changes were made, and our daughter remained with her class.

The outcome has been fine. The child has been challenged, is secure socially, and has thanked us."

- "As each child was born, we were more relaxed and confident. We progressively matured spiritually and relied more on common sense and intuition rather than on experts."

What is common sense? The phrase is bandied about so routinely that most people just assume everybody agrees on its meaning. This is not always the case. Before we talk any further about common sense, including its relatives—judgment, instincts, good sense—we'd better give these words a working definition. Let's call common sense the ability to make a reasonable decision based upon what we know about a situation and what end we want to achieve. Even with this broad definition, there are those people who suspect that common sense isn't so common. Fortunately, most of us have developed at least some common—or maybe uncommon—sense, even if just by virtue of having lived a few decades. We depend upon it every day in making choices about our careers, finances, marriages, and our families. Common sense in childrearing is deciding on a course of action based upon *our* value system, *our* family, and *our* kids. It can be applied to something as major as whether to permit Mario to buy his own car at age sixteen or to something as everyday as trying to reduce Gale's temper storms to three an hour.

Plain, old-fashioned common sense has slipped somewhat from the parenting scene these days because, with all the "new, proven effective" childrearing theories floating around, parents begin to believe that good sense just isn't good enough anymore. In fact, good old common sense is a primary route that "proven effective" parents choose to take. Suppose that during one of her temper storms, three-year-old Gale is venting her rage on your shins with her feet. Now, some theories would advise you first to identify Gale's anger for her, "Gale, I'm sensing a lot of frustration," and then to let her know how you feel, "I'm not comfortable with your foot hitting my shin at forty miles an hour." If Gale is immediately subdued, "Gosh, Father, I didn't realize that hurt. I've been so impulsive," you'd better do either of two things. One, throw away this book. You don't need it. You have a rare parenting magic the rest of us can only marvel at. Or two, take Gale to the doctor; she's got a fever. On the other hand, if your attempts to reason with Gale are having about as much impact as ping-pong balls against the hull of a battleship, common sense would dictate that you stop Gale from kicking you, move away from her flailing feet, and then discipline her for her nastiness. Nothing psychologically fancy, just definite action based upon your appraisal of the situation. Common sense means looking for the most simple, straightforward solution to solving a problem.

Then, too, sometimes parents are uneasy about trusting their instincts where their families are concerned. They feel that, with so much at stake, maybe they'd better look for something more "sophisticated" than instincts. They get nervous about the possible emotional repercussions of a bad decision. Shortly, these families will help us calm these kinds of worries. For now, putting more confidence in our judgments begins by remembering what some uncommon parents say. It is all right, even desirable, to listen to yourself more than anyone else. Susie from Wyoming concludes, "The best [childrearing] activity for me was to come to my own personal faith. As I am more confident in my judgments and intuition, I have become a better parent."

THE PERSONALITY OF A PARENT

What qualities make good parents? This is a question we asked these parents. At first glance, their answers may seem a bit surprising, but the more you ponder them, the more sense they make.

Mention the word *childrearing* to someone, and you're likely to call to his mind words like *consistency, positive reinforcement, parent-child bonding, active listening.* A pervasive image of childrearing the past few decades is that it is largely a series of techniques one applies to a particular child in a particular situation to achieve a particular result. Put another way, competent parenting is the smart application of a set of "proven" childrearing principles.

Nobody would deny that a fundamental of good parenting is knowing something about kids and their development. With so much attention given to substance, though, style is being pushed into the background. That's unfortunate for parents, because while possessing certain parenting "skills" is important, the real value of those skills depends upon the person who practices them. A wise parent is willing and eager to put into action words like *consistency* and *active listening.* An even wiser parent realizes that the effectiveness of any parenting approach is inextricably tied to what kind of person he is. In essence, our personhood sets the tone for our parenthood.

- "I would rank patience among the highest childrearing qualities. Larry always treated others, young or old, with patience."

- "The best thing a father can do for his children is to love their mother."
- "I believe that part of what makes a good parent has to do with personalities, the ability to deal with unknown situations, and the unexpected. I think the single most important thing that makes Stephen and I good parents is our role with each other. We are good people, I think, and good friends."
- "I didn't look for any parenting qualities in Bruce whatsoever before marriage. I viewed him in light of his personal, humanistic qualities, how he related to me and other people. Those qualities I admired most were a sense of commitment, a sense of adventure, a sense of humor, and a sense of trust."
- "She's as good a mother as she is a companion and friend to me."
- "I had no idea how strict Bill would be as a father, but I did know he would be loving because of the way he treated me. I was right."
- "The qualities I looked for in a spouse would naturally be good child-raising qualities: kindness, warmth, gentleness, intelligence, good humor, honesty, selflessness, integrity, courage, common sense, wisdom."

Finally, a dad who is a dentist said he valued "mental stability, intelligence, and good teeth."

These observations convey the feeling of virtually all the parents: The "heart" of a parent is more vital to family success than her childrearing "mechanics." What kind of person you are will have far more impact on your children than the fact that you can reflect feelings with the precision of a counselor or that on your better days your discipline consistency rate hits sixty-four percent (exceptionally high if raising kids under ten years old; unattainable if raising kids over ten). Stephen, father to Sarah and Emily (aged thirteen and eleven), from West Virginia, asserted, "My parenting style has evolved out of my personality. To act any other way would be a form of faking it, and children are unbelievably sensitive to fakers." Giving her husband her ultimate parenting compliment, a wife said, "He has qualities that make a home happy on a general basis, and not necessarily child-specific."

On the whole, these should be comforting observations. Most of us are good people. We have our rough edges, maybe a lot of them, but we're working to smooth them. And certainly we're striving to be better parents. Your picking up this book is evidence of that fact. If someone were to ask you, however, "Are you a better person or parent?" what would you say? If you'd answer "person," you'd have a lot of other parents for company. Many parents these days have much more confidence in their ability to be good people than to be good parents. Part of the reason for this is that everybody—the experts, media, other parents—tell parents how to be parents. You are so relentlessly bombarded with all you should be saying and doing in the name of childrearing that you simply can't measure up to it all. Who could? No wonder so many parents feel they can't master all the basics of childrearing. There are a lot more basics than there used to be.

Many parents wonder if they even have the personality or makeup to be a competent parent. For instance, they might consider themselves too emotional or too reactive and not laid-back enough. These kinds of worries are unfounded, for a couple of reasons. First, there is no perfect personality for a parent, just as there are no perfect parents. Each of us has characteristics that are natural for raising some kids and not so natural for others. One mother observed, "A mother or father cannot be all things to all children, so there are bound to be weak and strong areas in a child's development." In essence, no parenting style can be "right" for all children. Second, nearly every personality characteristic affects childrearing in many different ways. For example, your emotionality may trigger you to shoot off lines like, "I can't wait until you have six kids just like you" (Watch out, you'll be the grandparent of those kids!), but it also is the very trait that underlies how easily you show affection or how quickly you sense how little Newton feels after he's failed his first math test.

To begin relieving any doubts you might have about your childrearing skills, remind yourself of what some good people are saying: The basics of good parenting evolve from the basics of good personing. Sharpen up some of your childrearing "techniques" while you strive to become a better person, and you've got an unbeatable combination for raising kids.

Common sense, instincts, childhood memories, hang around and listen, pick and choose—key phrases to keep always in mind. They will direct you to more self-assured parenting. They will also help you take maximum advantage of all the parenting experience and advice of others. There is, however, one more group of childrearing specialists to consider. They are the most obvious, yet most overlooked. We'll hear from them next when we ask the question PARENT AND CHILD: WHO'S RAISING WHOM?

Chapter 7

Parent and Child: Who's Raising Whom?

"Children are vocal and as they speak their minds, you learn. Listen to their sounds, to the way they're behaving, to the way they're reacting. It's an incredible way to learn."

Mother, Middlebury, Vermont

*P*arents, family, friends, experts—plenty of people are ready and willing to give you their counsel, solicited or not, on how you should raise your kids. As we noted last chapter, some advice can be indispensable. Some adds only a little to basic common sense. And some is outright useless, even self-defeating. After all is said and read, you must decide on whom and what to heed and how to put any suggestion into practice in your home. In the extreme, you could ignore everybody and venture totally on your own into that unpredictable turf called childrearing. Though unwise, you could do it with relative ease since, most likely, none of these other childraisers live in your home.

There is another group of childrearing consultants—some parents consider them the leading experts—whom we haven't yet identified. These individuals can't readily be ignored. They do dwell in your house, and in your backyard, your car, your basement—in short, everywhere you do your parenting. They are your children, the people on the "receiving" end of all that we older folks call childrearing. Most everyone else who gives us advice is similar to us, that is, they are parents or at least adults looking at kids through adult eyes. It seems safe to say that ninety-nine-plus percent of all the childrearing advice ever written originates from adults. The kids are rarely sought out for their opinions. And that's surprising, because only the kids live every day with what we do, and only the kids can give a childlike perspective to childrearing. It's only natural that they could teach us much, whether they mean to or not.

Nearly all of these exceptional parents looked to others to help them improve their parenting. How much each parent took from anyone else was primarily a matter of choice and style. Without exception, every parent relied heavily on her own children to help her progress day by day as a parent. According to Connie from Ohio, "I think our children are constantly teaching us to be better parents. This is a give-and-take relationship on both sides. In one sense, every time you observe a child's reaction to your action, you learn to be a better parent. You learn what is effective and what isn't." Never-ending feedback from her children was Connie's main tool for sharpening her childrearing skills.

Ernie, a father to seven, thanks his children for guiding him gently in his emotional development as a father. They are responsible for much of his ongoing self-inspection. "With each child, I have personally grown in terms of being a better parent and in terms of being more understanding and more sensitive. It isn't easy to be a parent, but each child helps you to adjust and make changes."

Perhaps Jay from Phoenix summarized best the feelings of most mothers and fathers, "We had to learn how to be parents at the same time our kids were learning how to be kids."

From all parents, the message was similar: Children are natural-born teachers of childrearing. Hear what they say. Listen to what they don't say. Watch their actions and reactions. There is no limit to what we can gain from children. We are bound only by our willingness to pay attention and let their words and behavior guide us. If we often don't pick up on the kids' lessons, that may be because they hold up pieces of our personality we don't want to see. So we resist seeing them. Unfortunately, the longest-lasting lessons are those most painfully learned. By that standard, kids are consummate teachers. Their lessons are hard-hitting, but critical to our maturation as parents, and to their maturation as children.

What follows are the most valuable lessons some skilled parents have learned, sometimes reluctantly, from the minds and mouths of their children. Reading how the lessons were delivered should help us be more sensitive to our own youngsters' attempts to teach the same things.

LESSON #1: SHOW AND TELL: UNCONDITIONAL LOVE

At the heart of all quality parenting is unconditional love. No matter what our child does, our love for him will never cease. Nor will it rise and fall with his behavior. Our anger fluctuates, so too our joy, our hurt, our disappointment, and every other emotion, but never our love. Love is constant.

Unconditional love is the basis for every parenting decision and action. It is the driving force behind all discipline. A Montana mother, who prided herself on being a solid disciplinarian, declared, "Without unconditional love, discipline is irrelevant." Unconditional love is so central to effective parenting that it will be dealt with in more depth in chapter 13, "The Will to Discipline." For now, let's hear what these parents have discovered about children's capacity for unconditional love:

- "What comes to mind is how the children are so forgiving. If I have had a bad day and have been a grouch, I apologize to the kids, and they *always* say, 'That's okay, mom.' They also display great capacity to love one another. Sometimes when I think they could kill each other, I observe that, if one is in need, they automatically come to his rescue."
- "Parents need praise and encouragement, love and approval, just as children do. So often the children reinforce parental decisions, show love and approval of us, and even offer praise. When that happens, we become better parents with a better family."
- "Our children always display their love and affection for each other, traits not at first inherent in our family. Our feelings and emotions were usually silent, but we found it became easy and natural to adopt the ways of our children."
- "Our oldest daughter is a very affectionate and loving child. She writes little notes to us, hugs us, and tells us she loves and appreciates us. She has sensitized us to be more openly loving and affectionate."
- "The kids are supportive and understanding in so many ways—when we scold them before we listen, when we are sick, they offer to help. It seems no matter how bad our mistake, they still love us."

Unconditional love is an attribute every person worthy of the name "parent" possesses. Our "like" for our children may disappear for a few minutes, hours, even days, but our underlying love always remains. It is ever-present, even though we don't always express it, because we're tired, or upset, or just not thinking. By being so ready to forgive and forget, the kids are modeling unconditional love in action. Every parent in these families, no matter how loving, will confirm that *nobody* is better than children at reminding us to show and tell the love we feel inside. A mother from Nebraska concludes, "There is so much all of us could learn from the children as far as trust, faith, and most of all, love."

LESSON #2: LOOK IN THE MIRROR

Want to hear what you sound like as a parent? Want to see what you look like? What you act like? Look in your personal mirror—your child. Kids are a near perfect reflection of our childrearing style and habits. Like sponges, they absorb our everyday actions—good and bad—and like mirrors, they reflect back at us what we are, sometimes when we most need to face it. Few techniques for self-improvement are more revealing than the opportunity to watch oneself in action, even if in miniature replay.

Betty, mother to three daughters, twins aged thirteen and a seven-year-old, has long since realized the worth of watching herself in her girls. Their actions speak louder to her than do her words to them. "You tell your children the way to be, but they model their behavior on the way that you are. That is constantly, sometimes happily and sometimes painfully, reflected back to me. If I am acting a certain way and the kids are giving me feedback, I try to be open to it and let it be instructive. Regardless of how I think I am, what the girls see may be different." Betty listens with her eyes.

Jay from Phoenix says that his son Jason "has taught me some things about myself. He has shown me some of my weaknesses. For example, once in a while he loses control for a few minutes. I see that in me. I see me in him." Witnessing his son act independent of reason provides a vivid picture for Jay to consider each time his own temper threatens to control him. The angry image of himself, years younger, has a potent braking effect on his own emotions.

Not images but words give Julia, mother of two from Wisconsin, her most undistorted portrayal of herself. "The most enlightening times for me are hearing my own words come back. I remember one time when David was in the third grade. He was trying to talk to me and get me to listen. He finally said, 'Mom, you are listening to me, but you are not hearing!' I stopped in my tracks. That little person was able to be that sensitive and say, 'Hear me.' " Kids are wily little beings. They know that if they bounce our own words back at us rather than use their own, they have to say much less to get our attention.

Then, too, sometimes children don't even resort to words. Their faces alone reflect the effect of our actions. "Sometimes, I will see that look from my kids, especially the littler ones, that lets me know I blew it. It usually involves a temper outburst or me not acting rationally, either saying or doing something I don't mean. Looking at the kids, I'll know immediately that, instead of teaching them something, I just hurt their feelings."

And finally, how many parents have been audience to a childlike reenactment of their own discipline style? Becky from Las Vegas, after overhearing her five-year-old and eight-year-old at play, realized it was time to make some adjustments in her approach. "They interact with each other using words and a tone that sounds all too much like me."

Anybody can give you his personal impression of your parenting personality and technique, but nobody can present you with a more lifelike image of you than your own kids. If you want firsthand, realistic feedback of your childrearing style, watch and hear your kids. They'll show you what you are without the distortions that can accompany someone else's subjective opinion. So say parents who have encountered themselves in their children so many times that they began to wonder who was the real parent and who was the image.

There's a bright side to being forced to confront ourselves. While our children's portrayal of us may not always be flattering, it does prove one thing: They are absorbing our lessons. The fact that they are able, with such precision, to parrot our weaker points, is solid evidence that our stronger points are living in them, too. It's simply not possible for our kids to be keenly aware of our bad sides while being oblivious to our good ones. Kim from Pennsylvania said she finally realized this when her nine-year-old son, Nicholas, at a time she least expected, turned to her and said, "If you wouldn't have told me to do that, I would have done it by myself anyway because I know better." So there, mom.

LESSON #3: PRACTICE WHAT YOU TEACH

Anyone who advises you on childrearing is telling you how and what to teach your children. Unless that person lives with you, though, he or she can't know to what degree you yourself live what you teach, or if, as one Alabama mother phrased it, you "make your walk match your talk." Conscientious parents understand well that teaching by example is a cornerstone of successful parenting, but understanding does not translate perfectly into action. Many of these mothers and fathers confessed that living their own lessons was the unending challenge of their parenthood. They freely admitted to needing constant reinforcement, and so they turned to the only people present every day to monitor whether or not they were making their walk match their talk:

- "My kids are very inquisitive. If they hear something, but they don't catch it all, they ask me further. If I tell them, 'No, not now,' they will say, 'You have always told us to talk to you, and we are asking you a question right now.' They are telling me that the morals and the values we set for them, we have to set for ourselves, too."
- "Three years ago, Hans and I went fishing with three other fathers. We had gotten lost in the morning and were back in some real hard undergrowth, carrying canoes and getting frustrated. A lot of energy had been lost. Finally, we came to a lake and were ready to fish. Hans got snagged up in the rocks again, and I swore at him. He said, 'Dad, don't cuss at me. I want you to raise me good!'"
- "One of the characteristics that my father had was a terrible temper. I have some of that, and my children have helped me with it. If I say something that is out of line, the littlest one will tell me about it. If even my littlest one recognizes that I'm saying something I shouldn't, it really helps."
- "I have a tendency that when I get hurt, I strike out. I talk about people [behind their back], and that is not a nice trait. In fact, my children have talked to me about that. Kevin is particularly good at pointing out to me what a useless waste of energy this habit is. He has made me a better parent for it. Kids see things in you that you don't see in yourself sometimes, and they'll point them out."
- "Our eldest is a person who cannot stand tension between family members;

therefore, he will apologize sooner than anyone. He has taught me humility."

- "We always said to our children, 'We don't compare you to other children,' but yet we would ask our children to compare us with other parents, of course to make us look better. Our daughter pointed out this contradiction to us."

This mom and dad were brave. Most parents won't chance asking the kids to compare them with other parents. We already hear daily that we're the meanest, strictest, most old-fashioned parents in North America.

Children will not tolerate us getting away with less than we ask of them. If we curse, smoke, lose our temper, put down others, avoid worship services, leave our half-filled glass on the television, walk through the house with muddy shoes, and these are all things we won't let them do, we're going to hear about it, even if it's under their breaths, with their backs to us, on the other side of their locked bedroom door. If we require our kids to save part of their allowance, complete projects they start, call friends when they've promised, scrub behind their ears, then we'd better be prepared to follow similar paths in our own lives, or once again be prepared to have our inconsistencies pointedly held up for us, or for anybody else nearby, to see. Should we try to ignore them, the kids will be relentless. Nielsen may "forget" to turn off the TV during supper, but he'll never forget that we just forgot to turn off the TV during supper. In a way, that's fine. Who of us doesn't need to be regularly reminded that the best teaching is living a positive example?

Perhaps more often than most, these parents heard plainly from their children when they were pursuing a double standard—one for them and one for the kids. In fact, it was this constant feedback that helped them become the parents they are now. To be sure, being a parent conveys major rights the children don't have, for instance, the right to discipline and to make certain decisions for their welfare, but being a parent doesn't convey the right to close oneself to whatever validity lies in a child's observations. If we aren't too quick to defend our actions with, "I'm the parent here," the kids will, using our own lessons, make us better parents, indeed better persons.

LESSON #4: LISTEN BEFORE YOU LEAP

"Now you listen here, young man"; "When are you going to listen?"; "You're not listening to a thing I'm saying." These lines share two qualities: One, they're phrases parents probably deliver thousands of times per child. Two, each contains some form of the word *listen*. All are outspoken evidence of just how much we parents want our kids to listen to us, be it our request for Hazel to dry the dishes before the all-night movie station signs off, or our lecture to Winston about smoking, or our opinion of Faith's fickle friend.

Obviously, communication travels in two directions. More effective parenting doesn't only mean finding ways to make our kids better listeners. It also means making ourselves better listeners. Over and over, good mothers and fathers consider a parent's ability simply to say nothing and listen to a child as a key to encouraging two-way communication and to improving their own parenting. Paul and Sandy from New Jersey have discovered, "At times, a child's insight is a lot more genuine and not as tainted as an adult's. When you're dealing with children, and you listen to what they're saying, not being rigid in your thinking, you are learning and improving on your parenting all the time."

Preaching silence, however, is much easier than practicing silence, especially anywhere in the near vicinity of kids. Fortunately for us, the kids stand ever-ready and willing to inform us loudly that if we expect them to listen, we'd better do our share of shutting up and listening, too.

Robin from California learned early in her motherhood that she would not be allowed to carry on the pretense of listening. She'd better give her three-year-old some legitimate answers, or else. "Merritt was at her always-ask-why stage. We were in the kitchen together, and I was not paying full attention to her questions, but instead adding umm's and oh's at random. Finally Merrit said, 'Would you please stop that and grow up and talk like a mom!'" It may seem like we're appeasing the kids if we react absently to their questions or comments, but they'll eventually catch on, though it may take them all of five seconds or so.

Robin learned another lesson in listening from her older daughter, Mandy, then aged six. "Mandy didn't want a permanent. I made her get one. Afterward, she told me again that she didn't like it and didn't want it. I asked her why she didn't say something before. She said she'd tried, but I wasn't listening, so she finally stopped trying."

Toddlers and preschoolers are most grateful for our attention. What they are saying to us may be no more earth-moving than, "Mommy, I moved the chair so I could sit better," but to them, the action is momentarily at the center of their world. Good listening does not mean ceasing whatever we're doing to give our little one our full concentration each and every time he makes it obvious that's what he wants. Other demands on our life don't allow that. Good listening is attempting, whenever possible, to keep an ear open to what a child is asking or saying, even if he takes several hundred words to get to the point.

One mother said she raised her listening potential by keying on particular phrases used by her children when younger to add weight to their words. These were: "Mom, I'm talking"; "Listen to me"; "Did you hear me?"; and her favorite, "Mom, I'll stop if you answer me." She believes that parents are wise to tune out or call an end to relentless nagging for the sake of their sanity. She also believes that children have special ways to tell us they know we're only going through the motions of listening. When mom heard these signals, she asked herself, "Am I really listening?"

A youngster in Ohio, when he was not yet two years old, would take his father's face into both hands and pull it toward his own as if to emphasize, "Hey, I'm talking to you." Dad said he didn't allow this practice to evolve into rudeness, but he admitted it often made him stop and acknowledge his son's presence. Little children don't worry about subtleties when it comes to grabbing a parent's attention.

Young children don't usually worry about our opinion of what they're saying. They just like having our ear. Older children know we have our viewpoint and will probably give it. They prefer that we listen awhile before we do. Pat, a single mother of Laura and Charla (eighteen and seventeen), said that her daughters have taught her to control her mouth during those times when her words are only getting in the way. "I have a tendency to lecture. The kids teach me that sometimes I just need to listen, to learn that I can't protect them from everything that is unpleasant and sometimes to give them the freedom to make a mistake."

Debra, a mother of six (ages two through twelve), needed repetitions of the same theme from more than one of her children to hear what they were saying. She said their message eventually sunk in. "Many times one of our daughters has come to me wanting to talk about something and, as an introduction, has asked me not to say anything until she is all done so she can express everything she wants. Usually, she is asking something she knows we will say no to, but the lesson is still there. The kids want us to listen and not always be interrupting or cutting short conversations with all of our 'advice and counsel.' "

Anger is an emotion that parents contend with often. If we listen before surging ahead with our words, we may discover that what we thought we were upset about didn't exist. "Sometimes we get mad at the kids before finding out all the details. But if we just listen before the emotion hits, we find out things weren't that bad, and we learn not to jump to a hasty conclusion. Listening has also taught us to tell the kids when we are wrong." A father in Kansas was similarly grateful to his son for providing a safety mechanism for his "jump-to-a-hasty-conclusion" style. "The oldest son will often say simply, 'Stop and think about that, Dad.' Of course, he's right."

When children teach parenting, they emphasize the basics. Instinctively, they realize that the foundation for good communication is elegantly straightforward: Listen first, talk later. Kids don't get caught up in all the fancy, sometimes artificial-sounding intricacies of communication. They aren't concerned about us phrasing our questions with just the right words, or whether we say umm-hmm after each of their sentences to convey we're "comfortable with where they're coming from." Their main request of us is: "Hear me out."

Of course, to make sure we do hear them out, kids often get pretty agitated. Sometimes they'll try to overwhelm us with the sheer number and volume of their words. Sometimes they'll repeatedly interrupt us if they think we haven't given them a fair hearing. Sometimes they'll trick us into believing they'll eventually wind down if we just listen to them drone on a little further. Knowing firsthand the incredible verbal stamina of the average child, these parents are offering a caution. Listening does not include allowing Polly to argue endlessly, to abuse you verbally, or to become nasty. Such reactions don't fall under the heading of open communication. Quite the contrary, they are definite signs that the discussion should be closed. Polly certainly isn't paying attention anymore. By allowing the debate to drag on, we're doing little to foster the skill of listening for her or us. Open communication does not mean open season to blast parents verbally. Retha, mother to Clay and Cole, spoke for most parents when she said, "I let my kids tell me if they think I've treated them unfairly, *if* they say it in a respectful manner." Otherwise, until they decide to treat mom with the respect they themselves are asking, they've temporarily forfeited their right to be listened to.

A parent of three said her favorite method for teaching her youngsters how to speak with respect began when they were preschoolers. The instant mom felt the kids were not being polite, or at least civil, she said, "Go to the thinking chair until you can find a nicer way to talk." The thinking chair was an overstuffed chair in the living room. If the kids came back and still didn't speak politely, mom escorted them back to the chair, and she determined when they could leave it. The thinking chair had fewer occupants as the kids learned to speak their mind diplomatically the first time around.

While acknowledging kids' innate tendency to get overzealous in making their points, the better listening parents we heard still agreed: Kids teach the art of listening better than anyone. They'll inform us that to be heard more, we usually have to talk less.

LESSON #5: KEEP A YOUTHFUL PERSPECTIVE

Children do not see parenthood through the eyes of parents. This is a most basic truth of childrearing. If we overlook this truth for even one minute, as the next chapter will show, anxiety and frustration will follow, as we struggle in vain to make our youngster understand our parental intent, something he's not easily able to do simply because he's a child. There is a positive side to kids' not looking at life from our perspective. Sometimes their childlike slant is just the fresh angle we parents need. Rather than exasperate us, their view may actually help us form a more complete picture, and thereby make our parenting a little easier. Bob, a father made more open-minded by living for years with his sons, commented, "Sometimes my sons saw something good in a thing when I didn't. Sometimes they saw humor when I didn't. They've made me slow up and look at things with a different perspective." Here's what some other mature parents have learned about the value of a youthful perspective:

- "In New Orleans, where I was working my way up the academic ladder, I became obsessed with writing papers on my work with CT scans of the spine. I found myself at the hospital every weekend seeing the patients I couldn't get to during the week. Finally, our Emily, then about three years old, asked me if I loved my machine more than I loved my family."
- "By really listening to what Michael and Kristen had to communicate— both verbally and by their manner—they were often telling us how the world impacted on them. When Kristen was about seven, two of her friends' parents were in the process of getting divorces. One day Kristen asked if her dad and I would be getting a divorce. That was a real shocker, but it made us realize how events outside of our family could threaten her sense of family security. By trying to be sensitive to these, we learned to monitor and adjust our actions and methods as parents."
- "It was during the 1970's. The style for boys was to let their hair grow

fashionably long. We were not used to long hair, and the parents who had 'control over their children' seemed to be able to control the length of their teenager's hair. I did *not* have this control. I guess we were on Carl a lot over this. Then, one day he said to us, 'Exactly what do you want from me? I make good grades. I go to church. I'm not on drugs, and I don't smoke or drink!' After that, we accepted or tried to accept the antics of teenagers in as calm a way as possible."

- "My children teach me not just to be a better parent, but a better person. I was complaining about a basketball coach, and my middle son, who is on his team, looked up and said, 'Mom, he's doing the best he can do, and I don't want to hear any more about it.' "

Observing life through a child's eyes not only will make us more sensitive parents, but will also calm a few of our worries. Every loving parent wants to shield her children wherever possible from hardships and pain. Typically, we hurt for the kids more than they hurt for themselves. If we give credence to their perspective, though, our children will give back to us some peace of mind, because what they are often saying, with or without words, is, "Give us credit. We're made of tougher stuff than you think."

Jay and Mary's daughter, Meisha, underwent major surgery when she was nine years old. Understandably, they were frightened and feeling very sorry for her, that is, until Meisha showed them how to handle pain. "Our daughter has taught us to be stronger parents through her heart surgery. She was such an example of strength. She never complained, even after going back to the hospital again because of complications. She always had a smile, while we had to struggle not to be gloomy around her. My wife would say, 'She is acting great. Why are we acting like this?' Even today my daughter quietly lets me know if I'm getting out of hand."

Vallie from Florida has met a similar challenge with her son, Chip, now eighteen. At age seven, Chip was diagnosed with a brain tumor that threatened his life. Vallie might not have been able to cope with her son's illness and its continuing effects had not Chip, as a young boy, put his mother's hurt into soothing perspective for her. "I have to give my son, Chip, four shots a week because he has a chronic illness. He has helped me get through that. When I first started giving him the shots, I would just cry. He was about eleven years old, and it was killing me to have to do this to him. He would just say, 'Mom, don't worry about it. You are not hurting me. You are helping me.' "

Children size up life with an innocence that can frighten parents. Yet, often it is that very innocence which makes us confront our own locked-in notions about the world. "The children's fresh viewpoints have often taught us to be better parents. One instance that comes to mind is the time I heard from a third party that one of my sons had been discussing his early morning paper route, being out alone in the dark delivering papers. When commenting on this, he said he felt the streets were better off because he was out there on them! On hearing about this remark, I learned a little more about trust. It taught me, too, something about letting go of children when they are ready for it."

Sometimes, we parents require continuing reminders of our children's emotional recuperative powers—powers that often exceed our own. Jane from Oklahoma recalls, "The boys were on a basketball team that lost a lot of games. I remember one time they came home from a game and there were tears. Willie and I hurt with them, and we cried right along with them. The next morning they were over it already, and we were still hurting."

Kids are not only more durable than we think, but some have an innate gift for quickly simmering down a near-boiling situation. Too busy being mad right along with us, they don't always use their gift, but when they do, with minimal words they supply a quiet lesson about the futility of overtalking.

- "My son will sometimes quietly point out to me during an argument, 'Your negative self is coming out.' He often gives messages that help put things back in place. For example, when I get excited, I tend to yell without realizing it. He'll say, 'You don't have to yell. I'm standing right here.' "

"Negative self"? "Messages"? "You don't have to yell"?—I think this youngster is headed for some kind of career in counseling. He's already familiar with the basic lingo!

- "Karen was having a problem with a subject, and we went into the back room to talk about it. I was getting upset with her not telling me what the matter was with this particular subject or class. Diane, her sister, was just sitting there with tears in her eyes. I said, 'What's the matter with you?' I can't remember her exact words, but she said something like, 'Well, you're just going to sit there and yell at her.' That upset me. I think about that even now."
- "They teach me to be a better parent precisely when they bring my

attitude to my attention. For example, 'Mommy, why are you mad at me?' always startles me and makes me stop, think, and zero in on what is really bothering me."

- "One time I was hollering at Kevin, and he said, 'Mom, I think you are hollering at me because you had a bad day.' I said to him, 'Kevin I think you are absolutely right.'"
- "I think I push Neil too hard sometimes. I am a little too critical at times, and I have to back up and put my arms around him. . . . I think of my youth and what type of person I was and the things I would like to change. Consequently, there are times when I jump on him a little too hard. He will say simply, 'Dad, I don't know what you want.'"

It stings enough when we're on a verbal roll and the kids jolt us to a dead stop with a few accurate, softly spoken words. Sometimes, they don't even need words to make us reassess our style. "We had gone inside to buy a snack and wander through the gift shop. One of the twins [aged three] accidentally knocked over a rack of merchandise. I reprimanded him and had him help me pick it up. I was surprised to see how embarrassed he was. I realized right there that discipline had not been needed because what happened was an accident, and that even if discipline were called for, it did not have to include embarrassment."

Of course, the elite of parenting instructors not only say nothing to get their point across, they do nothing. "When the boys are asleep at night and look like little cherubs, I always regret having been short-tempered with them or not so understanding. It reminds me that they're just little boys—and a very precious gift." And crafty, too, lying there sweetly just so mom will take stock of her behavior that day. Always thinking, those kids, even when they're not thinking.

If you want to raise your patience threshold a degree or two every night, after the kids are asleep, quietly spend a few moments in their rooms pondering how much they mean in your life. Carlene, the Delaware mother just quoted, believes this will strengthen your resolve to be slightly less uptight with them in the future, even if that resolve only lasts until they wake up tomorrow.

One closing comment before summing up. No matter how open-minded we are as parents, on countless occasions we and the kids will not be of one mind on an issue. And that's to be expected. In fact, more often than not, a child's perspective is not a good one upon which to base parenting decisions.

Routinely, we must make our judgments over Perry and Mason's vehement objections. After all is said and heard, we are older, usually wiser, and overall better equipped to be parents than kids are. Given this thought, fix in your mind the main reality underlying this whole chapter. That is, much childrearing can be learned from children. These days, it is so easy to overlook their input, since nearly all childrearing instruction—whether from books, television, friends, or parents—comes at us from adults. The more experienced parents have learned an invaluable lesson throughout their childrearing careers: In many respects, children are the most grown-up of teachers. Furthermore, they're always available to guide us, every day, living directly under our noses, and our feet, and our coffee tables, and sometimes under our skins. Look to children often. They are the forgotten experts.

Competent parenthood is a blend of learning from others, whether they are four times our age or one fourth our age. To make the most of any childraising advice or child advice, two phrases are vital to remember as we mature through PARENTHOOD: PACE YOURSELF, BRACE YOURSELF.

Chapter 8

Parenthood: Pace Yourself, Brace Yourself

"If I had it to do all over again, I think I would relax and have more fun. Things that were so important to me then, for example, how old they were when they learned to tie their shoes or read, were really not all that important. Finally, I was just smart enough to realize that."

Mother, Califon, New Jersey

*P*arenthood is like a marathon race. It's long, demanding, and exhausting. Few pursuits, though, give a greater sense of accomplishment or "high." To carry the analogy a little further, three quarters through the race, marathoners get to a point called "hitting the wall," when their body is screaming, "Stop, I'm out of gas," just prior to getting their second wind and moving on strong again. Parents, too, hit the wall—sometimes literally—most often about three quarters through the race, when they're raising teenagers, although it can happen at any time with any age child. You can reach the limits of your energy to cope raising a baby with colic, a two-year-old whose every third word is *no*, or a ten-year-old who has decided schoolwork isn't for him. As we will soon see, strong parents, like strong runners, have found that if they can persevere past the point of near-exhaustion, a smoother going often follows. Stamina is a core quality of successful parenting.

Good distance runners know that to run successfully, you must pace your-self. Push too fast and hard, and you're spent before the race is over. Each racer must find the pace, or stride, that's best suited to her. She must brace herself for "the wall" or any other obstacles to be expected in such a long-term endeavor.

The length of a marathon race is 26.2 miles. The length of an "average" parenthood is about 26.2 years, give or take several years. No question, when compared to parents, marathoners are out for a Sunday stroll around the block. All the more critical, then, that to run the best parenting race possible, you must learn to pace—and brace—yourself.

TRAINING COMES NATURALLY

The rookie runner isn't sure what is a comfortable pace for her. She needs a few races under her feet to find a rhythm. So, too, the rookie parent. She needs a few years, or maybe a few kids, to develop a comfortable stride. Nearly all the veteran parents we interviewed said they naturally mellowed and more fully enjoyed childrearing as they received parenting training, courtesy of the kids. With the first child, they often were overanxious to do everything perfectly and, consequently, shot off threats like, "If that car comes home fifteen minutes late, A.J., you'll walk to the drive-in until you're thirty." On the other hand, by the time the last youngster rolled around, the older parents were more likely to force out tired lines like, "Please, Mario, I told you before, don't park your car on the front porch." Not really, but they did admit to being less excitable with the passage of time.

Then again, applying the logic of "more kids = more mellow" to its limit would mean that after five or six kids, mom and dad would be near comatose. While some of the larger families smiled at the grain of truth to this, overall the parents agreed that it takes only a little parenting experience to relax a lot:

- "As a brand-new parent I tried very hard to do everything just right and was very precise. Everything was of monumental importance. So I was hard on myself and on Michael as well. With Kristen, I was much more relaxed, realizing that my expectations were pretty unreal and that some things were just not all that important."
- "All stages of the first child were really a first for us and were probably more

of a crisis, more anxious, more intense than the same situations with
succeeding children. We really learned and were trained on the first child.
God bless her for surviving us."
- "You are always hardest on your first child. You expect more at an earlier
  age. You probably discipline a little more strictly. Willie and I have often
  later laughed about some of the things that happened to our older children
  back in elementary school that we thought were just going to ruin their
  lives. Now they don't even remember those things. We agonized over
  them, and they didn't affect the kids at all."

Even after growing more relaxed with each succeeding child, a few parents
still wished they could have been more easygoing. Jerry from New Hampshire
said, "We might not have allowed ourselves to get caught up in the American
life-style as much as we have. Although we had some goals to become more
self-sufficient, we kind of got caught up in that achievement life-style, with
more working and less fishing. If I could go back, I would probably spend
more quality time with my children in leisure."

His wife, Rita, concurred simply, "I would go fishing more."

A Michigan mother, when asked, "If you could do it all over again, what
would you change?" left no doubt as to what she considered vital to content
parenthood. "Relax. Relax. Relax. Be quiet. Be quiet. Be quiet. Wait. Wait.
Wait." I think she must have three kids.

Parents pass through developmental stages as do young children. As they
mature, we mature. As they get more settled, we get more settled. If you're
a young parent, what these mature parents are saying should be encouraging,
that is, "Hold on. Time and experience can soothe even the worst case of
parenting jitters." Ron, a father of nine, quipped, "We played it by ear. After
the first two or three, it was easy."

Of course, counting on several years, or kids, to relax your childrearing is
taking the long route. There are ways to parent more calmly *right now.* And
that's fortunate, because time doesn't always bring ease of mind. For some
parents, more kids means more anxiety. Along the way, they get a Spike or
Spikette, and whatever composure they've gained with experience is offset by
their new little spitfire. So, let's look at how you might better pace yourself
in your present situation, whether you've been a parent for one or twenty-one
years.

The more experienced the parents, the more they realized: Enjoyable childrearing begins with accepting several parenting facts of life. These are truths at the very heart of parenthood. Always keep them in sight, and you will develop a comfortable stride much sooner than you otherwise might have.

PARENTING FACT OF LIFE #1:
THERE ARE NO PERFECT PARENTS

Ask any parent, "Are you perfect?" and you'll hear an are-you-kidding laugh, followed by something like, "There are no perfect parents." Verbally, we all recognize this reality, but our actions regularly indicate that we overlook it. At times, we become obsessed with saying and doing all the right things. In other instances, we second-guess and third-guess our decisions, struggling to make sure we've found the absolutely correct one. Or, we may pick and choose our words so carefully that we lose some of the freewheeling banter so natural to interacting with kids. In short, we overlook parenting fact of life #1 when we overanalyze everything we say and do in the effort to be perfect parents.

Certainly we're striving to give our best to our children. There is a point, though, where our desire to do everything perfectly can be the very thing that hurts our effectiveness. We try too hard. We overdo. As a result, we miss out on much of the spontaneity of raising kids, with all of their imperfections and with all of ours.

- "One of the things that I have told young couples, particularly young mothers, who have come to me is that you bring to parenting exactly what you are and you give it your best shot. You are not going to do it all perfectly. There is no way you can. What you have to do—wherever you come from and whatever you are to start with—is give it the best you have for the years that you have."
- "There is a lot to be said for the old adage 'If only I knew when I started raising them what I know now. . . .' I was very tense when I started having kids. I wanted to do everything right. Things got out of control for me because I had so many children so fast, and I couldn't be perfect, and I couldn't do everything right. Really, that was the best thing that ever happened. I was forced to learn to relax and say if I get through today, and everybody is healthy and functioning, then we have learned

something. I think you have to give up the image of what a perfect parent is."

- "There are certainly parenting skills and personality traits in which we are lacking, but the important thing is that the kids know we are trying hard and know we care about them and their future. With that foundation, kids can compensate on their own for our deficiencies."

Todd from Wisconsin believes that parents might be able to reach perfection occasionally, but can't remain there because kids, and thus parenting, are always changing. "It would be hard for any parent to be perfect for their child every year of their life. They might be perfect when the kids are three or four, but when they get to be nine or ten or older, they wouldn't like the kids that much. The parents would have to change a lot. If they could change with kids just a little with each age, then they would be good parents." Todd is twelve years old.

Even if we could do everything perfectly, there simply are no guarantees in parenting. What kids become depends a lot on us, but also on the world they experience outside our homes, and on their own individual personalities. Bobbie, a parent of three, stated, "I don't think you should *ever* be graded on how the kids turn out, because that is assuming they are a blank slate and everything depends on what you do."

Ron from Ohio agreed, "There's a lot of luck that goes along with parenting. There are people who do everything well, but they are not lucky. Their kid is a maverick somehow or other, and bad things happen."

Rita from New Hampshire concluded, "There comes a moment around the time the kids leave home or go to college, when you come face-to-face with yourself and say, 'Here I am. I'm done. I did all I could do raising this child.' You hand the ball over to them and from then on it is their life."

To be a better parent, stop trying to be perfect. Perfection is not only a myth, it is a dangerous myth. The pursuit of perfection will leave you feeling inadequate and guilty. Instead of sticking with decisions based upon your best judgment at the time, you'll endlessly rethink and rehash, searching for that one "best" answer. Nearly always the end result is confusion. Too much thinking doesn't enhance good judgment. It clouds it.

Striving for perfection is like beginning a marathon race in a sprint. After fifty yards or so, you're exhausted, and there are still over twenty-six miles to go.

PARENTING FACT OF LIFE #2:
MISTAKES ARE AS MUCH A PART
OF PARENTING AS KIDS ARE

Not only are there no perfect parents, but no parents are even close to perfect. Though some of the kids did give their folks perfect marks, theirs were highly personal and loving opinions. When the parents were questioned about parenting imperfections, they freely admitted to inconsistency, errors in judgment, and overreaction. When asked, "Did you ever fail as a parent?" Kathy, a single mother with two children and two master's degrees, replied simply, "Every day."

Excellence in childrearing does not evolve from making fewer mistakes than everybody else. It evolves from making plenty of mistakes and learning from them.

- "All parents fail at one time or another. There will be times when you don't even like your children. You always love them, but there will be times you don't like what you see in them, like selfishness or rudeness, or times when you should trust them and you don't, or don't encourage them when you should. But parents are only human, and sometimes you have to think of yourself. You have to give yourself a little time and space. I don't know of any other job in this life where we don't make mistakes."
- "Even when the kids did things against the grain or did things to disappoint us, I don't think that was because I failed as a parent. It was just part of their growing up. I came home one day, and my wife, Alice, told me that she found some bad words written on a door in Stephanie's closet. They weren't for anybody to see because they were out of view. This was my daughter's way of being angry—either at us or at something she had done. We confronted her with it, and she said it was her way of taking out her frustrations. To me, if she was willing to do that, I was satisfied. It was better than her hurting her hand or hurting herself. I thought it was an unusual way of doing things, but it satisfied her."

Judy, a teacher who had guided and disciplined hundreds of children over the years prior to her motherhood, still felt unsteady as she walked into the classroom of childrearing. "Even with the formal education in preparation for teaching and the actual classroom experience, I found I was not adequately prepared for parenting. Most of what I learned was on a cope-as-you-encounter-the-situation basis."

Without fail, successful parents are emphasizing that mistakes are not a mark of failure. They are to be expected, as they are a natural, indeed necessary, aspect of a parent's maturation. Parenting is a process, one in which we make decisions, assess the results, keep the useful ideas, and discard the useless ones. Parenthood is, in a sense, trial-and-error-hood. You learn much unintentionally or accidentally, trying things out—usually on the first child, as these parents have noted—and over the years "tinkering" with your style to improve it.

More than just accepting mistakes as an inescapable reality of parenthood, good parents welcome mistakes. They consider them invaluable opportunities for growth, for themselves and their children.

- "It seems that problems and conflicts are inherent in the whole process of a child's moving from being totally dependent on parents to being a capable, independent adult. Some problems—especially of control and who has it—are necessary for children to learn to be responsible adults. For us, childrearing was lots of trial and error, give and take, pushing and pulling. It wasn't a clean, straight line. We had lots of I'm sorry's and I love you's."
- "Somewhere along the line, if I made a blunder with what I did, I could *see* the results, what effect it had—positive, negative, or something other than what I had expected—and then, could change what I was doing if necessary. I was amazed that the kids were not like some of the ceramics inside our cabinet. They are not something that will shatter with one drop."

Don't fear mistakes. That's what nearly two hundred fallible parents here are telling parents everywhere. Honest mistakes made by loving parents do not damage children psychologically, not now or at some unknown juncture years down the road. They may make life a little tougher for a while, for all involved, but they don't ruin "psyches." Kids were built to withstand being raised by human beings, with all of our shortcomings and inconsistencies. As Bob observed, children are "not something that will shatter with one drop." Quite the contrary, children are more like hard rubber—with steel belts on both sides. They are remarkably resilient, some capable of not only surviving the most emotionally turbulent environments, but maturing against all odds into well-adjusted adults. If kids can weather the worst of conditions, and a good many do, they will weather us. We love them. We're trying to do what's best for them.

One final point needs emphasizing. *Mistake* can be a misleading word. It implies "wrong" or "psychologically incorrect." But since there are no right ways to parent, how can we know when we're "wrong"? According to whose opinion? According to what expert's theory? To be sure, no one would deny that acting neglectfully or playing favorites or disciplining with personal put-downs is poor parenting practice. We could label those actions wrong. Much of what parents consider mistakes, though, are no such things. Their actions are not nasty or hurtful or even thoughtless. Rather, they are decisions made with a child's welfare in mind. "I feel we have done what we thought was best for the children. Maybe I learned afterward that I could have done something a little differently, but at the time I thought I was doing the best thing, and I don't think I would ever consider [those past decisions] mistakes, or that I have failed," said Connie, a mother of four from Ohio.

Perhaps Michael, father of five in Florida, has the most reassuring words for parents afraid of making one-too-many childrearing blunders. "I don't think you can ever fail as a parent until you completely quit." So go ahead, make "mistakes." They are not examples of failure. They are examples of love. And from them good parents learn to be even better.

PARENTING FACT OF LIFE #3:
THE BEST PARENTING IS DONE RIGHT NOW

Raising kids is a moment-to-moment affair. Each day demands on-the-spot decisions and judgments without full benefit of all the facts. Keeping up with "right now" is work enough for most of us. That is why successful parents say: Parent in the present. Don't look back, except to learn. Don't look ahead, except to plan.

Looking back can breed guilt and regrets that will only hinder a parent's maturation. It can emotionally drain our energies from the present, where they are most needed, and keep us mired in blame over a past event or course of action that didn't turn out as we had hoped. Looking ahead can create needless anxiety and worry over what may come to pass, but which very often doesn't. It can paralyze the will to make decisions and stand by them for fear of causing some as-yet-unknown repercussions far into the future.

Let's first hear what these parents have learned about the importance of not relentlessly second-guessing themselves.

- "If you looked back and measured everything you did, you probably wouldn't survive. You certainly wouldn't have child # 2. We may castigate ourselves over past 'wrongs,' but most of these kids do survive us. We think they are more fragile than they are. Also, there are certain kids with certain personalities that will have problems no matter what we've done, good or bad. I'm at the point now where I'm only going to take the blame for so much—I'm saying this and hoping I mean it!"
- "Instead of being upset, carrying guilt, or beating our chest with a mea culpa, we have simply admitted to our children that we are human and sometimes we do—and will—make decisions that don't work out. You just can't keep apologizing for certain periods of your life."

Gloria, a mother with a healthy appreciation of the many thousands of judgments required in a childrearing career, has some particularly soothing words for any parent walking beneath a cloud of old, undeserved guilt. "Whenever we went through our bad times—academic, social, or whatever—I always kept in perspective that whatever I did I believed was for the best. It's hard to imagine a parent making a decision having to do with a child's future in which she would say to herself, 'Well, I know this isn't going to be good for him, so this is what I will do.' This is so important to remember to help avoid the guilt about anything long-term."

To repeat, parenting is a process, one in which we mature from what we try, good and bad, effective and ineffective. It is a process filled with overreactions and blunders—like verbally blistering Amanda because she left the refrigerator door open, or punishing Mario for riding his tricycle through the flowerbed again when for once he was telling the truth about it—the neighbor kid did do it. No matter what we've done "wrong," or think we've done wrong, hanging on to the past will severely erode our ability to act "right" in the present, that is, to act with confidence. And confidence is a quality our kids need to see in us. Otherwise, they'll make too many decisions on their own, against our best judgment.

Even the most successful parents would change many things if they could turn back the calendar, but they can't. What they can do is derive some lessons from the past and try not to let guilt from yesterday filter into their parenting today. And they've discovered this: No matter what you've done wrong in your life—as a parent, as a spouse, as a person—your ability to give your children a quality upbringing comes from what you do now. The battle against guilt from the past can be an ongoing one. After all, we're making new judgments every day which can be fuel for tomorrow's guilt. If you accept that parenting is learning from the past, you can give more of yourself to your kids in the present.

PARENTING AHEAD Just as emotionally exhausting as parenting in the past is "parenting ahead," as one father called it. He was referring to looking too far forward in one's parenting and "seeing" problems that aren't yet here, and may never be. Rita, a mother of seven from New Hampshire, strongly warned against expecting troubles because others expect them for us. Another's experience need not be our own, and we can waste precious moments waiting for it to be.

- "When you are raising children and have a new baby, people say, 'That is a nice little baby, but wait until you get it home!' Then you get it home and they say, 'That is really nice, but wait until the terrible two's.' You can go through your whole life knowing that at any moment this child will turn into some kind of horrid demon. 'Wait until they go to school'; 'Wait until they become teenagers'; 'Wait until they leave home.' We have found every step of the way that this horrid demon never came."

Joanna from Indiana, a mother of four boys, formed some early images of parenthood based solely upon her first son. She found out with her second son that each child brings unique challenges, and sometimes they are much milder than we anticipated. "Our first child took twenty-minute naps and had a cry that made your head vibrate. I was anxious and unsure I could cope with that in a second one. However, he took four-hour naps. I worried in vain."

Unquestionably, conscientious parents plan for the future. Our goal is to guide our youngsters toward independent and responsible adulthood. Implicit with all discipline is the question, "What lesson about life am I trying to teach my child, now and for the future?" There are ways of parenting ahead, though, that only hamper good parenting in the present. The first is to anticipate trouble that may not come to pass. As Rita and Joanna caution, we can squander much time conjuring up problems that we can do little to prevent or avoid, and which may never occur despite our best efforts to worry them into being. For instance, your lovable, innocent Melody will be attending kindergarten next year with some not-so-lovable, not-so-innocent other kids. Worrying about what negative influences she'll meet is one sure way to rob yourself of enjoying Melody's sweetness right now. Unless you're planning to sequester her at home, Melody will bump into children less nice than she, to what effect you can't predict. She could just be sweet enough to be a positive influence on a few of them. Similarly, you could fret yourself into a frazzle waiting for your easy-to-get-along-with Delbert to hit his hormone-dominated teens. Even though most kids do become a little more immature as they mature into adolescence, not all do. Some even become easier to get along with. All your apprehension will not in any way make Delbert more pleasant throughout the next few years. In fact, it may breed a self-fulfilling prophecy. Delbert might well become what he thinks you think he'll become. Looking too hard for problems that don't exist can be the very thing that gives them birth.

Another way of parenting ahead which is even more unnerving is to overinterpret what a particular piece of misconduct portends for the future, to look too deep and too far ahead for the meaning of a behavior. Let's say four-year-old Rob has just stolen a match box Corvette from a toy store. Does this mean he will steal a real Corvette fourteen years from now? Absolutely not! It is impossible to predict the psychological future of a child from one, two, or even several incidents of misbehavior. And trying to predict will torment our parenting. How can we calmly deal with a here-and-now incident of petty thievery when all manner of "What if?" and "What does this mean?" are swirling around in our heads? Secure parents have learned that no one, except God, can know what any given behavior will lead to years from now. What's more, most misbehavior means *nothing* for the future. Today's misconduct must be handled today. Peering ahead to guess about the long-term ramifications of a disturbing incident will only leave us needlessly frightened and guilty.

Parenting ahead is like beginning a marathon race thinking, "I wonder if I'll still be moving at the twenty-mile marker." Our thoughts may become so fixed on some point three hours hence that we'll be oblivious to the sign on the route now that says, "Water, next right."

PARENTING FACT OF LIFE #4:
PARENT'S AREN'T ALWAYS POPULAR

All children—no matter what their temperament, intellect, or talents—share one characteristic: They can be so childish. Preschoolers can really act immature. Don't you sometimes have to stifle the urge to cry, "Oh, come on, grow up!"?

Such childishness underlies the central truth of parenting: Kids do not see parenthood through the eyes of parents. They don't understand our actions, our motives, our method in our madness. Though we know this, we ignore it every day. We ignore it when we endlessly reason with Holmes, struggling vainly to make him understand that we don't like his sister more just because his sister needs less discipline. When we frustrate ourselves because Faith won't accept that our curfew is for her safety. When we feel like a failure after Conan has wished the dog were his mommy because we marched him to the corner for smacking his sister with his rubber sword. Every day we make decisions our kids find disagreeable. The only way to stay in complete agreement with our children is to make no decisions at all.

Part and parcel of parenthood is being disliked by our kids at times, often because we are acting in their best interests, which they won't realize for years to come. When was the last time Igor walked out of his room after serving an hour there for nasty talk and said, "Mom, I was doing some thinking while I was staring out my window, watching those guys play football outside without me, on the last nicest day of the year, and I realized something. You're not trying to be mean. You're trying to teach me self-control. And this is going to help me when I'm grown up. So if it's OK with you, I'm going to go back in my room for another hour because I want this lesson to last. Oh, by the way, is it OK if I write you a two-hundred-word apology while I'm up there?" If this, or something even remotely similar, has happened to you, please write us. We're interested in unearthly childhood phenomena.

The parents in this book are very well liked by their children. No matter how high a child's overall performance rating of his folks, though, he frequently reconsidered his opinion at two times: during enforcement of rules and discipline, and during any age with a "teen" on the end of it.

Let's first face those moments when we, acting as good parents, are neither understood nor liked:

- "I think one of the first lines kids learn to use on parents is 'I don't like you.' I expected my kids, even as little toddlers, not to like me sometimes. That's the way it will always be for parents, as long as we don't let children do everything they want."

- "They've called me old-fashioned, not with the times, accused me of not understanding. These were all times when they were upset at my decisions and me. If I really felt 'gut-deep' about something, and I didn't necessarily have a reason for not letting them do it, then they'd really get mad. But I had to weather that. I'd much rather have them dislike me than to let them do something I don't feel is good for them."

- "Were there times when the kids didn't like or understand me? Where do I begin? I can be tough on the kids. I don't bend to go with the crowd, and they often get angry at me for that. An example: There is a popular program on at ten P.M. All of the kids in my daughter's class watched it and were talking about it. She couldn't because I wouldn't let her stay up that late. She is in the third grade; she doesn't need to stay up that late. . . . I try to give the kids what they need, not what they want. Sometimes that gets me disliked. Kids need to see that a parent's not afraid to stand up and take an unpopular stand. They see you do it, even if it affects them, and they may be more likely to do so in their own lives."

All parents, even the most popular, face occasional spells of unpopularity, but, for the most part, these are short-lived. Eventually the kids forget, forgive, or at least accept our blind unreasonableness as just part of our misguided parental duty. There are times in a parent's life, though, when the brief bouts of unpopularity seem to string themselves together into a nearly unbroken band of disfavor. Tammy, Teri, and Tracy, three sisters from Washington, describe a shared sibling dip in their relationship with their parents:

- "I think my bad times were when I was a senior in high school. I wanted to be independent, and I was rebellious toward my parents. I stayed out late and didn't want to do family things. I think this is an awkward stage that most kids go through. Looking back, I can't imagine wanting to do some of the things I did, but I think that is part of what growing up is all about."

- "I suppose the worst would have been during our teens. Mom and dad were never right, and we figured they were too strict. They said no, and we would fight against it. But, to look at it now, I am thankful for the no's."

- "The worst times happened sometime in high school. I resented being asked where I was going and when I would get home because I was sixteen and 'too grown up for that.' I didn't understand why they wouldn't let us go to the ocean for the weekend when I was seventeen and everyone else's parents were letting them go. It made me mad when I was eighteen, and if I didn't go where I was going, they would be disappointed in me. But as Erma Bombeck said, 'They loved me enough to say "no," even when I hated them for it.' "

Of course, the kids weren't the only family members aware of these turbulent times. Every so often, even mom and dad noticed that they weren't as admired as they were a few years back. Ironically, the nature of adolescence may be the one thing that parents and teens agree on:

- "I don't think the adolescence of the child is the child's adolescence for his or herself only. I think the parents go through an adolescence of parenting. I don't think you are the same parent for a baby as you are for an adolescent. I suppose if you have had fourteen kids, adolescence might be easier to get through. You would probably just ignore it completely, realizing you had no control over it. But the first time through is a bear. You try to do different things and none of them work. Finally you just forget it and wait."
- "Early adolescence—ages twelve, thirteen, and fourteen—with my son has been the worst for me. It seems like he hit me at the early stage, and he hit Dave [his stepfather] at the later stages, in high school. Looking at it now, I think he was just being an average child. We were always pretty structured in what the kids needed to do, and they have always known what they needed to do. But all of a sudden, my son didn't think he was supposed to do it. Sometimes, David and I used to have to get away. My mother would come over for the weekend to help."

From different angles, these parents and youngsters are converging on the same point. It is a fact of parenthood not to be liked sometimes by those you love most, and by those who most love you, even if for the moment they're not showing it. In fact, it is a fact of good parenthood. Good parents base decisions on the long-term welfare of their children. Children, not generally being long-term-thinking creatures, not only don't like those decisions, at times they don't like those who hand them down. If you seldom take an unpopular stand or enforce a misunderstood rule, your kids will grow accustomed to your ruling in their favor, becoming less tolerant of any disagreeable decisions on your part. One mom became uneasy if too much time passed without her children getting upset at her. "That's a sign I'm raising them like they think I should, and that's not good."

Teen turbulence, however common, is not inevitable. As some parents observed a few pages ago, it is neither helpful nor comforting to peer ahead and expect that your parent-pleasing nine-year-old is destined to evolve into a parent-pushing fifteen-year-old. Actually, some families contract only a mild case of the "tenth-grade syndrome," as one mother tagged it, while still others pass through the inflammation untouched. Linda, mother to Kevin (fifteen), Heather (twelve), and Megan (eight), is glad to say, "We consider ourselves lucky because Kevin still gives himself to his family. Many children his age don't even want to bother with their families. Kevin doesn't like anyone to interfere with his family times." Susie, too, finds her children more delightful with teenhood. "As the children have become teenagers, we have most enjoyed the late-night discussions about politics, philosophy, life goals, our faith, and the silly little things a family shares. These are such good times because they reveal to us our children's character. We are able to instruct, correct, and enjoy them as individuals."

Don't look ahead with trepidation to what *might* be coming. Instead, bask in your overall popularity now, but don't be surprised or discouraged if your stock as a parent briefly drops several points as the kids get older and much smarter in their own eyes. The best of parents pass through such periods. So do the best of kids. If you brace yourself for these times, they won't knock you over. They may push you off balance a little, but they won't have the power to convince you that all you have to show after all these years of love, effort, and sacrifice is a feisty, I'll-do-it-my-way sixteen-year-old who appreciates you only for your car keys and credit card.

There is added reason for optimism. Did you notice the last lines from the kids' descriptions of adolescent life? Without exception, these older youngsters looked back, shook their heads, and said in effect, "I had some growing up to do." Furthermore, the kids eventually became quite grateful for their folks' disagreeable actions. Recalled one recent high-school graduate, "The worst of times with my parents I actually now look back upon with thanks. Once in the eleventh grade, I was grounded for the last month of school to get my grades up. Every afternoon I would sit outside, pouting, with all my books. But by the end of June, I had gotten great test results and a much-improved class rank."

Some closing words of reassurance come from Will, the father of eighteen: "Not one ever told us out loud they hated us at certain points. We found out later they all did. But they're back to loving us now."

PARENTING FACT OF LIFE #5:
PARENTING IS TOO IMPORTANT
TO BE TAKEN TOO SERIOUSLY

Parenthood is a serious calling. It does come complete, however, with built-in safety mechanisms to keep it from getting too serious—kids. While being a mother or father may be the most important of life's occupations, it also is the most humorous. Kids make sure of that. They can act silly, goofy, crazy, zany—and these are their more subdued qualities. If we let them, kids will teach us to laugh while we are parenting, so say some fun-loving parents. "Probably the only way you can be a good parent is to realize that none of this is as serious as you think it is," said Susan, a mom of three entertaining youngsters, aged ten, twelve, and fourteen.

Learning to smile more, even during discipline, results from adjusting our perceptions some. It comes from telling ourselves that what seems unnerving—maybe even alarming—now, most likely will take on a lighter tone with the passage of time. "Some of the mishaps and incidents that drive you crazy when you are raising them make great stories in later years," said Joanna, an Indiana mother who has gathered a treasure of great stories over her nearly thirty years of parenthood.

Overlooking the light side is easy to do, particularly if you're worried that whatever behavior little Sigmund is displaying may have a dark side. That is, it may contain some psychological "meaning" you're missing. In reality, very little of kids' day-to-day mischief and misconduct is the stuff of psychological trouble. It is the stuff of growing up. Resisting overinterpretation is the first step to being able to laugh more often and heartily.

Dennis from New York acknowledged that while the humor in childrearing isn't always obvious, if you look hard enough, you'll usually find a glimmer of it hiding somewhere. "Our basic rule of parenting is that there is something humorous in just about every situation. If everything else fails, laugh." A three-year-old's temper display can be a shell-shocking, not to mention embarrassing, experience. But if you step back a few feet (a few miles?) and study it objectively, temper tempests can be comical. Melody's hands are flailing in a north-south-east-west direction simultaneously. Sounds never before recorded in nature are pouring from her mouth. Her eyes are darting in opposite directions. It really can be laughable, so long as you keep in mind that absolutely no emotional damage is occurring, just the reaction of a child who doesn't agree *at all* with how you or the world is acting. When little kids get mad, their motto often is: "Look as wild as you can look." One parent, at the first rumble of a temper quake, brought out a small mirror, and without a word, held it up for her little firebreather to get a close-up reflection of himself. Still another, with more energy to spare, flung herself to the floor and mimicked her youngster's every move until they both started laughing at how ridiculous the other looked.

Older kids, too, lend their brand of levity to life. Among all their editorial comments on discipline are lines with the makings of a television sitcom. "Dry the dishes? They're still wet!"; "Music nowadays is meant to be played loud. Your music was for softer times when there were a lot less people on the earth"; "Sure, you knew all the state capitals when you were in junior high. There were only twenty or twenty-five states then." Everywhere you listen in childrearing, there is amusement. What parent hasn't heard glum pronouncements like: "Mom, he looked at me," or "She put her finger on my side of the car"?

Jay from Pennsylvania admits, "A lot of times I'll say to the kids, 'Have fun.' I'm not just telling them that. I'm telling myself, too. I take these words and put them back on me because I don't want to get caught up in too much heaviness."

When you're not in the mood to find some small, cute aspect to a particular antic, try to reassess it with a lighter slant once it's resolved and has safely passed. A Nebraska mom's main regret was, "I wished I would have laughed more when the kids were younger and not taken things too seriously." Another parent, looking back over her parenting, more adamantly asserted, "Everything, *everything* seems funny after it is over."

The kids, too, think things are funny after they're over. Here's how one son described a "rejection" nearly all parents face, a threat that can sting the first time around.

- "When I was four or five, I ran away from home because I couldn't have an ice-cream cone or some other similar crisis. My mom helped me pack so I wouldn't forget any important items like clean underwear. I suppose I made it about two hundred feet to the bushes behind the house when I decided I'd gone far enough and this would be my new home. I sat out there for about three years, or about two hours, I forget, when I decided my mom had been taught her lesson. I gathered up my things and went back inside to announce that I was going to give her a break and come home. All mom had to say was that she missed me and she was glad I was home, but that I didn't have to stay if I didn't want to. My decision to stay was one of my smartest moves as a kid."

Did you ever notice that kids seldom know where they're going as they're preparing to leave? They just know that anyplace—including Antarctica and the Gobi Desert—is better than home. A veteran mother of eight used a twinkle of humor to help her roll with her daughter's promise to put up stakes elsewhere.

"One day one of the kids decided to run away. She was about four years old. Got up in the morning and announced, 'I'm running away.'

"I said, 'Oh, why?'

" 'I'm just running away. No one cares for me around here.'

"I just looked at her, and out she went. I told my son to keep an eye on her from the second-floor hall window. In case she left the yard, I'd get her. We have a three-car garage apart from the house, and she stayed behind that for about half an hour. We could see her, but she didn't know that.

"After a while she came back. 'I'm home.'

"I said, 'What did you say, Hope?'

"She said, 'I'm not Hope.'

" 'Oh, Beverly, what did you want?'

"She said, 'I'm not Beverly, either.'

"And I called her every name except hers, which was Sherry.

" 'I'm Sherry,' she said.

" 'No.' I smiled. 'Sherry ran away.'

"Oh, she didn't like that at all, but she never tried running again."

Such incidents remind me of my own mother's response to my first-time runaway notice. Looking at me earnestly, she begged, "No, Raymond, please don't go. Please stay. I'll go."

The no-nonsense advice of caring parents is: Laugh a lot with your kids. Find the humor in their behavior. They can be absolute characters sometimes. Learn also to laugh at yourself. Sometimes we grown-ups are bigger characters than the kids.

How fully we enjoy our children is directly related to two factors: a relaxed attitude toward childrearing and being prepared for the inevitable rough times that every parent faces. Still, no matter how well paced and well braced our parenting, we can gain even more family stability if we are willing to place ourselves and our children under THE SPIRITUAL UMBRELLA.

Chapter 9

The Spiritual
Umbrella

*"If I had one wish for my children, it would be for each
of them to know God, to know themselves, then to be
the best that this relationship creates. When one is
grounded in faith, no matter what life brings, there is
a stability, an eternal perspective, and help always
available. I can't give this to my children. God can."*

Mother, Casper, Wyoming

*S*trong family life has many components. Successful families are not in
complete agreement on the relative importance, or ranking, of these components. Foolproof formulas for family success don't exist. Rather, certain
themes are prevalent among healthy families, for example, reliance on common sense, teaching through example, give-and-take communication, and the
will to discipline, to mention a few. One theme to emerge most prominently
is spirituality, or the belief in a Creator and in living by His guidelines. Nearly
ninety percent of the families pointed to spirituality as a significant, if not
dominant, guiding force in their lives. Although the words varied—faith,
religious beliefs, Christian principles, moral foundation, church family—the
idea was the same. Spirituality is the umbrella which encompasses and fosters
a more loving, close-knit family.

In many homes, the presence of spiritual commitment was obvious to the interviewers even as they entered. You might recall from chapter 1 that the Love family requested to begin their interview with a prayer. The walls of other homes were liberally adorned with religious symbols and pictures. To be sure, these alone do not make a spiritual life, but the meaning of their presence is corroborated by the way these families live.

During the first ten interviews, no questions explored the relationship between spirituality and family life. The relationship surfaced so spontaneously that all subsequent interviews included specific questions on this theme.

The range of religions underlying these families' spirituality is diverse: Catholic, Baptist, Jewish, Latter-day Saint, United Methodist, Presbyterian, Episcopalian, Christian Buddhist, Pentecostal, Congregational, Christian Scientist, Lutheran, Fundamental Evangelical, Christian. No matter what their particular religious affiliation, almost with one voice the parents and children emphasize that it is the *spirit* of one's beliefs rather than the *specifics* that is most integral to a family's well-being. "I believe the most important thing we've done to foster spirituality in our children is to look upon them as spiritual. Rather than viewing them as little mortals, I've striven to see their true identity as spiritual—in the image and likeness of God, who is spirit. They have a true spiritual identity now, not just later," said Connie, a mother of four from Ohio.

Eighteen-year-old Ginger from New Hampshire likewise focuses on the spiritual aspect of her upbringing. "Primarily, my parents have put great emphasis on my relationship with the Lord. They have not necessarily stressed the idea of religion. We switched churches a few times in my life. Especially now that I'm older, they don't pressure me into declaring a religion or into being faithful to one particular religious group. What they have taught me—what they have given me—is a strong relationship with God. They show me the importance of knowing Him and making Him a part of my life."

In a number of families, mother and father are not of the same religion. Nonetheless, they work to blend any differences into a uniform set of spiritual principles. "My husband and I are two different religions, Presbyterian and Catholic, but we attend church as a family. We alternate churches, but always go together. The congregations of both churches work with us as we teach our children what it means to be Christian," shared a mother from Kentucky.

Carol, mother to Travis (twelve) and Troy (fifteen), relates a similar mentality. "Although my husband is not Catholic, he has always attended weekly mass with us. We both feel that faith has been a unifying and stable part of our family life. It seems to solidify basic moral values we hold dear. It is the one thing we all share equally."

A number of parents do not actively pursue church or religious involvement. Still, most allow their children the opportunity to reach a personal level of spiritual comfort. An Alaskan parent explained, "As time has gone on, we've done less and less about religion. We feel the children should have some exposure, though, so we do attend church some. The boys, even now, sing in the church choir, and we remain open about the subject of religion anytime."

Given the religious variety among these families, there are similarities overall. Nearly all the parents place a high premium on imparting to the children a set of spiritual and moral values. The following are testament to the powerful presence of spirituality in stable, contented families.

- "Our spiritual teaching to our children can be summarized by three principles: one, ask God for guidance in every decision; two, thank God for all successes, regardless of their magnitude; three, trust God that He knows what is best. One-hundred percent happiness doesn't exist, but if our children follow these principles, we don't believe they will ever have to go anywhere else to find the formula for happiness."

- "Our whole way of raising Kristen and Michael is founded on our religious faith. We believe we are saved by God's unconditional love and acceptance. In turn, we have tried to convey to Michael and Kristen that our love for them is as unconditional as we humans can make it. Hopefully, this has freed them to become the best they can be. If they can believe in themselves, in turn, they can show love and respect to others."

- "I've told my children that I love God first, then Don [husband], and then them. We've tried by example to let them know that faith was the most important part of life. If children know they have a heavenly Father who loves them, they are better able to relate to their earthly father. And if they have a good earthly father, they will better understand their heavenly Father."

- "We try to teach our children to analyze the framework of a situation, a story, or comment with: Is it honest? Is it kind? Does it follow the rules of the Ten Commandments? Does it follow the rule of the great commandment to love God above all things and your neighbor as yourself?"

Striving conscientiously to nurture spirituality in one's family will rarely go unnoticed by the children. To the degree that these parents talked *and lived* a spiritually based existence, the kids almost always mirrored similar values. Contrary to widespread worry that too much religion turns off children, especially teenagers, these families experienced the opposite effect. Almost always, the children firmly embraced what they learned and observed in their parents' life-style.

- "I don't think religion has made us a success as a family, but as individual human beings. Being successful humans makes you a successful family." [Katy, aged fifteen]
- "Our strong religious background is the center of our family, because if you're a Christian and you trust in God, then everything else will fall into place. Our parents really believe that God is the one that is going to see us through and that we should seek throughout our lives to trust God and to find out what God really wants us to do." [Kimberly, aged eighteen; Chip, aged sixteen]
- "If you look at the Ten Commandments, those are the values my parents stress. If we always keep in mind these values, life will be easier." [David, aged thirteen]
- "My parents have stressed a *strong religious background.* We always have our morning devotional, and we enjoy our church activities, but most importantly, we have been taught to place all of our worries in the hands of the Lord and to remember that everything has a purpose—'Thy will be done.'" [Jacob, aged sixteen]

Older children can more eloquently express the emotions within them, but younger children can speak their truth with exquisitely few words. Ten-year-old Tyler observed, "The Lord, I think, is who holds this family together." That says in ten words what most of these families believe.

LIVING EXAMPLE

Proclaiming to be spiritual is easy. It's as easy as talking. And anyone who raises kids knows how easy it is to talk, and talk, and talk. Living what you proclaim is not easy at all, but therein lies the surest way to a spiritually grounded family life.

Teaching by example is a theme that has surfaced previously in this book.

It will surface again, for it is vital to imparting anything to children, who sometimes seem built to repel guidance and wisdom. Nowhere is the need for example more evident than in teaching morals and spirituality. If your words shout one thing, while your behavior whispers something else, your words will be drowned out by the roar of your actions. For these families, dropping the kids off at church or Sunday school while mom and dad head for breakfast or back home to the paper is not part of Sunday routine. If the kids are sitting in worship services, the folks are sitting with them. If the kids are attending religion classes, mom and dad are at similar adult or fellowship classes at the same time, and sometimes teach those classes. In essence, spiritual growth involves all family members.

- "I teach third grade C.C.D. [Catholic religion classes]. Our family prays in the mornings together. We go to church on Sunday together. We believe in total religious education all the way through. Christmas is Jesus Christ's birthday. We don't open any gifts until we all sing happy birthday to Jesus."
- "Sunday is our family day. Nothing interferes. No birthday parties, no playing with friends, no ball practice. We have family council meetings each week for planning, decision-making, sharing, rewarding."
- "We call it family home evening. Every Monday night we do something as a family. We have a religion lesson which is given on a rotating basis among all of us. Then we do something fun, like bowling or going to the park and then out for a treat."

Sharing service and church-sponsored activities is an essential of home life for most of these families. It is the minimum daily allowance. These parents agree, while religious involvement is basic to fostering spirituality, the day-to-day conduct of one's life is indispensable to it. Here again, mom and dad must take the lead. Kathleen, from Illinois, a mother of five, whose ages range from twelve through twenty, commented, "While all four boys were altar boys, lecturers, and attended teen club, as did my daughter, I tried to instill in them that although attending church is important, just attending doesn't make it. They have been taught to live first by the Golden Rule." Betty from St. Louis repeated the sentiment, "We have always taught our children that they always have God, that they should always live Christian lives, and that they should always turn to Him for guidance. We have given them formal religious upbringing, but feel example is much more important than anything they can be told in a classroom." Susan and Stephen from West Virginia stated, "Judaism is a way of life for us, not just a religion. Our Jewish identity and knowledge of our heritage are very important to the well-rounded education of our children."

We observed previously that if we don't behave as we expect our children to, they will notice it. Take, for example, throwing our coat over the stair rail when we won't allow our youngster similar freedom. Even if Taylor can't *do* anything about this, he will, at the very least, grouse loudly about our inconsistency. "When I have my own house, I'm never going to hang my coat up. I'm going to throw all my coats, and underwear too, on the stairs, and make you hang your coat up before you even walk in the front door." A double standard of discipline will make our discipline much slower to sink in. Living a spiritual double standard carries more far-reaching consequences. Not only will the kids grumble about our dual set of moral expectations, they may gradually close themselves off to our wordy lessons, failing to absorb what our mouth is saying, because our behavior is saying something quite different.

Some parents have chosen a rigorous path of teaching by example. For instance, Jerry, father to seven children, two of whom are now in their mid-teens, has made an agreement with the kids that he will not drink alcohol at all if they too don't drink until legal age. Betty and Richard from Missouri never watched any movie which they considered unacceptable for their children. Other parents have quit smoking because, as their children have gotten older and become more exposed to peers who use smoke to look grown-up, they've realized that any stand against cigarettes would be a lot less clouded if they themselves could speak (and breathe) more clearly on the issue. One daughter recalls, "Values weren't stressed. They were lived. There was never any kind of alcohol, smoking, or cursing in our home. We, as kids, were never exposed to those things, at home anyway."

If we make Angel write ten reasons for clean language every time she curses, but four-letter words are favorite adjectives for us, what are we really saying? It's okay to swear when you're a grown-up? If Webster knows that, at the most merciful, he'll be shot at sunrise should we ever find out he cheated at school, yet he listens to us lie about his age to get him into a movie for half-price or to get reduced air fare, what will he think? In such instances, which speaks louder: "Neither you nor I will live this way" or "You can't, but I can"? If we think the kids aren't picking up on our mixed messages, we're fooling ourselves, because kids are incredibly perceptive. They may not be as sophisticated as we are, but their young life's work is figuring out how we operate. It's why they're so good at getting what they want from us.

Speaking on the need to impart values through example, Lois, a mother and high-school counselor in Minnesota, claims, "We parent more by what we do than by what we say. I did and continue to do lots of self-examination, so my behavior reflects what I believe and am. If I believe it's important for our children to share feelings, then I must be willing to share mine. If I think it's important for them to become independent, I have to be willing to give up control and allow them to make choices—this isn't always easy, especially if I feel they are making wrong ones." Lois further notes that, beginning very young, children raise questions when our behavior doesn't quite fit our words. "Since death and loss are a part of living, we made a conscious effort to take the kids to funerals with us when they were young. Kristen, at about age four, attended the funeral of an elderly lady we had befriended. One of her questions was, 'If she's with God, why is everybody crying?' " Even the youngest among us are sensitive to when our words and ways don't quite match.

Certainly, as a parent you have much more flexibility in your behavior than does Rutherford. The question, "Dad, why do I have to go to bed at nine o'clock, when you can stay up as late as you want?" can be answered with some explanation of the changing sleep needs from childhood to adulthood, or the differences in household routine for you and Rutherford. Any bedtime nagging tomorrow night from Rutherford would probably best be addressed with the eloquent, "I'm dad; you're son," or the ultimately eloquent, "Because." Likewise, on matters such as finance, transportation, marriage, your rights and privileges far exceed your children's. On matters of morality, however, conscientious parents work hard not to demand one set of values for the kids, and a second, more "adult" set of values for themselves. Day-to-day duties and freedoms are realistically different for parent and child. Morals are not, if we genuinely desire to instill the most solid spiritual foundation possible for our children.

THE ULTIMATE EXPERT

There's a maxim that describes the essence of raising kids: From birth to six, you teach them; from six to twelve, you guide them; and from twelve to eighteen, you pray for them. Good parents stretch this maxim some. They know that teaching and guiding never completely cease, no matter how old the child, and praying really begins at birth, even though it does tend to rise dramatically with the teen years. For many of these parents, God is the ultimate childrearing expert, the One sought, not just during uncertain, trying times, but daily. "Our expert is our Heavenly Father. We continually pray for His guidance for each child and know that we have been helped by Him. He knows them and how to meet their needs. We listen and try to follow," said Ross and Julie, parents of four from Utah.

A father of eight children aged ten to twenty-three spoke of his main source of childrearing support. "I had the Bible. I trusted the Lord and would ask Him to direct my life." With a clan that size, he believed the Bible was the only parenting book powerful enough to keep the household in one piece. Often parents, when asked about their single most helpful childrearing activity, said simply, "We prayed."

A willingness to seek divine guidance, by going straight "to the top" or through others with similar values, was common:

- "Turning to God for inspiration has helped me many times. Teaching my children to value their spiritual nature and to try to express it has made me feel like a better parent. Every night at bedtime, I remind my children of all the good things they have said or done that day, even if it's been one of *those* days, and thank them. This way we both are acknowledging and appreciating their goodness."
- "Richie went to summer school this past year. It's been a rough summer for him. His tics have been worse [Richie suffers from Tourette's syndrome, an epilepsylike condition]. He had a couple of crises because his anxiety reached a level where he didn't sleep well all night. On the first night, I prayed with him, and the next day went much better. This again happened a few days later, we prayed again, and the next day went well again. Since then, Richie asks me to pray with him to help him through difficult periods. I know I will not be available to him all the time, and I believe this has helped him to turn his problems over to a higher authority, to someone who understands better than I do."
- "The parenting advice that was most helpful to us came from an older couple in the church with whom we got to be friends. Even though all of their children were grown and married, they were all so close, lived lives

of good morals, and were a tremendous testimony to Richard and me."

- "One day I packed my things to run away from home. Mother came into my room, discovered what I was doing, and asked me to reconsider. Then she said a prayer out loud that I would not hold resentments and that I would stay where I belonged. I stayed." [From a daughter]

Childrearing is not for the faint of heart. It can be a chancy, at times frightening, experience. A parent's emotions can ride a roller coaster for days, sometimes weeks, or longer. Most of these parents, therefore, don't venture into uncertainty alone. They look to God to walk with them and their family.

Asking God for direction increases these parents' self-confidence. They know they are no longer facing a difficult decision by themselves, be it whether to enroll their young son in kindergarten this year or next, or whether to permit their oldest daughter to attend her first Strawberry Asphalt rock concert. Mom and dad may not be sure which course to take, but they believe there is One who does. So, they seek Him. A mother in Ohio believes, "A wise parent listens constantly for wisdom and guidance from God. The fact that we are willing to ask sincerely for guidance usually means that we are ready to listen and obey." And when a decision is a child's alone, frequently these parents will ask the Lord to give their youngster His guidance. "My children know I will always pray with them and for them," said Lucille, the mother of eighteen, in Nebraska. With that many kids, I wonder how Lucille got anything other than praying done!

REACH OUT TO REACH WITHIN

A central theme of spirituality is service to others. These families believe reaching out strengthens a family's bonds. Sharing one's family with others is both a cause and an effect of spiritual growth.

One aspect of church attendance is offering some form of financial support. Most churchgoing families give a part of their income to their denomination. A number of these families go a step further and require the children to set aside a portion of their money for church or charitable organizations. Not only is this a child's responsibility, say these parents, but the earlier he begins, the more naturally he will develop a sense of charity. *Tithing* is not a word with meaning only to parents. It also touches the children.

The spirit of volunteerism is likewise prevalent in strong families. When asked what they did to foster a child's sensitivity toward others, the parents repeatedly underscored the value of donating time and talent. The children were not only encouraged, but expected to spare a little of themselves for others.

- "We have adopted an older man in our community who has Parkinson's disease. We try to bring him to our home once a month, and the evening requires patience of all of us because of his speech impairment and physical disabilities. The boys are learning to be good about physical assistance as well as conversation."
- "One Christmas the children couldn't think of anything they really needed, and so we as a family decided to use the money we would normally spend on ourselves to instead buy a new bicycle for one of my very poor students. On Christmas Eve we took it to him, and we all agreed not to discuss it with anyone because it might embarrass him. It was a wonderful Christmas for us."
- "We try to make cards or write often to our elderly friends and relatives, especially those who are sick. We include the children in the card making or visits as often as possible."
- "Before Christmas, we pick out a neighbor or friend, someone who is usually alone. Twelve days before Christmas, we put one item, such as a cookie, piece of candy, in a Baggie and write a note with, 'On the first day of Christmas, my true love gave to me . . .' on it and hang it on their doorknob without them knowing it. We do this every day, adding one more item for each day of Christmas—two cookies for the second day, three cards for the third, etc., until Christmas Eve, when we bake a cake and go reveal ourselves to the person. We find that the person looks forward to each day and then finally to finding out who their 'true love' is. The boys have fun and they learn a little about true giving."

A sense of commitment—to relatives, friends, or the community at large—is a characteristic of healthy families. What follows is a gathering of suggestions for nurturing this sense in our own families. These are taken from these families' most common volunteer activities.

- Arrange regular visits to a nursing home to sing, play games, do puzzles, eat ice cream with residents. "Adopt" a resident who has no living family or few friends. The nursing home staff will have suggestions here.

- Sit with a child who is in the hospital so that his parents can rest for a few hours, or arrange to keep his siblings at your home to give his parents time with their hospitalized child.
- Make a meal and deliver it to an ill person or someone who cannot leave home.
- Give a free baby-sitting coupon to parents on special occasions, such as an anniversary, baby's birth, or a move to a new neighborhood.
- Put together fun bags, composed of small games and treats, to be delivered to children who are hospitalized.
- Drive a blind, elderly, or handicapped person to doctor's appointments, shopping, or dinner.
- Volunteer in a special-education classroom or school as a teacher's assistant. Or, be available to chaperon for field trips.
- Create holiday dinner baskets to be delivered to families on Christmas or Thanksgiving.
- Help serve food at a local missionary house, church, or community agency.
- Whatever your occupational talents—lawyer, plumber, teacher, carpenter—perform occasional services free of charge to those who need but can't afford.
- Invite a relative, friend, or family who will be alone on a holiday to your home for dinner.
- At Christmas, buy a gift for a needy child the same age as your own.
- Organize a backyard children's circus, inviting both adults and children. Allow the children to devote the proceeds to a local charitable organization in person.
- Every six months or year, sort through closets and drawers for clothing that is seldom worn or can be given to shelters for the homeless.
- Donate all proceeds of a garage sale to a local charity chosen by the children. Have the children write a letter offering the money to the agency.

Spirituality is an umbrella which protects while it nurtures a family's well-being. It builds cohesiveness through shared beliefs and values. It empowers a parent to teach by example, the most durable form of childrearing. It provides comfort through faith in a Creator who can guide one's parenting.

To nurture spirituality, as well as other components of rewarding family life, a parent needs TIME: THE ESSENCE OF PARENTHOOD.

Chapter 10

Time: The Essence of Parenthood

"Have children only if you want to share your life with them. If you don't think they are going to be the best people in the world to spend your time with, don't have them. There are other things you could do."

Mother, Califon, New Jersey

*T*ime. The four-letter word identified second only to *love* as a cornerstone of family cohesiveness. Excellent parents leave little doubt just how critical to a family's well-being they consider the willingness to spend time with and for the family. John, a father of four boys and a girl, minced no words in saying, "There are no tricks to parenting, just hard work. It starts with sacrifice and then goes to ultimate sacrifice. It is total commitment." Bobby, a mother in Idaho, seconded that perception more succinctly, "The family has always come first with me. That is where everything begins and ends."

The saying "Time is of the essence" can be rephrased slightly to describe strong family life. Time *is* the essence. Time provides the context in which all other family successes occur. The quality of relationships, the effectiveness of discipline, the openness of communication, the depth of spirituality—all are inextricably tied to the investment of positive time with one's family.

Love is the foundation of a family. Time is the medium for love.

Jerry from New Hampshire will be ever-grateful that as a young father his "my-life-first" attitude was permanently altered by the hard-hitting words of people assessing life after seven or eight decades of experience. "What changed my whole philosophy about having a family and believing in family was listening to old people—people who have retired, people who have gone through their lives raising their families, either successfully or not so successfully. When I was so active and wanted to be in everything—City Council, a singing group, Boy Scouts—I thought I had the perfect existence. But these older people kept saying, 'Just enjoy your children. Love them and be around them now.' Those words hit me like a rock. These people were close to death. They knew what is important. They didn't say, 'Be active in the community'; 'Be a success at work.' They said, 'Be with your family.' That, for me, is the salt of it."

Betty, mother of Judy, just recently graduated from college with honors, and Rick, who "isn't graduated yet, but is trying hard," always believed her time was the most durable gift she could give her children. Having this affirmed by her son was something she'll cherish forever. "Once, after our son had grown beyond the baseball and soccer fields, he and I were in a discussion, and I remarked that a neighbor boy, who had given his parents no end of problems, was now on his third car, having wrecked two others. I regretted not being able to afford one car for our son, who had never given us a problem in all of his twenty-one years. His response was, 'You and dad gave me something more important, something Steve never had—parents who were always there.' These words were, and are, my greatest gift."

Bill, father to Travis and Troy, aged twelve and fifteen, learned the preciousness of time long before becoming a parent. It was a lesson thrust upon him during childhood, and it's a lesson that's guided his fatherhood since it began. "The death of my dad when I was twelve was absolutely the worst thing that's ever happened to me. To this day, it's difficult for me to even think about it. Because of that loss, I try never to put off spending time with my kids. I realize it will not last forever."

Few of these parents entered parenthood with an ingrained realization of the degree of commitment involved. The value of time to a rewarding family life is something they've come to appreciate more with the years. Many admitted that as their family evolved, their priorities evolved with it, sometimes out of necessity. Not uncommonly, outside interests, hobbies, even job promotions on occasion, were cut back or bypassed altogether. The choices were difficult at times. On looking back, putting family first was a decision that none of the parents regretted in the end.

- "One of the things I used to do was to go into my own darkroom, put on my stereo headphones, and work. I could shut the whole world out. But when my daughter [aged two] wanted to come in, I couldn't shut the door. I wasn't home all day long, and when I came home, she would want my attention. I just couldn't go into that room and close that door anymore. So I sold all my darkroom equipment and haven't done it since."
- "It took me a while to realize that when children walk into a room and give you a greeting, they're asking you to turn around, recognize their presence, talk with them a few minutes, and see what they are doing. There have been times when I would say, 'I'm too busy. Don't follow me around. I'm really tied up.' [If I could go back] those are the things I would change. The kids have to be first on my list."
- "My teaching career took a backseat when my kids came along. I felt that time spent with my children was more valuable than any career for me. In order to give my best, I wanted my time devoted to my children. I haven't regretted it for a minute."

Patricia, a teacher's aide and mother of two boys, put it most bluntly. "You have to give up some of your own life when you have children. You have to know that, in many ways, you are living for them now."

Time is precious because it is limited. There is only so much of it to spread around, especially for parents. Big chunks of your day are gobbled up by the basic demands of running a household. The larger your family, the less discretionary time you have. Not one of these time-generous parents advises anyone to blindly follow the dictum of "At all costs, allot every minute of your free time to your children." Such a one-dimensional existence will fry your parental circuits before your firstborn cuts his first tooth. Even if you could relish being with or near a child every spare second, she wouldn't be real grateful for a hovering, ever-watchful parent. In the long-term, she'd be slow to grow up, and in the short-term, how could she ever get away with anything?

Involved parents recognize the importance of keeping some space in their togetherness, for their mental well-being and their children's. Nancy, a mother of three, aged twelve to seventeen, said, "I try to be where my children need me. Sometimes that's been at home, sometimes that's been as a Sunday school teacher or scout leader, and sometimes they have needed me

to be physically apart from them so they could become more independent."
And also so mom could regroup.

Parents from Omaha, Nebraska, concurred, "I think we are real careful about not overloading the children's circuits, about giving them time to be kids and giving them quiet times to themselves, but I am not sure we do the same for ourselves. I don't think we guard enough time for ourselves, and that is probably why we both lose our temper sometimes."

A father in Colorado asserts that every parent must find a comfortable middle ground between giving time to family and still fulfilling other responsibilities. " 'Balance' is the best word ever built in my opinion. It's not good to have too much of one thing or too little of most everything. If you give all your time to your kids, you would never get your work done. If you give all your time to your work, you would never see your kids. Someplace in there is a balance to life."

Obviously, families have widely varying flexibility in their schedules and lives. Some families can exist financially on one income, allowing a parent the choice to remain at home full-time to raise the children. Others need two incomes to pay the bills. Large blocks of their family time are spent coming and going between work, school, and the baby-sitter. Still other households are headed by one parent with one income, so "free" time is at the highest premium. While ultimately it is every mother and father's decision how best to allot energy and resources, these parents state wholeheartedly: Of whatever time in your life is negotiable, give much to your family and children. There is no substitute for your presence.

Sometimes when you can't be present in body, with a little creativity you can be present in spirit. Norman, who did a lot of business traveling when Kim, aged eighteen, and Chip, aged sixteen, were younger, devised his own personal way to reach out and touch them. "We would do things like work out math problems on the phone from my hotel room. I tried to overcome a lot of ostensible obstacles to keep my priorities where they should be. I believe these are the kinds of things that, by example, send messages a whole lot louder than you will ever state them."

Someone from somewhere once said, "Nobody ever looked back at the end of his life and said, 'I wish I'd have spent more time working.' " Several of the older parents, with children now raised, witnessed the swiftness of time's flight. One couple remembered, "Time passed so quickly. It cannot be recaptured, and we realized that our business [a restaurant] often had priority over our personal lives. It was especially difficult to try to be patient, to listen to a child, and to focus on his concern or problem when the business continued to make demands. We both wish we had known better how to avoid our business upstaging our personal lives."

Lucille and Howard felt no regrets, only a compelling realization of the quick passage of parenthood, even one that stretched out over eleven children and nearly thirty-five years. "We think that the hardest part of our parenting was the children leaving home one after another, even though we knew we couldn't keep them forever. When our nest was empty, we could hear every tick of the clock; the phone seldom rang; there were no more lines for cookies, bread, or chicken. We could have heard a pin drop in our rambling country home. I guess we didn't have to wait in line for the bathroom anymore."

In varying amounts, time is the one commodity we all have—or can make. If we let it slip away, we can't get it back. Of all ways to be generous with our children, the gift of time is the most worthwhile.

TIME—A CHILD'S PERSPECTIVE

These parents acknowledge that time is indispensable to a cohesive family life. But what do the kids think? After all, they do disagree with us grown-ups on more than a few facets of parenting. Maybe they don't consider our involvement in their lives as desirable as we do. Maybe to the kids, it doesn't matter that much if we're even in the same state, much less in the same house, car, or school auditorium. One way to find out, of course, is to ask them. They'll tell us what premium they place on our presence.

- "They, God love them, always seemed to have time for me or to take themselves away from what they were doing for me and the interests I had. I kind of wish I knew then what I know now because I didn't appreciate them like I should have. I kind of feel sorry for my friends because their parents were always 'too busy' to get involved in their interests, whereas, I can't say that I didn't have at least two fans at every one of my sporting events or class performances." [Daughter, aged eighteen]
- "My parents were always involved in what I was doing. For example, during high school, my mom would drive me and my other teammates to a baseball game or track meet, and my dad would take off work early to avoid missing my first at-bat or my first race. It wasn't because they had to or because they weren't busy. It was because they wanted to." [Son, aged nineteen]

- "What other people see is that my parents raised four decent, happy children. Some may think there was a trick to it or some magic was employed to make us turn out the way we did. The truth is they worked at it." [Son, aged twenty-seven]

- "This is the man who brushed our hair, made tire swings, and hit a thousand fly balls to his eleven-member outfield. This is the man who took his wife and five daughters shopping, who would spend the whole day patiently waiting, offering an occasional expert critique [I like the red one], until we found the perfect outfit." [This description was written by an adult daughter as part of a family scrapbook given to her mother and father on their fortieth wedding anniversary.]

- "My parents are the most unselfish human beings that I believe I will ever run across in my entire life. I don't believe there was a single instance where they put their own needs above ours. They were always sacrificing for us, and it was never because they had to. It was because they wanted to. My parents knew that raising responsible, caring children was constant work and sacrifice. They believed that children need consistency, and so this meant putting aside what they wanted in order to give us that consistency. I only hope I have enough guts to put all of my strength and energy into raising my children as they did in raising one." [Daughter, aged twenty-four]

The children's interviews are filled with intense appreciation for mom and dad's presence, emotionally and physically. While the most moving testimonials come primarily from the teens and older, the younger children, too, in their own way made plain their feelings. Eight-year-old Adam said, "The best time I ever had with my parents was at Disney World. We went on a roller coaster. My mom sat in the back because she was scared, and I sat with my dad. I liked that so much because we were all together." To Adam, all of Disney World didn't rate as his best time. Being with mom and dad did.

Ten-year-old Christian said, "When mom helps me with my homework is our best times because she spends time alone with me, and I understand it better." Even schoolwork is tolerable if it's paired with the presence of a parent.

Ten-year-old Tyler recalled, "Once when we were at the water slides for my first time, my mom and dad went down with me, and when I would get scared, my dad would say, 'Tyler, don't be scared, I'm here.' That's why my dad is the best dad." As Tyler says, if you want to be the best, be there.

We cannot overestimate what it means to children to share warm moments with us. The activity around which those moments are wrapped is secondary. What is primary is the togetherness. Strong parents understand the immeasurable impact of time, but nobody reinforces that impact more clearly than the children themselves. When considering his most precious memories of childhood, one young man in his middle twenties said quietly, "My parents took turns being unselfish while I was growing up." And there is no better way to be unselfish than to give of yourself.

OF QUALITY AND QUANTITY

Parenting in the past few decades has seen the emergence of a concept called *quality time*. Many experts now contend that the real value of any time spent with children depends on its quality rather than its quantity. In other words, when you interact with kids, especially if your opportunities to do so are limited, make the most of those opportunities. Make sure they are mutually positive, stimulating, and emotionally satisfying. Play games, tell stories, walk, talk, share, care. All these are worthy goals. It does little good to average five hours a day with Felicity, if three-and-a-half hours are mutually irritating.

Good parents agree that time shared with kids is best when it's good time. These parents part company with the experts on the notion of quality superseding quantity. They maintain that quality time depends on quantity time. The more time spent with or near a child—be it playing a game, drying dishes, or reading quietly in the same room—the more quality time is likely to occur.

Becky, mother to Ben and Emily, at ages nine and six representing the youngest family in this book, said, "Just being there to give a hug or a reassuring word right when it's most needed, or to see a smile that is so special, these are moments that make parenting worthwhile to me. I know I'm experiencing something I'll always treasure." For Becky, catching everyday "pieces" of her kids' growing up is what puts the quality in her parenting.

Connie, a mom of two from Delaware, felt similarly. "It's not easy to create an atmosphere conducive to a quality experience, whether you're dealing with a two-year-old or a fifteen-year-old. It just seems to me that the quantity of time spent together increases the odds of those spontaneous quality times which everyone appreciates."

Some parents were uneasy about the whole notion of quality time. They felt it was a phrase that could mislead. A mother and father from Mobile,

Alabama, stated, "We question the concept of quality time spent with children. It is too easy to use this as an excuse not to spend time with children on a regular basis. The presence of a parent, regardless of what might be taking place at home, is a major factor, in our opinion, in the stability of the family."

To Ron and Candy from Hot Springs, Arkansas, *quality* was not the guiding word, *equality* was. After Becky (now aged twelve) was born, requiring Ron and Candy to divide their time between her and her older brother, Jacob (now aged sixteen), they made some parenting adjustments. "Instead of 'quality time,' we planned 'equality time.' Since I spent more time with the baby, Ron spent extra time with big brother." This workable compromise continued after Abby (now aged seven) was born. Ron and Candy strove for equality; it was their way of ensuring quantity.

Finally, one father from Omaha didn't dally over diplomacy in his stance on quality and quantity: "Forget about quality time. Just be there." Indeed, "just be there" was a pervasive parenting theme. Quantity time is not measured solely by how many fun hours are shared with the kids. If this were so, some of us could only enjoy quality time. Out of necessity, our schedules don't offer large open blocks for frequent family activities. Besides, as the children move into their teens, they typically become less excited about hanging around us older folks. We embarrass them. Given these realities, most parents considered quantity time to include a passive presence, a willingness to make ourselves available for support, if and when the kids need us or are ready to talk. And when kids want to talk, they want to talk *now*, even if it's to us parent-types, even if it's because we're the only ones around.

Sometimes parents feel badly that their financial state doesn't allow them to give as much as they'd like to their children materially. If you've had such feelings, words from parents in Massachusetts should hold some comfort. "Our most important contribution to our children is giving *ourselves* to them, giving them all the time we can. We feel they can't ask for anything more than that." Not that kids won't try to ask, but conscientious parents maintain that time will more than compensate for a lack of designer labels, video games, cars, or extravagant allowances. Should the kids complain a little about our priorities now, they will appreciate them more fully some years from now, and that's what counts.

Making ourselves accessible to our children forges more than a durable family bond. It also provides them with a sense of security. No matter what life away from home deals them, no matter what risks they take and lose, no matter what outside supports they watch crumble beneath them, the unquestionable presence of their parents remains. The certainty that there is always a place to gather and regroup will bolster a youngster's self-confidence as he prepares for another run at the world. Sherry, a mother of three, aged ten to seventeen, said, "By being available to the children all the time, I think we have helped them know they have a strong home base. As they reach out into unknown areas and projects, they won't feel so anxious. They know we will support their endeavors." Lois, a high-school counselor and mother of two college-aged children, agreed, "I hope we were able to provide the guidance and the security in their at-home years so that they could like and believe in themselves. I believe that security for children comes in knowing that you are always there for them, physically and emotionally. We've tried to be there, whether as scout leader, Sunday school teacher, tear wiper, cheering section, confidant, hunting buddy, fashion consultant, disciplinarian." Nothing can more quietly and surely build a child's self-confidence than knowing his parents will be present and supportive, whenever, however.

Attentive presence is a quiet way to say, "I love you. You're most special in my life." Michael, now in his twenties, recalled, "My parents always made me feel like I was somebody. They would sit patiently and listen while I stumbled through some stupid joke I heard at school, even though most times I blew the punch line." How easy it is to affirm our child's worth to us simply by looking up from what we're doing and listening to a choppy version of a joke we first heard twenty-four years ago. If we laugh, the compliment is even nicer.

"You're worth my time" is a message made more memorable by spontaneity, that is, when we unexpectedly turn from our interests for our youngster's sake. A seventeen-year-old girl told how loved she felt when her parents, after seeing her sadness one day over some troubles with friends at school, changed their evening plans, not to deliberately stay home and work out the problem, but to be nearby just in case she wanted to talk. A son remembered, "Dad would be sitting on the front porch reading the paper. I would look over his shoulder and say, 'Why don't we go fishing or play catch?' There were times when he would want to keep reading the paper, but there were also times when he would say, 'Good idea,' and he would fold up the paper, get up, and do something with me. It was the greatest thing in the world to have him stop what he was doing and do something with me."

Of course, we can't drop whatever we're doing every time Fester makes it apparent that's what he would like us to do. Contrary to what the kids might believe, we do have a couple of other requests and demands on our time. We have to find a healthy blend between parent time and parent-child time. An Oregon father of four confessed, "I am often too task-oriented and don't willingly enough drop what I am doing for 'kid time.' It's a fine line to walk because the basic work of a household has to be done. I struggle with when I should stop what I'm doing and when it can wait." Normal feelings for parents. When we can give ourselves to our kids, and if we do, we are sending them a love message more plainly than anything we could say. It's a love message we may forget, but they rarely will.

JUST YOU AND ME, HUH, MOM AND DAD?

To think of family time as involving every family member would be to constrict the spirit of the idea. First of all, as kids get older and naturally pursue their own interests, gathering everyone in one place at one time can be about as common as a full solar eclipse. Second, and more important, whole family time doesn't always offer the kids a chance for a parent's undivided attention. The more brothers and sisters there are, the more mom and dad have to be shared. Throughout their interviews the children made it abundantly clear that while they value full family fun, they truly treasure one-to-one moments with parents. When asked, "What were the best of times in your relationship with your parents?" the kids quite often said things like:

- "My most precious times were when I was alone with either parent. In the winter, my dad and I would go out and watch men ice fishing on the lake. These were my most wonderful memories of my dad because he was all mine, and he was able to enjoy just me."
- "The very best times I can recall are those times I have spent alone with one or both of my parents. While there have certainly been good times with the entire family, and while I certainly don't advocate favoring one child over another, there is something about those individual times which have made me feel special, and which have allowed an individual relationship to develop between me and my parents, which is different from the relationships they have with my brother and sister. An example of one of these times was taking a leisurely walk around town one evening, talking about my college experiences and listening as they reminisced about theirs."

- "My relationship with my parents can also be seen in terms of those activities that I share specifically with one parent or the other. My father instilled in me a love for nature. He always brought me along when he went hunting or fishing. Our time together out in the hunting blind or fishing boat was some of the most enjoyable and memorable of my growing up. There was a lot of conversation and the feeling and mood involved in sharing, as father and son, the experience of doing something we both loved.

  "With my mother some of the most enjoyable times have been spent doing nothing more than just sitting down talking, whether it be at home on a Saturday afternoon or at a restaurant over lunch. The time my mother and I set aside to be together isn't centered so much on a specific activity, rather, it involves enjoying each other's company in conversation."
- "There have been lots of good times, but I'd say the best is when I go on a date with my dad and he takes just me roller skating. We have a lot of fun." [Daughter, aged eleven]
- "I love it when I'm sick; well, only because mom babies me so much, and I feel so protected."

Laura, the teenager just quoted, wasn't alone in her sentiment. Several children drew parallels between being sick and being content. Feeling under the weather could make them feel on top of the world because of the special attention it drew from the folks. One daughter said it well: "Undivided attention feels so good!"

What the children are saying is reassuring. It isn't easy for parents to arrange whole family activities, especially given that older child or two who always seems to have other plans, or who would lunge at the chance to talk unhindered on the phone all night while the rest of the family is out somewhere. When we can't orchestrate everyone's schedule into one, don't worry, the kids have stated we don't need to. They regularly prefer our company alone.

Every parent in this study has at least two children. Most have three or more. They know well the importance of putting extra effort into finding ways to make parent-child time:

- "If I were to write a book on parenting, I would advise parents to make special times with their children. As a young parent, I would be at home with the kids all day, and when I finally put them to bed, I could relax.

As soon as they got in bed, my husband, Roy, would want to go in and play with them. There was a time when that really bothered me, but then I realized that Steven was getting the one-on-one attention he needed from dad, and when Steven would fall asleep, Roy would go into Stephanie's room and have one-on-one time with her. This happened at least five times a week."

- "I make sure we have private moments. I do certain things with my son only and certain things with my daughter only. For example, Tuesday night is library night for my daughter and me. When my son was born, I didn't want my daughter to get upset because she had to suddenly share all of my time. She was one-and-one-half years old when I began taking her to the library on Tuesdays. She is nineteen now, and we still go to the library on Tuesdays when she comes home for the summer."

- "Shopping with one child provided the opportunity for one-on-one conversations. There were no interruptions from family members; this child had my complete attention. And the shopping itself was the pause needed for additional thought before conversation was resumed."

- "When we had several kids at home, for instance, we assigned a special day of the week to each child. On their day, only that child could stay up from her nap, or go to bed later at night, or spend time alone with mom or dad in some project."

Many families have similar ideas for making one-to-one time with each child. What follows is a gathering of these ideas for use in your family.

- Create for each child a never-ending story. Using him as the main character, each evening before bedtime weave a tale about him and his adventures. Ask him what things he'd like to do, see, explore, and learn about in his own ongoing fantasy.

- Whenever a young child shows you proudly what she did—a puzzle, a picture, a house of blocks—ask her if she'd like to do it again so you can watch.

- While you are enjoying a hobby—gardening, woodworking, crafts, painting—invite a child to watch and introduce him to the basics. Provide him tools of the craft with which to copy you. One mother described herself as "an avid gardener. All my kids, even the two-year-old, know how to pull a carrot."

- Use a tape recorder to produce a sound diary for each child. Record his earliest sounds—laughing, cooing, crying. Continue with his first words, songs, counting. In essence, create a permanent time capsule of his development through language. Set aside "recording sessions" for each child to tell his diary what he's learned recently.

- Allow a child to select her own special day of the week. On that day, show or teach her how to do something; for instance, sing a song, write a poem, plant a flower, bake cookies, fry an egg, make toast, tie a ribbon, wrap a gift, sew on a button, sort laundry, pump her own gas, discriminate a weed from a flower, identify a tree by its leaves, bait a hook, read a road map, program the VCR, tie a tie, play tic-tac-toe. Said a youngster now in college, "Thursday was dad's day off. He would always do something special with me. He taught me to tie my shoes on a Thursday."

- Periodically pull out the family photo album and tell a youngster about himself from his birth forward. Describe his antics as a toddler, his early questions about life, his first days in school. Kids love time trips into the past through pictures, especially about them and all that makes them special to you.

- Carry a camera with you or keep one nearby so as to catch a child in her own special moments with mom and dad.

- Take a child to visit your workplace. If possible, let him spend time with you as you move through your day. Indeed, the chance to "see where mom/dad works" was ranked at or near the top of favorite parent-child activities by these children.

- On a rotating basis, ask each of the children if she would like to go with you as you run errands, go to the store, visit a friend, or take a drive somewhere. The car is a prime vehicle for moments of privacy between parent and child. The destination of the trip is typically less important than the time taken getting there. Said a son about car trips with his father, "I loved my times *alone* with him, regardless where we went."

- Establish a weekly walk day during which you and one child take a leisurely walk. "I'll never forget how my dad would just let me stop and smell the flowers, look at the trees, pick up the stones," said one daughter. "Start young" is the advice of these parents. Introducing a walk day to a fifteen-year-old who fusses about taking the trash thirty feet to the end of the driveway may trigger a look that says, "Walk? I'm ready to drive in six months."

- Ask your daughter or son, depending whether you're a mom or dad, on a "date." Agree on the day, set the time, and plan the evening to its completion. Said a seven-year-old daughter obviously in love with her daddy, "When my daddy gets me flowers and we go out is the best, because he loves me!"

- Pick a day, say the third Monday of the month, as breakfast day, to spend with your son or daughter. Before school or work or athletic practice you and your child go to breakfast together. Or let each child choose a lunch day or ice-cream day. Many of the children spoke enthusiastically of a parent coming to school to eat lunch with them or taking them out to lunch.

- If your child practices a musical instrument, every so often quietly sit and listen. Your attention, punctuated by a complimentary word or two now and then, is a motivator and a display of pride. "If I had to choose one memory with my father, I'd say it was the time I came home from college on spring break and told him about the opera I was in at Indiana University. I remember relating to him the entire story of *Rigoletto* as we listened to the music. He'd never had any exposure to opera, but I was so pleased he shared with me this lovely discovery I'd made."

- Step in occasionally and help your child with his chores—drying the dishes, raking leaves, shoveling snow, doing laundry, dusting, setting the table. In addition to giving a lesson in cooperation, you will stimulate some natural camaraderie. "Working in the garden or yard with my parents was a lot of fun for me. Other kids used to ask me why my parents made us work so much. If they only knew what fun we had at those times." It's not the chore that's fun, it's having you there, if only because you're not thinking up something else for the kids to do!

START A TRADITION TOMORROW

Tradition—a word once associated with only positive qualities, such as character, durability, and roots. But now, in our modern, fast-moving society, the word is sometimes associated with *old-fashioned,* or a rigid adherence to custom solely because "that's the way it's always been done."

Excellent families view tradition in a most favorable sense. To them, traditions are predictable and reliable times for togetherness. They are a medium for time well spent. Traditions also foster a sense of security. No matter what forces shake the family, no matter what its members endure, traditions are something around which to wrap a sense of belonging. They can insulate from life's uncertainties. They are a constant.

Traditions need not be handed down through generations. Many families' traditions began spontaneously and gradually evolved into an integral part of their identity. Three youngsters from Wisconsin, aged ten to fifteen, summarized the traditions that added meaning to their family life:

- "With our birthdays, we have cake in the morning before school, and we open our presents. Molly's birthday is sometimes at spring break, so we go do whatever she wants to do, like go to a museum. We also get to pick a place for dinner for our birthdays. For Christmas Eve, we always have an international dinner. Last year it was German, and once it was French. We always have a Christmas party with cookies and eggnog for the people from our dad's clinic. Sometimes we go Christmas caroling. On Easter, we hunt for eggs in the house. On some holidays we go to parades. We put up the flag on the Fourth of July. On Memorial Day we usually have a picnic with our friends and our relatives from out of town. We have a friend that my dad bowls with, and we alternate holidays with them. Labor Day we go to their house, and then they come to ours for New Year's Day."

To children and parents, tradition was synonymous with family time. A now-adult son described his father's storytelling as the source of his most enjoyable family hours. "My dad could talk in pictures. It was like a movie going by in front of me."

Sixteen-year-old Frieda remains grateful that years ago her family established a weekly night out. "Friday night dinners are very important to me. There are those times when we can't go, but they can only be missed for special occasions. I'm so glad my parents raised me to be there for Friday night dinners."

The composition of the family traditions is varied: a father cooking breakfast for each child on his or her birthday; opening presents one at a time on Christmas Eve, beginning with the youngest and continuing to the oldest, then back around for round two; the yearly garden planting; popcorn and a video movie on Saturday night; cutting the Christmas tree; a child sharing lunch with her father at his workplace on her birthday; monthly family game night. The particulars of the tradition are not so much what matters. What matters is that the tradition is a family priority. It is a dependable event, not something to be bypassed without very good reason.

The younger a child is when a family tradition is begun, the more naturally she will integrate it into her concept of family. Younger children eagerly embrace moments with us. Older children, as a normal part of their emerging independence, have interests other than the family. Traditions started early are durable. As the older children point out, no matter what outside interests compete with family time, a long-standing tradition is the last thing to be crowded out.

Traditions are memories made warm by love. Seventeen-year-old Lori describes one of her fishing trips with her father. "My dad and my sister and I were out in a boat in a shallow area. The weeds kept getting tangled in the motor, and most of the day was spent untangling. When we returned to shore, a lady asked about our catch. My dad explained that we didn't catch any fish because we spent most of our time untangling the motor. The woman sympathized, saying she was sorry we didn't have a lucky day. I'll never forget what my dad said, 'No, we had a very lucky day. We caught a lot of memories.' " Traditions do more than create time that binds. They create memories forever.

RITUALS—LITTLE TRADITIONS. A form of family tradition is the family ritual. Rituals are things such as good-night kisses, a joke of the day, a bedtime story, meeting at the door (bus stop) after school, "I love you" in place of "good night," a "horseyback" ride around the yard after supper, a nightly walk, watching the evening news, a daily reading hour.

Rituals can be shared daily, weekly, or occasionally as the desire arises. For example, a few families liked to pull out old family photo albums and recall mom and dad's youth, courtship, and early marriage. They talked about the places they once lived, old friends, their first car, their high-school days, great-grandparents. These family portrait sessions foster a sense of family through its history. What's more, photos are black-and-white proof to the kids that mom and dad weren't always as ancient as they are today.

Like traditions, rituals are durable components of a family's well-being. They are its personal way of identifying itself and its members as unique. Rituals are the signature of a family.

THE GET-TOGETHER GETAWAY

The leading tradition in successful families is the family vacation. Here, *vacation* is broadly defined as a regular break from routine—annual, monthly, even weekly—that not only frees everyone from daily demands, but more important, frees them to be with each other. Vacations are seen as a form of retreat, a chance to relax, regroup, and reinvigorate relationships. Given top priority status, vacations are not something to be put off, bypassed, or relegated to an if-we-have-the-time spot on the calendar. One father described his family's protectiveness toward their vacation time: "We made it our business that whenever the kids were off school, we were off to somewhere. Sometimes it was unconventional, but it was always special." A flavor for the integral role of vacations in these families' togetherness comes from comments like these:

- "Vacations are the best of times for us because they are times together. We are able to relax; there is no TV, no basketball, no baseball. It is just us and the children. Around here it's hard to have much privacy. If we try to do anything, the phone rings or someone comes to the door. When we go away on a trip, there is nothing to bother us. We don't have the distractions, and we don't have to be anywhere."
- "The best of times are during our summer vacations at a beautiful mountain cabin. No telephones or televisions or radios distract us from each other. We share so many moments together hiking, fishing, playing, reading. These times are good for our children, as they are not exposed to peer pressure and can explore who they are and who they want to become in natural solitude."
- "The best of times with my parents must include our numerous family trips. The feelings of having a close-knit family became much stronger on these trips. I feel they were somewhat of a test of the strength and togetherness of our family. To spend days or weeks constantly together, and to call these the best of times, shows that the tests were passed." [Daughter, aged seventeen]
- "The best times are when we are on a vacation and know we can't leave. We fight or just disagree, and then know we're trapped and so we do fun things." [Daughter, aged twelve]

Parents who work hard every day at being parents realize: Families need to get away to get together. In one sentence, Julie from Omaha summarized her unwillingness to forsake vacations. "The kids aren't going to remember how clean the house was, but they will remember a trip to the state park."

As with all traditions, it's the spirit, not the specifics, that matters. Neither money nor several days are necessary to create a vacation. Some families, when money and time were at a premium, improvised. Instead of traveling, an Alaska family schedules "play days" at home, suspending routine and requirements for everybody. They enjoy twenty-four uninterrupted hours playing as a family. Thinking about this takes me back to the "snow" days of childhood, when schools had to be closed and several inches of snow temporarily halted much of my existence. Forced to be confined, I delighted in my unexpected freedom. The warmest memories can come from the coldest days.

Barb, a mother of five from New Jersey, has nothing but fondness for her family's budget vacations. "When the kids were little, we always did cheap things. We never took them anywhere like Disney World. Instead, we would go to the state park on weekends. Very rarely did we do anything that we had to spend money for. Consequently, we often ended up just hanging around and enjoying our 'boring time.' To us, that was an important kind of time. We sat around the table and played a lot of made-up games."

Neither do kids need money to make a vacation. Thirteen-year-old Matt from Oregon said, "The best times I have ever had with my parents are when we just go on small outings, like golfing and fishing. I think this is because I like spending time with my parents rather than going to Disneyland or a place like that." His eleven-year-old sister, Kara, was even more easily contented. "The best times I have with my parents are when we sit down and have popcorn together while we play a game or watch television. It's fun, and we can talk about things." More fun than Disney World? At least it's cheaper.

More so than their parents, the kids say: A break from routine is important to us. It isn't where we go, how much money we get to spend, or the size of the swimming pool that we'll talk about for years. It's the chance to be with our family, not bothered by anything or anybody.

Vacations are booster shots for a family's resistance to everyday strains.

OF TIME AND MONEY

In sharing his thoughts on money and childrearing, Stan from Hawaii said philosophically, "It is more important to have a high level of living than a high standard of living." Marilyn from Oregon agreed. "Buying things is no substitute for time and love. Kids can't be fooled. They would much rather have us attend their school program, for example, than miss it because we are working late so they can wear a designer label on their clothes." Seconding this perception wholeheartedly was a daughter from Washington. "Mom and dad made a mutual decision that mom would be a housewife. They sacrificed the tangibles, like a pool, new cars, or a boat for things that mean so much more, like spending time with their children and nurturing their growth."

One mother's opinion on overdoing the tangibles was blunt. "The more you give to children materially, the less they appreciate." On the other hand, she's noticed that the more time you give to children, the more they appreciate it.

If you are unable to provide your children the standard of living that you'd like, or the one that they'd like you to think they'd like, you needn't feel guilty whatsoever, according to these parents and their youngsters. It is time that heads children's list of most precious parental gifts. Whether you're short or long on money, the more you give of you, the less your kids will care about worldly goods or any lack of. Time *is* the essence of parenthood.

Time is the cornerstone upon which a family's well-being is built. *Involvement, presence, availability*—words that signify a parent's commitment to family success. Giving quality time in quantity improves every aspect of one's home life. An example will be found next in COMMUNICATION: THE BASICS AND BEYOND.

Chapter 11

Communication: The Basics and Beyond

"It doesn't matter if you're a nuclear family, a single-parent family, an extended family, or a step-family, you can have a good family if you start from the beginning with good communication."

Mother, Pittsburgh, Pennsylvania

Communicating with children is a skill that has tested the best of parents for countless generations. Two thousand years ago, a parent somewhere must have been lamenting, "These kids nowadays. They all want to wear shoes. I tell them, 'You mark my words. These things are a passing fad.' But do they listen?"

For all of its challenge and complexities, good communication with children can be distilled to two basic goals: Get them to listen, and get them to talk. The whole of parent-child communication can be summed up in these two goals. Though we cannot possibly delve into all the intricacies of the subject, we can concentrate on a few basics as practiced by some successful parents, parents who most likely wouldn't have been as successful had they not acquired knowledge of these basics over the years.

As these parents emphasize throughout this book, you don't need to be psychologically sophisticated to be effective. Simple, straightforward approaches are often the best means to a desirable end. So it is with communication. Master a few basic principles, and many of the finer points will naturally fall into place.

PRINCIPLE #1: TALK LESS TO BE HEARD MORE

The first step toward better communication begins with a step backward. Or, to explain more clearly, we must step back from how we presently communicate with our children and scrutinize our style. Despite our best intentions, are we doing anything that is only frustrating us and the kids? Many competent parents have learned the long-winded and hard way that what often sounds like open communication is the very thing that is closing a youngster's ears and mouth. These are the illusions of communication, as one father called them, and they can trap a parent into misspending thousands of hours and millions of words over the course of a parenthood.

THE LECTURE Topping the list of futile communication practices is the lecture. Few things shut down two-way dialogue more surely than a lecture, which is not surprising, as a lecture is essentially a one-way monologue. We talk on and Buster grunts every twelve minutes just to let us know he's still conscious. When asked what she thought was her worst parenting strategy, Pat, a single mother of two teenage girls, said without hesitation, "Lecturing."

Jay and Mary have a similarly disparaging opinion of lectures. In looking back at earlier years of trying to make themselves heard with their now nineteen-year-old daughter and seventeen-year-old son, they regretted what they called "overparenting." "I think if Jay and I made a repeated mistake, it was probably that some of our talks with our kids were too long and on a lecturing note."

As youngsters head into adolescence and become convinced that our views were outdated just prior to the Civil War, their definition of a lecture narrows. To teens, a lecture is any sentence over seven words, any compound sentence, or any group of words beginning with: "When I was your age"; "Now listen here"; "And another thing"; "You know, I wasn't born yesterday." Eighteen-year-old Kelley called lectures "*long,* one-sided discussions where my brother and I don't say much because we don't like these discussions."

Kids reflexively shut down in the face of a lecture. Their eyes glaze, their face goes slack, and they cease to register any incoming information except,

"Do you have anything to say?" To which they reply, "No." Our grown-up definition of a lecture is much broader. We grant ourselves a few thousand words before we consider ourselves lecturing. Regardless of which definition we use, lectures seldom bring home the points they were intended to.

To get a sense for how poorly kids hear lectures, listen to seventeen-year-old Stephen from Maryland. "I would come up with a problem and hear, 'I told you so,' or 'You're right; you shouldn't have procrastinated.' When I didn't need their opinion, I heard it. I *knew* I was wrong, but they had to make sure I knew. I always felt, 'OK, I was wrong. I admit it. Now could you help me out?' For instance, sometimes they would take me to the library the day before something was due, and I thought they might laugh and say, 'Great, you'll have this done by tomorrow. You owe me a lot for this one!' But it was usually, 'This will never happen again!' I admit, they were trying to mold me, teach me good habits for studying. If I had gotten C's instead of A's, I would say they were right. But I got A's by doing the project the day before it was due. I *know* and I *knew* that it wasn't a good way to do it, but I did it so well it prevented me from seeing their way of doing things."

In full agreement with Stephen was thirteen-year-old Sarah, who was even more strident as she described her least favorite times with mom and dad. "First, my parents scream. Then comes the we're-so-disappointed speech. After that, the I-never-did-that-to-my-parents-when lecture begins. After that, they realize how ridiculous they sounded, but they don't take back anything."

Strong stuff, but many youngsters feel similarly. And most every parent, especially those with older children, knows this. We've seen that same blank or turned-off look again and again from the kids. Why, then, do we continue to talk well after it's obvious our words aren't landing anywhere? Our drive to lecture arises from our drive to be good parents. We love with no limits, so sometimes our urge to persuade knows no limits. We so much want to make Dawn understand, say, the risks of being out too late at night, or to make Oxford realize the critical importance of education. Lecturing is our way of searching for the right words, the right logic, the right emotions to get our concern across. We believe that if we just press on long enough, something within our youngster will click, and he'll learn through our words and not the world's consequences.

Unfortunately, lectures are a classic example of the law of diminishing returns. The further we venture into a lecture, the less any of our words have meaning to the kids. Worse, whatever impact our first words had will fade away as they become more deeply buried beneath an avalanche of ensuing words. One mother confessed she finally realized how completely she'd slipped into the lecture cycle upon seeing that "here-we-go-again" look on her son's face immediately after she declared, "We have to talk." These words had so many times signaled a lecture that her son was now shutting her off before her first word.

To squelch her urge to lecture, Marcia from Kansas made herself follow one rule. It was her survival technique born during her years of living with three teenagers. "Don't intrude and wait until they come to me for advice." Regularly, responsible parents must assess a situation without a child's invitation to do so. When the matter is not urgent, Marcia's advice was to delay offering a wordy opinion. It gives the kids a chance to seek our input, although they probably still would like it in one hundred words or less.

Betty from Missouri developed an indirect approach that worked better than any word barrage. "My children sometimes would close their ears if they felt I was preaching to them. I found that my cautions and warnings were accepted more readily if I brought up a news article that concerned the situation I wanted discussed and called it to the attention of their father. He and I would talk about the hazards, consequences, implications, while our children absorbed the information and never thought I was preaching. This really helped when they began driving. Instead of constantly repeating, 'Don't drink; don't speed; don't drive with others who drink and speed,' I brought up articles I had read in the paper in which others had been guilty of these offenses, and I expressed my sympathies for the families of any victims. The topics were not limited to driving, but concerned any issue I felt needed some conversation." Betty made no deliberate effort to draw the kids into the conversation. She allowed it to occur naturally, counting on a teenager's compulsion to insert his opinions, especially if he thinks he isn't being asked for them.

An idea similar to Betty's comes from Don, father to a boy and two girls in Connecticut. Don's approach is more visual than verbal. "We try to show the kids examples of what can happen if a child doesn't follow directions or doesn't behave. For instance, if we are at a party or a gathering where there is a particularly ill-behaved child, when we get out to the car, we will discuss that child's behavior. We ask the kids if they would like to be perceived as that child was. Of course, they say no. But we are always looking for these kinds of examples to teach the kids."

Lectures arouse defensiveness, believes Stan from Hawaii. His close involvement with his church provides one gentle way to communicate collectively with his five children. "I speak at least once a month in our church, and many lessons that are aimed at everyone are heard also by our children. This is more persuasive than speaking to them individually. It is nonthreatening."

Few of us have the opportunity that Stan has. His methods, however, as well as Betty's and Don's, illustrate a principle supported by many psychological studies. Some communication, especially that which an individual doesn't want to hear, is more credible and persuasive if imparted indirectly, that is, if it is overheard or aimed at someone else—like a sibling—within ear range. In other words, kids will be a little more open to thinking like us if they think we're not deliberately trying to make them think like us.

To summarize—if we haven't gone on too long already—kids don't learn much from lectures. The children in these families realized this after the first few lectures or so. The parents realized it after the first fifty lectures or so. Everybody's advice is to drastically cut back on lectures and begin replacing them with other, more give-and-take communication practices, of which additional suggestions are coming shortly.

THE CLICHÉ "When you have children of your own, you'll understand why I do what I do"; "This is for your own good"; "You'll thank me for this someday." Lines like these have been solemnly stated by so many of us parents so often that they've pretty much ceased to have any impact on kids. They've been rendered clichés. Bobbi, a registered nurse and mother of three, aged eight to eighteen, believes her best piece of communication advice is, "Avoid the clichés. They turn off communication." She feels that clichés draw a child's attention away from the real issue. Contrary to what the kids think, we parents do have specific reasons, say, for our stance against dating in the ninth grade, or our rule that all homework be completed before phone privileges begin. By falling back on a cliché to justify our actions, we dilute the precision of our position.

Kids react to cliché's with the same excitement they reserve for lectures, not unexpectedly, as most lectures are liberally sprinkled with cliché's. Sixteen-year-old Kristine from Illinois considers her roughest times with her parents to be at the present because, "They think I act too smart and expect everybody to do everything for me. I hate getting lectured about my 'attitude problem,' especially after being told how my parents walked to school uphill in the snow both ways."

Remember your eye-rolling, dulled senses reaction every time you heard something like, "You know, young lady, you don't know how easy you've got it. When I was a girl, I used to get up at five o'clock in the morning—two hours after I went to bed—washed every wall in our house, and then split a cornflake for breakfast with five brothers and sisters." Nothing's changed. Such childhood comparisons, however accurate, will have no effect on our children until they themselves become parents and can say, "You know, young man, when I was a kid, I only had one TV in my room, and it only received seventeen channels." We can take some consolation that his son will give him the same blank expression he once gave to us.

Nearly every parent draws upon clichés to some degree, and probably always will. This is because clichés are true for the most part. Some day Webster will understand the motive behind our homework-before-phone rule, and Lola will see the rationale underlying our no-dating-in-the-ninth-grade "lack of trust" in her. Despite their truth for us, clichés hold no truth for children. Since kids are kids—we psychologists are trained to say profound things like this—they aren't able emotionally to grasp the meaning of child-rearing clichés. The far-off future or long-gone dinosaur days of our youth have no relevance whatsoever to them. Kids are creatures of the now. Therefore, good communicators suggest: Give your reasons for your actions in present language—I'm not letting you go to the party because I don't think there will be enough adult supervision. Resist drawing parallels to parties in your day, when lemonade without sugar was the strongest drink available. Forsaking clichés may not get you any more understood, but at least you won't have to weather that look that says, "Tape #104, 'When I was your age . . .'"

THE HEATED WORD There's a fundamental relationship between emotions and communication. The more upset parents are about something the kids have done, the more intense our desire to talk to them about it immediately, and the more likely we'll say something we'll later wish we could unsay. Knowing this from experience, some excellent parents advise that the less said, the better, when angry. It's wise to delay any discussion until we're settled enough at least "to see straight." Connie from Ohio observed that too much is said during high emotions that hurts when it hits. The keystone of their family's communication was "determining when to express one's thoughts and feelings and when to keep silent. We don't subscribe to the let-it-all-hang-out theory of open communication." In other words, when emotions are at high pitch, we release hot words we should have kept to ourselves.

A New Jersey mother has one cardinal rule for maintaining communication composure: "Treat your kids the way you would treat your best friend." Adults work hard to stay cool and collected with other adults. We usually strive to act with some measure of restraint, or at least civility, no matter how agitated we feel. This parent believes we owe the same effort to our children, who mean so much to us, even though she knows, as does every parent, that kids can exasperate us far more than most grown-ups.

Robert, an electrician and father of four, calmed himself during potentially explosive situations with these thoughts: "Never forget what you were like as a child. Never forget all the things you've done." For Robert, staying even-tempered comes from remembering that impulsive, foolish behavior has always been a normal part of growing up. It is not a sign that a child is straying from the values we thought he had.

"A three-year-old is the embodiment of the word 'relentless,'" said one mother. Knowing that toddlers and preschoolers can wear thin the patience of the most even-tempered parent, strong parents offer this advice: When you feel the urge to explode—in response to incessant nagging, whining, questions, or complaining—put distance between your ears and your little one's voice. A parent said, "When I feel I'm being hammered at, I tell my son to go into another room, either to play or just sit for a while. When my temperature drops back to normal, I ask him to come back in."

Another parent stated that he put a ceiling on the number of questions he would answer, questions like: "Daddy, why is there air?"; "Well, why do we have to breathe?"; "What happens if you don't breathe?"; "Why do people hold their breath?"; "Why can't I see air?" Dad said that not only do his four-year-old's questions make him feel ignorant, but that he can respond to only so many without getting exasperated. "No more questions for now, I'm out of answers" was dad's phrase, and he temporarily ceased answering, either by changing the subject or playing dumb.

A common viewpoint was that temporarily curtailing a dialogue with a preschooler is better than carrying it to the edge of your patience, and possibly saying or doing something regrettable. Take a bit of time to recompose yourself, and you'll be better able to explain patiently why clouds are white or why Dawn has to lie down because mom's going to.

From Alaska, where the air is cool, Susan shares a technique she used to pull herself through her minutes of hottest emotion. "Sometimes when the boys were very young and I was very angry at them, I would first read to them rather than raising my voice, which is what I would have done if I tried to talk to them immeately." Susan's opinion was that most problems weren't going anywhere if she didn't react instantly to them. After a short story or two, in a less perturbed state, she could turn her full attention to the disturbing matter. Although she wryly admits, there were occasions when a complete reading of the *Encyclopaedia Britannica* wouldn't have been sufficient to settle all her agitation.

Other suggestions offered for lowering the temperature of our words were to tell the kids:

- "I'm really upset, so I don't want to say anything right now. Go play, and I'll come and get you when I'm calm."
- "I'm going to sit in this chair for a little bit. You sit in that chair. We'll talk after we sit."
- "Your mother [father] and I have to discuss this situation first, then we'll all talk."
- "Write me a letter telling me what happened and why you did what you did. Then we'll talk about the letter."
- "I'm too upset to think clearly, so please go to your room, and I'll join you when I'm calmer."

With preschoolers, a delayed response is not always possible. First of all, they bounce so rapidly from one piece of mischief to the next that sometimes they're headed into a second and third round of trouble before we've even figured out how to deal with the first. Second, as a general rule, the younger the child, the more immediate our response needs to be to his behavior. Even a delay of a few minutes may be plenty of time for a two-year-old to lose the connection between his misconduct and our discipline. Therefore, while working for composure before we respond is wise, with younger children we have less time to do so. Balancing both ends of this equation is tricky, but we can take comfort in another general rule of childrearing: The younger the child, the simpler his misbehavior.

A few closing words about overheated communication. No parent exists who is calm all the time. Once we assume the name *mom* or *dad*, our emotions become inseparably linked to our children's well-being. As frightening as that can sometimes be, we wouldn't want it any other way. Furthermore, getting upset is not all bad. Anger is like a spice. If we don't pour it on, when we do use it, our children will have little doubt about the strength of our feelings on a particular issue. Still, strong parents assert that, on the whole, some of their weakest communication occurs during those times when their brain is overwhelmed by their blood pressure. They've learned that a soft approach leaves a more lasting impression than hard words.

PRINCIPLE #2: GIVE A FAIR HEARING

Curtailing lectures, clichés, and heated words will do much more than soothe your family's nerves. With fewer words automatically comes more silence. And silence is the forerunner of the skill most fundamental to communicating with kids: listening. In fact, *silent* and *listen* contain the same letters.

In chapter 7, the children gave us parents a basic lesson in listening. They said that they will talk more if we listen more. Sounds fair enough. So, picking up where the kids left off, these mothers and fathers will now add their thoughts on the art of listening. After all, contrary to what kids think, we parents are capable of coming up with a few ideas on our own, even if only by pure luck.

As do their children, good parents believe good communication starts with the willingness to pay attention. To Joe from Dallas, good listening means keeping his mouth closed until a child closes hers. "Listen to the end, no matter what you are being told. If you blow up before listening to the whole story, be ready to apologize."

To Lois, mother of two, listening to the end means "being quiet, attentive, and taking in what is being said. Listening is not having to put in the last parental two cents' worth."

From Augusta, South Carolina, Joanne and Curt listen more thoroughly by believing, "There is no such thing as a foolish question. Every question is important because a child wouldn't have asked it if he didn't feel it was."

To be sure, no parent can be the perfect listener, in large part because we are often so emotionally connected to what the kids are telling us. What's most important is to work at listening, even if we're not always successful. · When asked what she would change about her parenting if she could go back a few years, Sharon, a mother of three, replied, "I'd listen more and allow the kids more chance to talk before I gave my suggestions." She then added this advice gained from past inexperience: "Don't react quickly to whatever your kids are telling you, even if you're dying to react. Hold off even a minute. Hear what they're saying."

From Kentucky, Mary Jo confesses she doesn't always give her oldest son, aged thirteen, an open ear. "To Stewart, very often I respond yes or no when I haven't even heard what he asked. I'm busy doing something, and I will say, 'No, you can't do that.'" She does try to compensate for her reflex, however. "I have come back to him and said, 'If you feel I made the decision too quickly, I will sit down and talk with you about it.' There have been times when I've changed my mind. And times when I've said, 'After we discuss it, if I still feel the same, you'd better back off and let it drop.'" Don't mess with Mary Jo after she's reconsidered and remains unmoved.

Ron, father to Abby, Becky, and Jacob (aged seven through sixteen), reminds himself that a child's perspective is not an adult's. "A child has big problems as he sees them, regardless of what his age is. We may know something is a little thing, but to him, it is big. If he comes home with a bad grade or loses something that he likes, it is important to him, and we have to try to understand that." Recognizing that life's little problems seem bigger when you're little should add a few minutes to our patience threshold.

The younger the child, the less likely she is to tell us something that prompts parental advice or comment. She just wants to say what's on her mind. We can listen longer if we remind ourselves that putting thoughts into words can be a time-consuming, exhausting exercise for little ones. As they stammer their way through a meandering monologue, we sometimes fight the impulse to hurry them along, feeding them words and finishing their sentences. A mother of three said she always tried to remember that the younger a child, the longer she needs to make herself understood. By patiently listening, mom was giving her best compliment. Without words she conveyed, "You're important."

Some parents stretch their listening capacity by telling themselves that listening is safe. Nothing bad can happen while the kids are talking to us. If, for instance, Stanford has already skipped a class at school, he can't be skipping any more while standing in full view of us and telling us about it, not unless he's incredibly creative. Should he be planning more skipping, as long as he's voicing his intention, he's not yet acting on it. Of course, any seasoned parent knows that kids are ten to fifteen times more likely to tell us about trouble after it's over rather than before. Even so, some long-winded listeners suggest: Listen as long as you can. There's no rush to talk. You'll hear more of what a child is thinking, and when you do speak, you'll speak with more understanding and authority.

Good listening begins with silence. It doesn't end there. Betty, whose two children are young adults, feels that questions are a natural way to listen and understand, and she wishes she would have taken more advantage of them. "I regret not asking my children more questions in depth. I was a good listener, but I think I could have gotten better conversation with more questions. I was sometimes so intent on listening and getting them to express how they felt about something that maybe I missed some very worthwhile communication. I never realized this until our children were older, but now I'm looking forward to grandchildren and some very enjoyable conversations."

What are some worthwhile, exploring questions? Here are a few:

- What were you thinking when you did that?
- What else could you have done?
- Did you expect things would turn out the way they did?
- What can you do to make things better?
- How did you decide what to do?
- What will you do next time that happens?
- Any ideas on how we should handle this?
- What would you do now if you were me?

After sliding past your youngster's initial "I don't know," questions like these should provide a closer glimpse into his motives and thoughts. Brace yourself, though. Sometimes what you hear might be a little scary. Remember, while ignorance may be more comforting than knowledge in the short run, knowing what and how your youngster thinks will render you a much more effective parent in the long run.

Other suggestions for lengthening your listening stamina are:

- After your youngster has given you her side of a story or her perception of a situation, quietly ask her to tell you again what she said, so you can be sure you understood it.
- When your son has finished talking, rephrase for him what he just told you. Then ask him if that is essentially what he meant.
- Make sure you understand the five W's of what your child tells you—the who, what, when, where, and why—before giving your opinion, advice, discipline, or whatever action you take as a result of what you heard.
- Turn off the television, radio, stereo, even telephone, if necessary, to avoid potential distractions to giving your child your full attention when he is ready to talk.

Techniques for good listening apply to children of any age. Whether a youngster is two or nineteen, open communication begins with listening and continues with a genuine attempt to understand completely what he is saying. Even if we totally disagree with Justice, he deserves a fair hearing before we act.

PRINCIPLE #3: PRACTICE YOUR TIMING

Communicating with kids is as much a matter of timing as it is style. Just as important as *how* we talk or listen is *when* we talk or listen. Parents who've discovered the best ways to communicate have often done so by first discovering the best times to communicate. One father dubbed these "the prime times of communication." A child is likely to reveal more about her thoughts and feelings during one prime time than she will during a dozen communication sessions prompted by some misdeed or a family crisis.

The key, of course, is to know when these times are or how to create them. Excellent parents can help here. Through planning or fortunate accident, they've uncovered some of the most productive moments to talk and to listen to children.

Bedtime is the preferred time to share thoughts with younger children— once the kids are *in bed,* that is, and not during the forty-seven minutes of verbal, and sometimes physical, grappling it can take to finally get them there. A mom from South Dakota had a nightly ritual for hearing all about her children's day. "When the kids were being tucked into bed at night, we always asked them, 'What were the good times and best times of the day?' and 'What were the bad times?' We learned quite a lot." Parents from Montana, Bill and Carol, made bedtime their standard talk time with their sons. "When the children were young we alternated nights tucking in each child. Having two children, this meant that Bill tucked in Troy and I tucked in Travis on one night, and then we switched the next night. That was private, one-on-one time to talk. We are still tucking in our thirteen-year-old. He demands it."

Bedtime is a settled time that can relax a child's inhibitions and encourage her to share things she might not during the hustle of the day, when other pursuits—like running and jumping—can easily take precedent over stopping to talk with us. Most kids are anxious to say anything—they'll make stuff up if they have to—if it means stalling their bedtime off for another ten minutes or so.

Bedtime can stimulate communication even with older children. Several parents, rather than turning over in bed and trying to fall asleep upon hearing their son or daughter return home from a night out, invited the kids to sit on the edge of the bed and chat about their evening. Attempting to convey a genuine interest in their youngster's emerging independence, these parents avoided prodding questions. One seventeen-year-old daughter enjoyed her after-the-date dialogues with her folks almost as much as the date itself. "My favorite times with my parents are when I come home from a date and sit on their bed and we talk and talk and talk." Another teen said, "I think some of the best times with my mom were when I'd come home late from a night out, and she'd be waiting up. We'd stay up for a couple more hours, even though we were tired and just talk. She'd listen to the problems I was having at school or with friends. Most of the time we'd laugh, but sometimes we'd cry."

A word of caution. If you're thinking of initiating something similar after your youngster's next evening out, prepare to meet some suspicion. Teenagers can get borderline paranoid when asked extremely personal questions like, "Did you have fun?"

Meals are also a natural time for freewheeling banter and an exchange of ideas. Jay and Mary from Arizona said, "We have worked diligently to have an evening meal at least four or five times a week. We believe this has been extremely important in keeping our family close. We even take our phone off the hook so our conversations won't be interrupted."

Another family established a meal rule that no one could interrupt the person who "had the table," in other words, the person talking. This was their way of making sure each family member had a chance to talk about whatever was on his mind, and to carry all thoughts through to completion. Sometimes, though, mom or dad did have to intervene to terminate a dominating filibuster.

Pete and Elise initiated a family tradition they enjoyed with their three sons for years. "Every few weeks we had a round-table discussion at breakfast. We gave each person in the family five minutes to talk about what was going on and how they were feeling about those things. This five minutes had to be completely uninterrupted. If they needed another five minutes, they were given them. The most important thing was that this time was theirs and uninterrupted." Pete and Elise discovered that permitting kids an unbroken monologue, with no "threat" of parental comment or advice, has nearly unlimited potential for evoking their perceptions on matters. Of course, the real challenge for parents is to clamp our mouths at the end of the five minutes in which Cecil revealed he can't wait until he's twelve so he can marry the neighbor girl.

Jerry, father to four boys, takes advantage of post-meal moments. "We keep the kids [aged eleven, thirteen, and twins, aged seventeen] around the table a few minutes after everyone is finished eating. It's one of the few times everybody gets together and can share about their day." Jerry is smart. He knows that even teenagers will talk to us if it means they can leave when they're done!

It's not surprising that bedtime and mealtime are prime times for communicating with kids. These are natural opportunities for togetherness. Some mothers and fathers were pleasantly surprised to uncover another prime time for communication: while doing chores. In the last chapter, one suggestion for making valuable parent-child time was to share a chore, a household duty, or a work project. Not only do the kids appreciate our company, but they'll more easily talk about their interests and concerns, just to pass the time or because they're shell-shocked that we're helping. Either way, shared chores stimulate communication.

"Our dishwasher broke when the kids were little, and we couldn't find the problem. During that time, I found out how much each child would talk while drying the dishes as I washed. It's been over ten years now, and the dishwasher still sits there broken because I've refused to let go of that time I have with each child during dishes. The kids always seem to open up when they're stuck with drying the dishes." Is mom ever going to have the dishwasher fixed? "When the kids are grown and gone, and I'm stuck with washing and drying."

Elizabeth, a fifteen-year-old from Wisconsin, the youngest in a pastoral family of three children, enjoyed working side by side with her parents because of its potential for meaningful discussions. "Just doing a project with my dad or baking cookies with my mom makes me feel close to them both. It is during these times that I feel I can tell them anything. I remember a few times in particular with my mom that I have had the best down-to-earth chats with her."

Driving provides a good avenue for communication. "I find that when I'm driving my children to various places, it offers a nice time to talk," says Martha from Connecticut. "Often it's just me and one child, so we have the privacy we need. No radio, no tapes, no interruptions, just sharing thoughts."

Robin, mother of three in California, finds nighttime traveling even more revealing. "Many interesting discussions are discussed in the dark. Somehow it's easier to reveal personal ideas then."

In fact, any activity or time spent with a youngster raises the probability that you'll come away knowing her a little better, and she you. Every one-to-one activity suggested in the last chapter is a means for a mutual sharing of thoughts, feelings, and ideas. Barbara from New Jersey asserts, "I feel the most important factor in open communication for parents and children is to have quantity time. Productive communication might only happen ten percent of our time together, but the other ninety percent is necessary to set the stage for healthy discussion. Quality time, which gets good press, is certainly important, but it's just as important to be around each other enough to have boring times, too."

Sometimes you can help spur conversation by revealing a small, heretofore unknown, part of yourself. Julie, a now-married daughter from Nevada, said one of her fondest memories of her father arose spontaneously when she was about fourteen. "One day I was sitting in the middle of the floor, and dad just came in and sat down beside me. He talked to me for the longest time. He told me things about his growing up—things I'd never heard before." Julie drew closer to her father that day because he was willing to open up to her the same way he wanted her to open up to him.

Carol from Montana learned her most durable lesson about communication timing from her mother. Carol, now raising two sons, was one of thirteen children. Her mother had one overriding rule of communication: The best time to communicate is the instant a child wants to—not five minutes later, not even five seconds later, but immediately. "With thirteen kids, mom had a system where, if any one of us wanted to talk, she would drop everything and go to her room, where we'd close the door, and no one could interrupt. She said if it was important for us to want to talk, it didn't matter if she was stirring gravy, she'd be there."

A creative strategy for converting a child's thoughts to words comes from an Oregon family. Dad is a regional sales manager, mom is an executive secretary and homemaker, and their six children are aged three through thirteen. That's a lot of childlike perspective to elicit, so mom and dad arrange mock television interviews between themselves as interviewers, and the kids as "stars." Like reporters anxious to reveal stars to their fans, they probe each child's opinions on most everything, and the kids, ever anxious to act like stars, give elaborate and revealing responses. The two older children aren't quite so much into the TV interview scene anymore, but I think they're still willing to be guests on *The Dating Game.*

Chapter 10 called time the essence of parenthood. In this chapter, we can make a similar statement: Timing is of the essence in communication.

PRINCIPLE #4: SAY IT WITHOUT WORDS

Speak fewer words, keep silent longer, listen to understand—guidelines parents follow to enhance communication with their children. Each phrase reinforces the wisdom of a softer, less wordy approach to communication. The softest, least wordy approach may be the most prevalent in strong families: giving affection.

One mother called affection "the quiet language of love." Affection is continuous communication. It is an ongoing show of love, a constant affirmation that this spouse or this child is a most important person in our life. Affection takes little time and effort, yet its effects are immeasurable to a family's well-being. Affection builds a child's self-esteem and her sense of security. It nurtures her willingness to come to us with those thoughts, feelings, and fears she might otherwise hold close to herself were she not so sure of our love for her.

Not unexpectedly, many parents brought to their families the warmth they experienced in their childhoods. Candy, a mother from Arkansas, recalled, "My own parents openly displayed affection for each other and us. I remember how warm, safe, and secure this made me feel, just thinking they loved each other no matter what. I try to let my children see my husband and I embrace and cuddle on the sofa. I enjoy their happy looks. I know what they are feeling."

Barbara, a very expressive mother of four from New York, says, "I remember loving to watch my parents dance. My father loved being 'fresh' with my mother—well within a PG rating, nothing really inappropriate! My mother was always affectionate to me. Even as a teenager, I remember curling up on her lap. My father was less demonstrative, but I never doubted his love."

Some parents grew to believe in the communicating power of affection through its absence in their own childhoods. "The lack of affection in my own upbringing has had an impact on me today. It has actually taught me to be affectionate. My wife and I kiss, hug, dance in front of the children. We all but make love. We are comfortable expressing our love to each other."

Sharon, mother of three (aged seven to fifteen) from Wyoming, leaves no doubt about the role of affection in the emotional health of her family.

"There was no communication in my own upbringing, no display of affection with any of us. I came into parenting with the attitude that I wanted to be a different, *and better,* parent than my own. Therefore, I've strived to communicate about everything with my kids, to give them open affection and to tell them often how special they are to me. I never felt I got enough affection, so I hug, kiss, and tell my kids and hubby I love them all the time."

Stan, father of Julie (nineteen) and Hans (fifteen), asserts that affection can soothe and heal harsh moments. "In terms of open communication, there are times when it seems inappropriate to talk—when things are heated or words are just not enough. But you can still communicate by touching one another. It is so important—that physical expression of love. I always liked to hold my kids, even now." To Stan, affection is more than daily doses of expressive love. It is a silent sign that no matter what disagreements or conflicts arise, as long as people can touch, they can eventually talk.

These parents have strong feelings about the positive impact of affection on children. Do the children have the same feelings? Is affection as important to them as their parents think? Let's listen to a few of the kids.

- "I can't remember a day that I went to bed without getting hugged and told that I was loved. Affection is so natural in our family that I immediately notice a family that lacks it. Our slogan wouldn't really have been, 'If you love someone, tell them.' It would have been, 'If you love someone, show them.' It's still the same now that we're pretty much grown."
- "We feel sorry for all the people in this world who have never been 'bushel and pecked.' Mother and dad would sing and dance around the kitchen with us saying, 'I love you a bushel and a peck . . . and a hug around the neck . . .' with a concluding barrage of smothering kisses."
- "Affection is now and always has been openly displayed in my family. My father is one of the most masculine men I know, but he always kissed my brothers and me, and he would tell us verbally how much he loved us. A lot of the boys I grew up with had fathers who were extremely uncomfortable in expressing affection to them. I suppose they were afraid it was not a manly thing to do. I do not doubt their fathers loved them; it is just they were the kind of men who only knew how to say 'I love you' by getting up and going to work every day so they could provide the things their families needed. But, even now, a hug from my mother makes me feel good from the inside out, the way it did when I was five years old."
- "Our family has never been one to be stoic. Openly displaying our affection

for each other, whether it be in the form of a kiss or a hug, has never been seen as silly or inappropriate. I feel very comfortable in showing my love for my parents and sister. In fact, at age twenty-two, I still give my mother and father a kiss before I turn in at night." [Son]

• "I always knew my parents loved each other. They made no secret of that fact and, even though we would say 'gross' when they kissed and hugged each other in front of us, it gave my brothers and me a wonderful sense of security to know they were so firmly anchored in each other. Affection is the rock our family was built on. Even now, when I go home, I occasionally catch them kissing each other in the front room or holding hands when they walk out in the yard. It still makes me feel good inside, and they are the model that I follow in expressing affection in my own marriage. I know how to be affectionate to my wife and I am comfortable in doing so. I know how to hold and comfort her because I saw my father do it for my mother when she was upset or sad. I sneak up and steal a kiss from her, and I bring her flowers for no reason, because I saw my father do it for my mother. Through their example, I came to understand the meaning of mature love and how to practice it."

While touching—with generous hugs, kisses, pats on the back—was the most common affection in these families, the quiet language of love came in many forms. "To me the eyes are so important to communication," said Rita from New Hampshire. "I always make sure I look the kids in the eyes. If we are lacking that connection with the eyes, then something is wrong, and I can sense that. If you can't look each other in the eye, then there is a veil there that needs to be removed. I don't think it should last even a day. Removing that veil becomes the most important thing in my life, and everybody in this family will tell you that. They know that nothing else matters around here until I get the good feeling from the eyes again."

Some parents and children were not comfortable with a lot of touching. Still, they expressed themselves in other wordless ways. Sixteen-year-old Christopher's favorite mode of affection is "pseudo-punching," a good-natured boxing and shoulder punching between him, his brother, and his father. It is his rugged, yet demonstrative, display of feelings. Similarly, nineteen-year-old Michael considers wrestling with his brothers to be affection, "now that Dad is no longer a worthy opponent." Emily, aged thirteen, likes affection "not necessarily through hugs and kisses, but through water fights, hysterical fits of laughter, and cheering at the end of a winning baseball game."

Recognizing her son's uneasiness over his mother's public display of mushiness, Julie uses a silent signal to speak her emotions. "My eleven-year-old son doesn't want his mother to yell 'I love you' across the ball diamond, so when Tyler leaves to hit, I squeeze his shoulder three times. No one else is the wiser, but he goes out there with a smile. It works too when Jaime jumps out of the car pool for school. Three winks, three squeezes, all mean 'We love you.' "

Loretta from Colorado appreciates her mother's kisses, but equally respects her father's style of conveying his love. "Instead of saying, 'I love you' or 'I think you are great,' my dad shows affection in different ways. He expresses himself by fixing things around the house and trying to make sure that everything is working fine. He expresses himself in the cards that he writes for the holidays and my mom's birthday and our birthdays. He likes to sing and play the guitar, so he expresses himself in that way. He wrote a special song for my grandma when she died."

Linda, one of seven children from a Georgia family says, "We are not a hugging and kissing group of people. Hugs and kisses are not needed to prove how much we love one another. But we do show affection with cards and notes we write to each other." Her sister, Joanne, added that much of her family's warmth for each other comes from "joking and kidding around all the time and making up crazy names for each other, like Tumbleweed, Nibbin, Pop, Pea-head." Indeed, nicknames are a popular form of affection. They are little labels that convey big feelings.

Excellent families freely give feelings away, however they can, with kisses, cards, tickling, flowers, pseudo-punching, nicknames. While aware that every parent has his or her own level of comfort in giving and receiving affection, most of these parents agree: Don't assume your children know you love them. Find ways to show them. The younger the child, the more naturally he'll reach for warmth. And if you have a teenager who would think to himself, "What's dad up to?" if you up and hugged him, coupled with an "I'm glad you're my son," then ease into your expressiveness slowly. Shake his hand more frequently. Put a hand on his shoulder. Pseudo-punch him. Begin with the smallest, easiest displays of caring. You may be pleasantly surprised at the effects you'll bring about for the whole family.

The closing sentiment on affection comes from a mother in Arkansas, when she was asked, "What changes would you make in your parenting if you could go back?" She declared without hesitation, "I would be huggy more and hyper less."

The better parents are decisive. They know to persist in certain decisions, no matter how much the kids might disagree. Five-year-old Chip, for instance, if allowed, will ravage seven cookies before supper, in contrast to his mother's decision to permit him one after supper. Fifteen-year-old Eve will assign herself a Saturday-night curfew with enough stretch to reach into early Sunday morning, if her parents didn't impose a less flexible, 11:30 P.M. in-on-time rule. In determining how a household should be run or how a child should be raised, it's normal for parents and kids to be at odds, regularly. Being decisive means making and living with judgments that are in our kids' best interests, even while they won't understand that for years to come.

Being decisive does not mean ignoring our kids' input or never seeking it. Excellent parents regularly ask their youngster's opinion on matters that affect him, even if ultimately they don't move their minds one inch because of that opinion. Allowing children a voice in some family issues carries two benefits. In the short-term, the kids may better accept decisions they were at least consulted about. In the long-term, they will see themselves as a valued part of family decisions, and indeed of the whole family.

In the next few pages, we primarily will be listening to the children. The word *children* here is misleading, as some are really young adults, now in their late teens and early twenties. We asked them, "How are decisions made in your home?" Their answers revealed that the decision-making process in solid families parallels three forms of government: democracy, benevolent monarchy, and dictatorship. First, let's hear how a one-person, one-vote rule is used to formulate family policy.

Clay, the eleven-year-old son of Retha, a single mother, says that he, his brother, and mom vote on certain issues, for example, which restaurant to go to—mom provides the options based upon the limits of her pocketbook—or which television show to watch. Clay adds that sometimes they draw straws to decide who dries the dishes and who washes. Or they might flip a coin to determine things like who sits in the front seat and who sits in the back. At age eleven, Clay is already aware that chance oftentimes provides the most equitable solution among determined siblings.

Tara, aged sixteen from Wyoming, appreciates the fact that she, her parents, and her three siblings "every once in a while have a family schedule meeting. Since we are all so busy doing different things, we touch base with our schedules as we sit around the table. Usually, big decisions are made here. One or two family members may come up with an idea, and then introduce it to the rest of the family for an opinion." To illustrate, when the family was considering purchasing a home computer, the discussion centered on who would use it, when, and for what purpose. What features did the family want and need? How would computertime be shared? What uses would take priority? That is, homework comes before video games. On another occasion, as Tara's mother was preparing to return to work part-time, the family talked over changes in household duties, what mom could and couldn't do at home anymore, and how the new routine would affect each family member.

Family meetings were useful even with younger children. The littlest member usually sat on a parent's lap, oblivious to the purpose of the gathering, but his presence said much: "We are all involved in this decision." Typically, younger children enjoyed a voice in daily matters, such as what to eat tonight, whom to visit, what movie to watch, who would do what to prepare for a party. Family meetings are a forum for the smaller members to speak. One father observed, "Our sons didn't care what kind of TV we bought nearly so much as getting to vote on what show to watch on Friday night." It isn't the size of the decision that makes young children feel special. It's their say in the decision.

Brian, a sixteen-year-old from Ohio, says that everyone in his family gives input based upon individual talents and interests, and in his parents' case, also upon authority. "Who makes decisions? I think we all do that. Does this painting look better here or in the living room? Ask me. Should we take this in for repairs? Ask Marc [brother, science scholar]. May I have a friend stay overnight? Ask mom or dad. We all make decisions that count, as needed. So who is the authority in our house? It depends."

Pat, a son from Clayton, Georgia, also respects his parents' style of allowing each of their four children a vote on certain matters. However, mom and dad do have the veto vote. Why? "They pay the bills." Pat states, "The decision process in our family has been handled for the most part democratically, meaning family meetings and conferences, with a lot of influence coming from my parents. They have always been fair. We are all allowed and encouraged to give our opinions on any decisions."

To be sure, a pure democratic process is useful only for those issues for which any of several choices is appropriate, for instance, where to go on a weekend excursion, or what card game to play, or whether to open Christmas presents on Christmas Eve or Christmas day. As one father aptly pointed out, "No parent in his right mind is going to give the kids an equal vote on matters that are his parental responsibility and duty. If you have more than one child, you'd get voted down every time!"

The preferred method of decision making in these families can be likened to a benevolent monarchy. Mom and dad are the rulers, but the kids are respected members of the kingdom. When a decision affects any or all members, each is asked for an opinion. All feedback is considered, but the final decision belongs to the parent. The children endorse this system of family government over any other. Michael, the oldest of four sons from Indiana, said:

- "My mother and father make the decisions in our family. If it is a decision that directly affects one of us kids, we are asked how we feel about it, but the final decision is always left up to them. They have a partnership, and in turn, an equal vote. When we were young, they always cared about how we felt about something, but thank goodness they freed us from the responsibility and guilt often associated with having to make all of our own decisions. We were allowed to be children. As we grew older, we were given increasingly responsible roles in making choices for ourselves, but we were never abandoned to those choices. We could always go to my parents for help and advice. My parents taught me that making decisions was easy. It was the consequences that could be difficult to deal with."

Craig, at age seventeen, appreciates that his folks look from his viewpoint on such diverse matters as buying a car, a lawn mower, or allocating car privileges between him and his older brother.

- "When a decision, usually an important one, has to be made, like buying a new car, a step-by-step process is the most useful to the family. First, my parents will talk it out between themselves. Next, after weighing their choices, they may choose to turn the matter over to Brian and myself, asking us for advice. This has been occurring more frequently now, since we are older and wiser. After taking our advice and opinions on the matter, my mother and father will then make the final decision."

To Mark from Mississippi, being a respected family consultant was more than a chance to be heard. It was a means of bolstering his self-image.

- "When I was a young child, mom and dad made most decisions together. But as each one of us children got older, we were more frequently included in the decision-making process. Mom and dad were always interested in hearing our ideas and suggestions, even if they weren't followed in the end. I can especially remember being included as a near equal with mom and dad in many decisions associated with a house-remodeling project we carried out during my junior year in high school. That did wonders for the self-esteem of an adolescent quick to doubt his abilities."

The children's input here is clear: We like being a part of decisions. Even though our ideas may not be acted on, merely being asked adds to our sense of belonging in the family. Our opinion matters, and that's one sign that we matter.

Of course, as we noted early in this section, managing a household or enforcing discipline quite often entails decisions that rest solely with the parent. Here it is wise to be a kindly dictator. Now-grown Judy, one of seven children from Georgia, recalls, "Everyone could throw in his viewpoint, but dad and mom made the final decision. They had the power. For example, it was their rule that on Sunday you were at church. You had no choice." In other words, you were welcome to an opinion, but on certain issues, the folks rule, no questions asked.

If you have a house rule that all homework be completed before the television goes on, discussing this each and every evening with Holmes is only asking for conflict. You know he disapproves; he's disapproved since the rule's onset three months ago. Discussion will only lead to dead-end debates. Similarly, five-year-old Dawn is upset that, from this point forward, if she refuses to dress herself in the morning, she will head for bed half an hour earlier that evening. Why ask her opinion on this discipline? It's already obvious what she thinks about it. She earned early bedtime the first day the procedure began. To avoid endless word wars, quiet dictating is the best parental route. In no way does this mean you're blocking open communication. It means you're smart enough to decide when to close communication for the benefit of all parties concerned.

Democracy, benevolent monarchy, and dictatorship—three forms of strong family government. Each respects the children's perspective, the for-

mer two by eliciting their input, the latter by not, as sometimes it is benevolent to curtail communication.

Communication with children may be simple, but it is not easy. That's why
skilled communicators concentrate on mastering the basics: listening, timing,
affection, respect. Good basics are more than enough for excellent communication. They lay the groundwork for mutual understanding and a parent's
GREAT EXPECTATIONS.

Chapter 12

Great Expectations

*"I want my children to stand up and face the wind. It's
a reflection of the strength required to maintain themselves in society today."*

Father, Phoenix, Arizona

Excellent parents do not expect excellence from their children. They
expect their personal best. The emphasis is on fulfilling one's potential, upon
behaving as well as one is capable of behaving. Jane from Oklahoma observes,
"If we don't expect anything of our children, no one else will. We are the
ones they are counting on. No one else loves them enough or cares enough
to spend as much time and effort expecting something of them."

The children in these families have achieved much—personally, socially,
academically, athletically. Largely their successes reflect the cohesiveness of
their home life. When parents provide a secure, encouraging environment,
children are more likely to reach for their limits, often with excellence as the
result. Strong parents do much more than encourage and support. They
actively expect behavior equal to ability. James and Barbara, parents of four
from Mobile, Alabama, explained, "Our children know that average is not
good enough. God has blessed them with many great qualities and abilities.

We don't hesitate to tell them that they are special and that much is expected from them. This develops their sense of worth and potential."

Effective parents don't pressure or relentlessly push their children to achieve or to live by some unattainable code of conduct. They are acutely aware that driving too hard can throttle a child's desire to move forward. On the other hand, they are not squeamish about lifting their expectations to meet their children's capabilities. Debra from Oregon, mother of six children under age thirteen, said, "As we saw what a child could accomplish, we realized that we were underestimating abilities, so we raised our expectations some—in just little things like memorizing ABC's, doing daily jobs, or learning the piano. Overall, we wanted to expose the kids to lots of opportunities, so they could choose things they liked or were good at." Debra's initial mind-set is common among parents today, that is: Be cautious, don't overexpect. With experts debating the hazards of pushing kids too hard, many parents are understandably unsure how much expectation is healthy. Consequently, to ensure a large margin of psychological safety, many parents underexpect. To counter this trend, the better parents say: Don't be afraid to ask a good deal of a child who shows signs he's capable.

Strong parents are particularly unwilling to let their children drift along in their personal development, however much in step they are with others around them. Early on, Norman from Florida taught Kimberly and Chip to exhibit out-of-the-ordinary politeness. "It is what I call the Old South mentality—'Yes, ma'am'; 'Yes, sir'; 'No, thank you'; 'Yes, please.' The principal of their school once told me, 'I think your children got a lot of attention when they first came here because they had learned to say things like 'Yes, ma'am' or 'No, thank you.' That is so unique. It was like they were from another planet.' I wanted my children to be polite. It doesn't cost anything, and it produces incredible dividends. It delights people because it is so different." Norman's children at once stood apart from their peers because of some simple, if uncommon, courtesies. Had they not had them, they probably wouldn't have been criticized. Neither would they have been noticed.

Another social courtesy, manners, are never neglected by Clifford and Annetta from North Dakota. "The girls' (aged nine, twelve, fourteen) manners are expected to be the best. In public we quietly share proper etiquette. Even in the car, we will discuss what will be appropriate to where we are going. We have practiced etiquette at home before going someplace special. It's always a pat on the back to hear compliments on the girls' behavior, which we always share with them." Again, conscientious etiquette is not a widespread trait. While its absence doesn't mark a child ill-mannered or socially awkward, its presence shows much about her willingness to walk ahead of the crowd.

Bill and Pat from New Jersey used summer "social refresher programs" to bring out the best in their biological and foster children. "Like sending a salesman to a refreshing workshop, we tried periods of what others call Montessori program. These usually were put into effect in the summer and were used for anything that needed attention—manners, language, task completion. I remember one summer we all worked on answering the phone with a cheerful voice. To this day, the children will comment if someone sounds gruff on the other end of the line."

One mother commented on the criticism she heard from relatives because she expected her two-year-old to say thank you anytime he received anything from anyone, or else he'd have to return it. " 'He's only two,' they'd say. 'He doesn't know better yet.' How will he ever know better if I don't start teaching him? And it's easier to teach a two-year-old to say thank you than a ten-year-old who's never learned basic politeness."

Another parent echoed these thoughts. "Our kids know they are not allowed to hit each other. We started disciplining this when they were toddlers. If they smacked someone, they were set down right there on the floor for a little while. They learned what we expected at a very early age. That made it so much easier, on them and us, as they got older. They still fought, but hitting wasn't usually a part of it."

In talking of expectations, several parents used words like *nonnegotiable* and *unquestionable*. Their attitude was that some behaviors are not open for discussion. Sue conveyed nonnegotiable expectations to her three children this way: "Of course you're going to your brother's [sister's] program [concert, dance recital, school play], that's the way we support each other." Attendance at family functions was simply a given for all members, no questions asked.

Excellent parents will also give their children a firm push toward something they judge healthy for them, even if at first the kids' feet are dragging. Again, with all the experts' cautions against overdirecting children, it is tempting to be unassertive and hand a youngster near total freedom in choosing his pursuits. Many of these parents resist this temptation because they know that a child, be he six or sixteen, is not always the best judge of what's good for him.

- "One summer I told the twins I wanted them to go to our church summer camp one time before they got out of high school, and this was about their last chance. They didn't want to go, but I made them. I remember thinking all week that those boys were going to be so mad at me for forcing them to go. It turned out just the opposite. They had a great time. So often that happens to you as a parent. You stick your neck out, and sometimes it works great and other times it's a total failure. You never know, but you still have to do it. From camp, they gained confidence in themselves which they passed onto their brothers and sister. The decision I made to force them to do something they didn't want to do turned into a wonderful experience for them."

These parents aren't suggesting we railroad our children into always doing what we want for them rather than what they want. They are suggesting that parents need to judge when to make children choose our way. This is not parental domination. It is a legitimate recognition that even though the kids—and some experts—might disagree, sometimes we do know what's better for our children's development than they do.

Returning to the story just quoted, what if the boys would have stayed angry and disliked camp? That was a possibility their mother was aware of, but she considered the potential gain well worth any temporary risk. Besides, we cannot do our job as parents if we fear a child's reaction to our decisions. The only way to make no waves is to make no decisions.

Sometimes, even years down the road, the kids wish we would have exerted our will over theirs. From Tucson, Arizona, a father tells, "Once, this summer, a girl called Scott to play tennis. We told him afterward that when he was little we wanted him to take tennis lessons, but he just didn't seem interested. He said, 'Why didn't you just make me do it?' " Kids! They'll fight us when we force them, and then be mad because we didn't!

Twenty-one-year-old Sean fought his parents when they made him practice the piano, but ultimately was grateful they persevered past his resistance. "I remember starting piano lessons. There were some pretty rough times in there, and I remember sitting on the piano bench for two hours, saying, 'I'm not going to practice anymore. I don't want to do this!' Dad was sitting right there with me, saying, 'Yes, you are.' There was a period of time when I didn't do much with my music, but just recently I accompanied rehearsals and played in the band for a production of *Little Shop of Horrors*. I enjoyed that tremendously, and I owe so much of that to mom and dad for starting me

and encouraging me, and forcing me when necessary." Sometimes the repercussions of underexpecting can be as far-reaching as overexpecting. Sean is
grateful that his parents expected more of their son than he did of himself.

Every child is born with tremendous potential. Excellent parents believe
this. They also believe it is their duty to make a child explore his potential,
sometimes initially against his will. Regardless of their unique talents, all
children possess the ability to behave a cut above the crowd. Settling for
average—in morals, manners, or character—is not something these parents
are comfortable doing. They have too much respect for a child's resources to
allow them to lie unfulfilled.

GREAT KIDS NEED GREAT PARENTS

To teach children to reach for their best, parents must reach for their best.
Put another way, great expectations for a child begin with great expectations
for oneself. To be a successful parent, we must be willing to do more than
the average. We must be willing to supervise our children more closely, keep
better contact with teachers, work harder at discipline than do other parents.
Excellent parenting means striving continuously to improve, not to look
better than others, but because that's the only kind of parenting we're
content with.

Michael, looking back at his childhood from a twenty-seven-year-old's
perspective, now understands that the power of his parents' expectations for
him derived from their expectations for themselves. "My parents believed you
get what you expect from a child, and they expected a lot from us. But they
never asked anything of us unless they set the example we were to follow.
They practiced what they preached, and even when times were hardest, I
always believed we were all in it together."

It is a rare parent who navigates one full parenthood without hearing the
likes of: "Carson is allowed to go to bed later if his grades are good"; "Gypsy's
parents let her stay out past midnight as long as she calls them"; "Marlin
doesn't have to stay in the yard after supper." In flinging at us the name of
every parent in the Western Hemisphere who is "nicer" or more in touch
with childrearing reality than we are, a youngster hopes to bend us toward
other mothers' and fathers' practices. Fortunately, veteran parents are not
without comebacks to such comparisons: "Well, we don't run our house the
way Carson's parents run theirs"; "Gypsy's not my daughter, you are." Or
the childrearing classic "If Marlin jumps in the lake, are you going to jump

in, too?" In working to be a stronger parent, you will be subjected to more comparisons than most. Your parenting is indeed unlike many parents. And your kids won't let this slip by without comment.

Assume you decide to establish a one-hour reading time in your home from seven to eight o'clock in the evening, two days a week. The television is off, the phone is disconnected, everyone finds something to read. Page and Booker may immediately resist, "There's not another kid in the whole school who has a reading hour!" They may be right. So? What the majority, even the vast majority, does is completely irrelevant to your parenting when you are acting as you judge healthy for your children. It is true, you are out of rhythm with others, but in a most positive way. Kathleen, a nurse and mother of four boys and a girl, aged twelve through twenty, identified her stickiest struggle so far to be "not allowing the kids to follow the crowd. It is difficult for us, for instance, when other parents allow late curfews, letting their children go whenever and wherever they want and do things that our children are not allowed to do. Our kids would probably say that we've stunted their social life, but they are not allowed to do things we feel are not in their best interests, no matter how many other parents allow their children to. And interestingly enough, some of our children's peers have not fared well due to the freedom they experienced at too early an age."

Facing the prevailing winds as a parent takes both courage and stamina. You won't weather resistance from only your children, but from other parents as well, who may question, even criticize, your high standards. One mother related an incident involving a birthday party for one of her ten-year-old son's friends. Before giving her son permission to go to the party, mom called to find out if there would be a video movie for the kids and what it might be. A popular movie was planned which contained a fair amount of violence, gore, and rough language. While allowed to attend the party, her son had to exit when the movie began. Not only was this mother the only parent to prescreen the entertainment, but she subsequently received some ill will from the hostess, who misread her actions as a criticism of her own parenthood.

The mother above stood apart from fifteen to twenty other parents. The following parent from Rhode Island stood apart from several hundred.

"My son was in high school, and one day he told me, 'I won't be going to school this morning.'

" 'Why? Are you sick?'

" 'No, but it's national bunk day [otherwise known as senior skip day], and everybody will be out of school.'

" 'Well, everybody may be out, but you better be there.' And he left. We had an assistant principal who insisted that if your child was home, it'd better be by your permission, and you had to notify him. If not, he'd call you. About nine-thirty that evening the telephone rang, and it was the principal. He asked, 'Is John sick?'

" 'I don't understand. What do you mean, 'Is John sick?'

" 'Well, he wasn't in school today, and you didn't call.'

"Then it hit me, and I said, 'Well, he disobeyed me, because I told him to be in school.'

"The principal said, 'You know I'm going to have to discipline him.'

" 'You take care of him on that end, and I'll take care of him on this end,' I said.

"So I confronted John: 'Why weren't you in school today?'

" 'Well, nobody else was there.'

"I was angry. 'I don't care about everybody else. You were to be in school.' So I punished him by grounding him for quite a while.

"The next day he walked out the door angry and mumbling. When he came back that afternoon, I figured he'd still be sulking. He wasn't, but he just kept walking slowly around the house. Finally he said, 'Thank you.'

"I looked to see who he was talking to and said, 'Pardon me?'

" 'Thank you.'

" 'For what?'

" 'I stood ten feet tall today. The principal told me that he began calling parents at eight in the morning and finished at ten that night, talking to every parent whose child had skipped school. And he said, 'Your mother is the only one who told the truth.' Then John said, 'And I thank you for that.' "

In striving for excellence, expect that at times you may walk alone. Other parents will not agree with or understand your position. Initially your children, too, may not see the wisdom in your uniqueness, but eventually they will. And aren't they really the only ones who matter?

The remainder of this chapter will focus on three areas in which these parents consistently held high expectations for their children: academics, household responsibilities, and athletics. Don't be mislead by the word *athletics*. As we will see, the expectations are not for performance, but for the character-building aspects inherent in most sports, like commitment and cooperation.

Let's now find out where these parents place academics in the hierarchy of expectations for their children.

SCHOOL: A CHILD'S FUTURE

There are nearly four hundred children in the one hundred families we interviewed. The great majority of them are, or have been, honor students. On one hand, academic accomplishments reflect innate abilities. What you can achieve is in part determined by what you received at conception. On the other hand, success is also a function of motivation, of the desire to achieve. Desire, like talent, often needs an outside influence to bring it forth and to nurture it into a self-perpetuating quality. In most cases, that outside influence is a parent.

The academic profiles of some of these families are impressive. A Nevada family of seven children all have earned honor-roll status in school. Parents in Georgia, themselves with seventh- and tenth-grade educations, have watched each of their seven children graduate from college. From Wisconsin, Bill and Sue's three children have carried solid A averages through junior and senior high thus far. One might argue that a child who stands high academically entered the world with at least above-average ability. When all the children in a family consistently do well, part of the credit must go to the parents. They are the influence common to all.

Thirteen-year-old Kim from Tucson, Arizona, has a learning disability which has not stood between her and academic awards. Kim studies an average of three hours a night, often with a parent, because that's what she needs to do to stretch for her potential.

Hans and his parents work together to accomplish what his test scores predict he can't. His father says, "Hans' mother has been an absolute warrior in the school department. She spends hours sitting right with him and helping him." Mother reinforces the need for close involvement. "I have had to rearrange my own schedule from time to time, to supervise and assist with homework. But when there is a test or paper due, there is no question about priorities—homework comes first." In this family, both dad and son have learning disabilities. Dad has achieved his master's degree, and Hans, a sophomore in high school, is on student council and "holding his own in his studies."

Kim and Hans may have been born with what some might consider deficits, but they also were born to parents who have helped them more than counterbalance a slow start with an excess of drive.

School is the work of children. It is their primary childhood responsibility. But it is far more. It is their future. School forges the work of the adult-child—her career choices, challenges, even satisfaction. Excellent parents acutely understand this, so they are noncompromising in their expectation that their youngster reach for his limits. Gary and Marge from Colorado will not negotiate with Leigh Ann or Ty about school. "We really push them to do well in their scholastics, but we only do that because they are capable. If they are capable of making C grades, and they make them every time, wonderful. If they are able to make A grades, and they make those every time, wonderful. If they are making C's, and they should be making B's, or if they are making B's and they should be making A's, then we sit down with them. We spend a lot of time with the teachers and counselors, asking them what they think of the kids' abilities and how they are doing. We take time with them in their courses, and we can see their aptitudes or lack of them." Gary and Marge's philosophy about education is elementary: Get a good sense of what your children can do, and expect them to do it.

Excellent parents don't follow a hard-driving, get-that-grade-to-look-the-smartest mentality. They realize that blindly bulldozing a youngster into achieving at all costs will most likely only shove him into a retreat from learning. Nonetheless, they insist on effort commensurate with talent. Mary Jo, a mother of three young school-agers in Kentucky, says, "It is really the 'effort' grade that counts. It is not the academic grade. The children are all quite a bit more intelligent than I am; I recognized that a long time ago. So, to know what is going on and to make sure that things go how we'd like, we have to get involved. Education is not only the teacher's responsibility. A lot of educating is done in the home."

A question in the interview was, "To what degree does education impact on family relationships?" The answers consistently assigned education "top-priority" status, while underscoring the importance of close parental involvement.

- "There are a lot of things you can take away from someone, but you can't take away their education. I think we expected the kids to do a good job in school and encouraged them all the way through. It doesn't take a genius to recognize that if you have an education and some skills, you can make a better living the rest of your life. Education was vitally important, and we let the kids know that from the beginning. We were very active with parent organizations. If there was a parent's night, we went. If there was a parent/teacher conference, we went. We were not asking the kids to do *the* best, but we were asking them to do their best."

- "Education has always been a top priority in our family. Based upon the kids' achievement tests, we demand a certain level of academic work from them. We have stressed that their education will lead to opportunities in their adult life that they will always value. We will not be able to provide financial security, but their education will."

- "Academics are number one. If the children are sick, makeup work is done as quickly as possible. Appointments [doctors, work, etc.] are made before or after school hours. Vacations are planned at other times. We study together, helping each other. We have been PTA members for eight years."

At times, no matter how encouraging, how involved a parent is, a youngster still will not strive for his best. Even the most conscientious parents can face periods when they have to make a child learn.

From Connecticut, Martha nudged her son, Jason (aged ten), along in his motivation by letting him feel the natural results of his indifference. "Once Jason waited until the last minute to do a report. After getting nothing but grief when I asked him about it, I decided to let him sink or swim on his own. He got it done, but received comments from the teacher that were more negative than he's used to. I could tell that he realized he had made a mistake by rushing through it at the last minute. It was difficult to sit back and watch him flounder, but I felt it was necessary."

Some youngsters are like Jason. Slipping grades or other tangible signs of sagging scholastics are enough to restart their engines. Their parents don't need to do much other than let them dip temporarily until their academic gyroscope rights itself. Other children are not so easily set straight. Consistent structure and monitoring from their folks are what gets them back on level.

Norman and Vallie from Florida had occasions to sit down with their son, Chip, and together determine academic goals with backup consequences. "If Chip decides with us that he can make a 3.0, and he is capable of that, then we all decide what the consequences should be if he doesn't reach 3.0. Chip now knows what is expected. The standards are established, and the consequences are communicated." We'll read more about the power of rules with laid-out consequences in the next chapter.

In many homes, academic slippage is never given a chance to begin, as parents enforce a basic homework policy. "Our main rule: Homework is to be done immediately after school, before TV or play. There is no room for error on this one." Parents quickly discovered that endless inquisitions and proddings could be avoided by checking all assignments first thing after school and by linking privileges to accurate completion. A homework rule also lends a little peace to the evening. It short-circuits those close-to-bedtime exasperating interchanges that start something like, "Did you have any homework tonight?" "Oh no, I left it in the bushes again!"

Some parents give an afternoon break before homework time. Carol, mother to Travis and Troy, said, "We felt that the kids need to unwind after school, so they can ride bikes, play ball, whatever until five o'clock. At that time they must sit down at the table and do their homework before they may use the radio, television, or telephone. We are available to help if necessary." Furthermore, the work has to be done neatly. Carol continued, "We are somewhat demanding here. Many times we have seen a paper and insisted that it be rewritten."

Another common approach to schoolwork was to establish an evening study time. Routinely, television and radio were kept off, no phone calls were accepted, the whole house was quiet. Usually, this period lasted one hour, and if a child had no homework, she could read or study. In Florida, one father required his children to select a letter of the encyclopedia and write a report on a topic of choice.

Linking long-term privileges to academic performance was the preferred method of Olene and Oscar, parents of the seven college graduates from Georgia. Their standard outcome for below-potential grades was loss of television for six weeks until the next report card showed improved marks. They never tampered with their rule, and it's hard to argue with their results. Dave and Bobbie from Idaho set up a system of consequences and rewards. "Quite a while ago, we made up a table of what the kids would get for different grades. For instance, an A average would receive five dollars and a movie, while a C or D average received grounding, no television, the whole works. The kids were rewarded for good performance and got negative consequences for bad performance."

Perhaps the best illustration of how far strong parents will go to ensure their youngster doesn't shortchange his future is provided by Jane from Miami, Oklahoma, a mother of four sons and a daughter:

- "One time Bill was in the ninth grade and was not making a very good grade in a math class. I went to parent's night totally unprepared for what the teacher told me about Bill. He was entertaining the class with jokes and just being a clown. I was so mad that when I went home, I got Bill in a corner and I said, 'OK, Bill, I told the teacher that I will be working with you for the next three weeks and then I will give her a call. If things in the classroom haven't changed after that time, I will come to class with you every day until they do change!' You can imagine how he liked hearing that, but the important thing was that he knew I would do it."

Certainly personal circumstances might not allow you this kind of flexibility, but you have other options. You might request the school authorities to keep your youngster after school every day to work on his assignments until his grades rise. If feasible, you can let him walk home, or charge him mileage for picking him up each afternoon. Remember: The best parents take a strict stance on underachievement. They reserve some of their firmest discipline for it.

Another approach is the note-home procedure. Every day your youngster is responsible for writing down all assignments on a daily record sheet and having the teacher sign it if, and only if, it is correct. For younger children, the teacher can be asked to complete the sheet. You now have an accurate record each evening of all assignments. Work must be completed before any privileges begin. If the daily record fails to make it home, arrives unsigned, or without the necessary books, no privileges are available all evening. You might also want to keep an extra set of books on hand from which to assign your own work should any omissions in the record sheet occur. Make sure your assignments are longer than those of the school.

Responsible parents are not flexible about their child's education. Their expectations are sharply defined: Do what you are capable of, or we will make sure you do. They will not allow a youngster of any age to decide to limit his learning. He is not capable of understanding the long-term repercussions of such a choice. Where schoolwork is the issue, strong parents are at their strongest. Nothing less than their child's future is at stake.

IT'S OUR FAMILY'S HOUSE

"From the very beginning, it was 'our' house, so the kids knew they were expected to pull their weight in helping maintain it. Before anyone entertains—parent or child—everyone pitches in to get the house ready, doing yardwork, weeding, cleaning, whatever is needed."

Responsible parents expect a healthy, oftentimes hefty, amount of household help from their children. They are motivated by the attitude that this house or apartment is not mom and dad's, it is the family's. Living here is everyone's privilege, so it also is everyone's responsibility. Requiring children to "pull their weight" nurtures a sense of ownership. A child will better care for a place if she is an integral part of its care. Pat, a mother to five natural and dozens of foster children, related this story, "A second-grade teacher told us how she once went around the room asking the children what they received for allowances. When our daughter's turn came, she said she didn't work for money but for love." Pat feels her daughter's answer reflected her belief that her parent's house was her house, too. Either that, or she figured that as long as mom wasn't going to give her money for chores, she'd better find some other payoff.

"Start young" is the consistent advice of these parents. A two-year-old can learn to put away his toys, to give you his cup when he is finished drinking, even "throw laundry in the dryer for me," as one mother said. Walter and Martha, parents of two from Connecticut, stated, "We required reasonable chores from our children as early as possible in their lives. There is no play or television if the chores aren't done. We also give them responsibilities that they must do together to teach them to be cooperative with each other."

Upon returning home from work, a father in Vermont could always trace the whereabouts of his two-year-old daughter. He followed the trail of toys, clothes, and general debris left in the wake of a toddler. Working her way back up the trail and putting items in their appropriate place can provide a child an early lesson in responsibility.

Many housekeeping responsibilities lend themselves to a cooperative effort. Young children can help, certainly not in doing things perfectly or even remotely adequately, but it's the idea that counts. One mother began requiring her son to help make his bed at age three. Mom did the main bed making; he smoothed the blanket and laid the pillow on the bed.

Kids love to imitate parents. This fact helped one parent teach her earliest lessons about household duties. "I often made sure the kids were nearby when I was dusting, vacuuming, picking up, whatever. I let them push the vacuum with me, wipe tables, clear up clutter. They imitated me and we had fun together." In essence, you can create a positive tone regarding chores before your kids are old enough to realize they are working.

Naomi from Vermont agrees that children will more naturally cooperate if they are given family responsibilities from the outset.

"A relative was visiting and asked my young daughter, 'What are your chores?'

"My daughter said, 'Oh, we don't have chores.'

" 'Well, then, who cleans your room? Who puts your clothes away? Who sets the table?'

" 'Oh, I do that.' My daughter never viewed these as chores. In our house, there is x amount of work to be done, and there are x people. Everybody does his or her share, from the very beginning."

The policy of strong parents is: Start kids early before they become allergic to work and sweat.

Chores are also a natural way for teaching that work is an inescapable reality of responsible existence. Work at home is the forerunner of work in life. While the kids may not now appreciate our mode of instruction, as with most of our parenting moves, one day they will acknowledge our foresight. Sheri from Georgia said, "We always had to work around the house, and there were times that we'd fuss about it. Now that we're older, though, we respect all the work our parents expected of us. We learned not to fear hard work."

Household responsibilities are tools for building self-reliance, for making a youngster tackle jobs himself, without waiting for someone else to step in. A mother in Montana confirmed, "Requiring the kids to do chores is difficult. It seems to never end. I would rather do them myself, but that would be unfair to their development."

Twenty-two-year-old Michael from Minnesota seems to have successfully absorbed his parents' lessons in self-reliance.

- "My responsibilities within the family have undoubtedly changed as I have grown. As a young boy I was responsible for such things as making my bed, keeping my room somewhat clean, and taking out the garbage. As I matured, I was given more privileges and freedom, but with this also came more responsibility. For example, when I was old enough to drive, I could use the family cars. But I was expected to periodically wash and wax them. As a high-school student, I did a lot of yardwork and helped Dad with larger projects, like painting the house.

"My parents' goal was to teach my sister and me to be self-sufficient. Now that we are both in college, we are expected to pretty much take care of ourselves. If we need clothes washed, we don't wait for mom to come home, but do it ourselves. If mom and dad are late from work, we start preparing the meal before they get home. As young adults, we are expected to pitch in and help with family chores without having to be told. If the lawn needs mowing or the dishes need done, it's our responsibility to get it done. Everyone, including mom and dad, is expected to help out around the house."

When asked, "What are your family responsibilities?" eighteen-year-old Leslie didn't seem too upset while reciting a litany of chores longer than the average teenager's. She even looked upon them with an admirable note of humor.

- "Help with the dog—walking, feeding, washing, cleaning up any mess that she might make. Keep my bathroom reasonably clean—sink, floor, tub. Iron all my clothes. Help with meals—preparation, set table, clear and wash dishes, polish. Transport my younger sister to soccer games, errands, flute lessons. Keep my room free of fungi and infestation by insects and occasionally muck it out when it becomes impossible to discern the tops of desks, tables, beds. And, help shield my mother from stress."

Not just teens, but younger children too regularly detailed a full list of household duties. Seven-year-old Abigail said her family responsibilities were: "Feed the rabbit, dog, bird, and fish. Keep the fishbowl clean; keep the birdcage clean; make my bed; make sure my sister, Rebecca [aged twelve], gets up in the morning; get ready for school; Windex windows; keep my room clean. And, give mommy a morning hug."

Many families followed a dual-level system of responsibilities. On the first level were family chores. Not linked to an allowance, these were expected because a child was a member of the family. The second level included duties which youngsters completed to earn their own money. If the duties were shirked, allowances were reduced proportionately. A number of families did choose to separate household duties from money. Susan from Wisconsin said, "Although allowances were not tied to chores, the kids were expected to do chores each week. Their friends all knew they had Saturday morning chores before they could go out, and these included changing their beds, straightening, dusting and vacuuming, cleaning the bathroom, emptying wastebaskets. In addition, during the week they would help by feeding the dog, setting the table, mowing, shoveling snow, etc."

Carol and Bill followed a work-for-no-pay system, but they did have reservations about it. "We have never given the boys [aged twelve and fifteen] allowances. We feel that their chores are a family responsibility. We simply meet all of their needs financially. When they leave home, they may have a problem handling money for lack of experience. Only the future will tell."

Some parents' posture on chores was flexible. Still, their bottom line was unbending: They must be done. Barbara from New York admits her compromising approach with her four daughters, aged four through eighteen, is a reflection of her personal style. "Almost everything is negotiable as long as it gets done. No one has ever offered to put our home in *House Beautiful.* Chores don't go away, but you can do them later. If you've got a big exam, or a concert, *maybe* I'll do them for you this week, but next week you'd better plan on paying me back. Sometimes there's some screaming back and forth on this one!"

Pat was firm on most requirements, but retreated on a few stubborn ones to save herself recurrent migraines. "Our kids had to help in the family business a lot, so sometimes the home duties suffered. We'd use a chart or list of duties for the four kids and rotated jobs. If their room was a mess, no hassle, I just shut the door on it." To shield the rest of the family from the debris decomposing in some teens' rooms, the door had best be a nine-inch-thick concrete slab with an external deadbolt and alarm system. In describing her son's room, one mother labelled it the "Star Trek zone—to venture in is to boldly go where no mom has gone before."

From parents and children, the message converged: Household responsibilities are shared by everyone. On the whole, these children are expected to help more than most children their age. Of course, since kids generally are not born self-motivated, a parent often has to take action to ensure that jobs are performed within a reasonable time frame—like before the turn of the century. What follows are some of these families' strategies for getting chores finished more smoothly, with less work required of the folks.

- "The kids [aged six and ten] have their daily chores, which consist of such things as hanging up clothes, picking up toys, making beds. On Saturdays, they are usually given a list of jobs—about three each. The whole family usually cleans together. Sometimes the kids get to pick the jobs they'll do or they'll choose three from a list of six. They love to have their own list so they can cross off their jobs as they do them."
- "Dishes are divided up so that each child has one or two days a week in which he or she is responsible for *all* of the dishes. If the job is not done satisfactorily—that is, the floor swept, counter scrubbed, trash taken out—or on a timely basis, a child inherits the next night as well. In some cases, this has resulted in a succession of days for the offender, but the rules are set down in advance, and everyone is aware of them." [Four children, aged eleven through eighteen]
- "For weekly responsibilities, I usually make up a list of things needing to be done, and I pass around the list for the children to sign up, one duty at a time for a fair chance at the easier ones."
- "Any household responsibilities that are not done properly are redone until done right. This has led to a delay of privileges or being late for an activity. For summer vacation time, specific jobs and responsibilities are posted or assigned and must be done before any fun begins. Completed chores that don't need to be redone earn rewards of time to be with friends, a day of shopping or going out—movie, skating, or their choice of funtime."
- "The children [aged three, five, ten, twelve] are paid for their household responsibilities. If they want extra new clothes, birthday gifts for friends, games, whatever, they must buy them themselves. The chore problem takes care of itself because the kids eventually learn: no work, no pay, no fun."
- "When the children were younger, we had a chore wheel on the refrigerator. They'd spin it to get the room they were responsible to clean."
- "We finally came up with a solution for the boys' rooms. They must make their bed and pick up the floor every day or they are grounded for two days. We enforce this consistently, and it is *never* waived, regardless of their plans. They are grounded about once or twice a year, and it works beautifully."
- "Each of the children had certain chores, and simply were not allowed to

do anything else until they were done. If this meant it took all day, so be it."

- "All jobs are done in the morning before school. If not done, that job plus another is done after school."

ATHLETICS: A BLEND OF EXPECTATIONS

Some exceptional athletes are present in these families. Many sons and daughters play or have played varsity sports. Several have been accepted at colleges on full athletic scholarships. Fourteen-year-old Kara from Kansas is among the country's best gymnasts. Tom from Rhode Island has been drafted by a professional basketball team. Do such lofty athletic accomplishments reflect parental emphasis on sports? Yes and no. Yes, in that these parents view athletics as one medium for solid character development. No, in that performance and winning are considered among the lesser aspects of the game.

These parents don't possess a winning-is-paramount mentality. Their attitude is, "If this sport is your interest, we will support you." Perhaps the most tireless example of support came from Joanna and Carl, parents of four now-grown sons. Joanna says, "All four boys played basketball from grades four through twelve. We went to every game, except for a couple, whether they were playing or warming the bench. For a few years, I could even beat them at horse." Having watched several hundred games, it's surprising that Joanna couldn't beat them one-on-one, on the strength of basketball savvy alone.

A few parents did regret having at one time gotten drawn into a performance mind-set. John, father of five from New Jersey, admitted, "I used to push the boys into athletics. They wanted to play, but I used to try to get them to be as good as they could be. They didn't need that. I haven't pressured David [the youngest] at all, and he is probably the best player of all the kids. He has no concept of pressure. When he plays, he just floats out there with his confidence."

Norman from Florida also entertained athletic dreams for his daughter, but diligently avoided making his dreams her reality. "Kimberly ran like I always wanted to. Chip ran like I always did. I loved to watch her run and win. Although I had visions of Mary Decker, when Kim wanted to quit running, I said, 'If you don't want to do that with your life, don't do it for me.'"

Repeatedly, the parents pointed to benefits more worthwhile than competition. Michael from Florida says, "I think the importance of athletics is not so much that a child is learning to play a sport, but that he or she is learning to be more well rounded socially, how to work in a team, and how to work under some pressure."

Carol from South Dakota agrees. "All three of our children have been involved in athletics. It's brought many hours of togetherness for our family. I feel it has also taught them so much besides the ability to play ball. It has taught them to get along with their teammates, to take praise and criticism from their coaches, and to learn to stick with something instead of quitting when the going gets a little tough. The kids are good athletes, and we are proud of their ability, but more important, sports helped build good character."

The physical benefits of athletics were frequently cited. Many parents echoed Gary, a father of a son and daughter. "I feel that a good, healthy body is very important to the mind, and while I want both of them to do something athletically, I don't push them. I also don't necessarily push the traditional sports, which can take more time than the kids have, or which perhaps they aren't built for. I played a lot of football. I don't care if Ty plays football at all. If he learns to play racquetball or tennis or runs or bicycles, that's fine. I encourage the individual sport that builds stamina and gives time to think on your own a little bit. The kids don't have to do well. They are out there to build their bodies and have a good time."

Overextension was an issue that several families faced and resolved. In their enthusiasm to take on much, the kids sometimes took on too much, and parents had to restore balance. From a Montana mother:

• "Both boys are dedicated athletes and love their sports. But when we realized our life-style was becoming too hectic and schoolwork was slipping, we decided that the boys would have to choose a sport to drop. We remember our oldest saying that he would take a hot bath and make a decision. He came out looking like a raisin and chose to drop basketball. The younger boy dropped ski racing. We called their coaches and explained that these were family decisions. Things improved considerably around home after that."

Jerry and Susie, parents of four boys from Oregon, were well aware of the complications of overextension, so they took steps to avoid it. "A rule we decided on in early elementary school, and have used for all four boys, was that they could choose only one organized sport a year until they reached junior high. We didn't want them or us to get overinvolved and burned out on Little League sports. As a result, the boys may not have been as accomplished early in as many sports as other youngsters, but with a little practice, they still have done well."

A word connected with athletics was *commitment*. "What you begin, you complete" was a common parental standard, not just with athletics, but with most other activities. Clifford and Annetta enforce this rule for their three children, aged nine, twelve and fourteen: "If you start an activity, you finish it. If not, you pay for it." For many parents, a sports rule was: Upon deciding to play, a child owes one full season. Further, a commitment supersedes conflicting interests. "Once they sign up for a team, they have to be committed to it. Gabrielle had to play soccer in the rain on her birthday, even though she didn't want to."

Ron and Sandy from Ohio expected commitments to be honored, regardless of the consequences.

• "All of our kids who played sports had to sign a contract with the coach and the school. The contract says that they will not drink, smoke, or indulge in drugs. They signed and we signed under their name. We always taught our kids that this was a legal, binding contract. When Kevin was a senior, one boy on the football team dropped football. His parents left town for the weekend, and he threw the biggest blast. It started on Friday night and it was broken up on Sunday night. Half the football team went to this party. Somebody wrote an anonymous letter to the coach and said this party had gone on. All the football players were then called before a board and questioned individually. Five boys admitted that they had been drinking and, because of the contract, were kicked off the team. Their parents were beside themselves. They thought this was wrong. Since the boys admitted they were at the party, their parents didn't feel they should be kicked off the team because the other kids had lied about being there and were still on the team. My husband and I felt those parents missed the principle of the whole thing. When you say that you will do something, you should stand up and do it. It is a matter of integrity and character."

Carol and Bill made their sons, to their ultimate benefit, live with what at first seemed a misguided pursuit. "We believe that children should complete what they begin. An example was when the boys were young and started

Tae Kwon Do lessons. It was their idea, however once into it, the lessons were physically demanding. We thought the discipline was wonderful, but they decided it was too much. We felt they hadn't given it a chance, so we said we expected them to stick with it until they reached their first level belt, which is yellow. If at that time, they still didn't like it, they could quit. By the time they tested for yellow belt, they loved Tae Kwon Do and are now [nine years later] second-degree black belts. Troy is teaching it at school next year." Carol's story harkens back to an observation made earlier in this chapter: At times a youngster will develop self-momentum only after receiving an initial nudge from his parents.

Regardless how heavily a sense of commitment was championed, one area consistently overrode athletics—academics. Unanimously, these mothers and fathers placed scholastic pursuits well above athletic ones. Should the two collide, forcing a choice, there was no question which would emerge victorious:

- "Academic success has always been considered more important than athletic success. The younger boy was astounded when we called his soccer coach and said he would no longer be on the team. He was in the fifth grade. He cried and said, 'But, Daddy, you love to watch me make goals.' His father responded, 'But I love to see you succeed in school more.' "
- "More than one time, Michael has asked the basketball coach if he could be excused from practice because he had a lot of homework. The coach has always said 'Okay.' As a coach myself, I tell my players right at the beginning of the season that schoolwork comes first."
- "You can play sports as long as your marks are the way they should be—what you are capable of. That is our number-one rule. My son enjoys sports; he is a decent athlete, but that is not where his future lies."

Strong parents support athletics for the opportunities they afford a child's overall development. Their emphasis is on fitness, teamwork, cooperation, and commitment. In other words, the greatest expectations are for the character and physical well-being of the child. Competition and the drive to win are not highly valued. Athletics are encouraged for how they can broaden a child's personality. They are not allowed to narrow it.

Successful parents expect their children to succeed, not measured against others but against themselves. They expect a child to reach for his limits, in talents and in conduct, no matter what the prevailing standards say is acceptable. They demand a level of childrearing for themselves that stands out, not for appearance' sake, but for their children's.

Fulfilling one's potential depends upon self-motivation. And self-motivation is a quality that begins externally. A child learns to motivate himself by first being motivated by others. To motivate well it is vital that a parent possess THE WILL TO DISCIPLINE.

Chapter 13

The Will
to Discipline

*"If you can get things going in a positive discipline
direction, you won't have to chase after them endlessly
in a negative direction."*

Mother, Tilton, New Hampshire

Styles of discipline vary greatly. At one end of the spectrum is the permissive: "As parent, I'll allow you, the child, to follow your feelings and desires with few limits." At the other end is the authoritarian: "Because I'm the parent and the boss, you'll do as I say without question." In between these two extremes lies the authoritative parent: "I'll give you freedom within certain expectations and rules." No parents in these exceptional families considered themselves permissive. The thought alone made many of them shudder. Some parents wondered if their discipline was too demanding, but the more they spoke, the more obvious became the love which guided that discipline. Overall, these mothers and fathers can best be described as authoritative. Motivated by love, they possess the willingness to discipline quickly and firmly when a situation calls for it.

Discipline is indispensable to the smooth functioning of a family. This belief is shared by every one of these parents. To Betty, a writer and mother of twin girls and one son, "Discipline is teaching a child how to live in this world. It is constant directing." Betty understands that she is her children's first, and kindest, teacher about life. She must discipline them today, or someone else will tomorrow—a teacher, an employer, a landlord, a judge. No one will ever discipline them with even a fraction of her love and understanding. The quality of her children's future greatly depends upon Betty's resolve to discipline now.

The will to discipline, then, is one mark of a good parent. Yet, from our interviews, we concluded that these good parents actually do less disciplining than most parents. Two reasons account for this seeming contradiction. First, these mothers and fathers work hard to live the philosophies they profess throughout this book. Where family life is cohesive, the need to discipline diminishes. Second, the stronger a parent's will to discipline, the weaker a child's desire to test that will. Put another way, the will to discipline makes the act of discipline less necessary.

For most parents, discipline is the dirty work of parenthood. It often requires us to take action we'd rather not, to stand strong against the temptation to melt emotionally, and to persevere when "it's easier to let them go." The best of parents have these feelings. A mother from Hawaii, after twenty-five years of raising three children, revealed, "I felt badly about setting restrictions on each child's activity because I knew they would sometimes resent it. It was hard to say no, but when it had to be done, it was done."

Holding her kids responsible for their actions is a task that gives Nancy, a thirty-nine-year-old mother of four, aged five through thirteen, some of her more distressing moments. She confessed, "It breaks my heart when I have to discipline them." Her husband, Bob, teased her with a smile, "That's why I get the hard decisions!" Still, both Nancy and Bob know that, however difficult or upsetting for them, a little discipline now at their gentle hands will spare their children a lot of discipline later at the much rougher hands of the world.

Successful parents face problem behaviors familiar to nearly all parents. How they handle these is a topic for upcoming chapters. This chapter will present nine general guidelines which direct these parents' discipline. These guidelines are not secrets known only to skilled disciplinarians. They are commonsense, practical principles meant to strengthen your will to discipline. In so doing, they will lessen your need to discipline.

GUIDELINE # 1:
DISCIPLINE BEGINS WITH LOVE

"The basis of our discipline is unquestionable love. Without constant love, discipline is irrelevant," said Carol, a Montana mother of two sons. The children have already given us parents a fundamental lesson about love: If you feel it, show it. That lesson will now be applied to discipline by their parents.

In offering her foremost piece of discipline advice to new parents, Sherry from California, mother to Brian and Laura, said, "Most of all, love them to pieces, and let them know you love them to pieces. We are a loud family when we are angry, but we try never to part from one another angry, and no matter how much I have yelled at the kids for something, I also remind them that I love them and that there is absolutely nothing they can do in this world that would ever change that."

Michael, father to five children, aged five to sixteen, in Melbourne, Florida, repeats Sherry's sentiments, "I can't think of a thing that my son [Neil, aged sixteen], for example, could do in which I would shut the door and tell him not to come back. Conceivably, there could come a time when a parent needs to do that, but I can't think of anything my son could do in which I would say, 'Neil, don't ever come back into my home again!' " To strong parents, unconditional love means an unbreakable bond, one that will endure all misbehavior.

Susie from Wyoming follows this small bit of wisdom in disciplining her four large teenagers: "Discipline is the truth in love. Truth without love is harsh. Love without truth is compromise. Always give the truth in love." Of course, in sharing a household with several teens, Susie knows that kids don't always want to hear the truth, particularly where curfews and the car are involved.

Carlene, mother to Tommy (fourteen) and Billy (eleven), has taken her most valuable childrearing lesson directly from her own childhood. "I went through a period as a teenager where I wondered what it would be like if I were living with my natural father—my parents were divorced when I was two years old. I thought maybe I was missing something. When dad wouldn't let me go somewhere or do something, I would promptly inform him, 'You're not my real dad, and I hate you!' What a brat! He would look at me and say, 'Well, I love you. Now go to your room!' Looking back and now being a parent myself, I realize I must have broken dad's heart every time. But he's a wise man. I think he knew in time I would realize how much I was loved."

Parents from Michigan, Bob and Joan, believe that an atmosphere of love does much to alleviate childish accusations. "Sometimes when you discipline children, especially the younger ones, they get the impression that you don't love them. But if there's an overall open, loving relationship, they know different. They may say, 'You don't love me,' but they really know better than that." To Bob and Joan, unconditional love is the best way to respond quietly to the likes of, "You like being mean"; "Harmony's your favorite"; "Why'd you ever have me?"; or any other misperception of the meaning of our actions. Kids may accuse us of not liking or loving them, but every day they see in countless ways where most of the care, affection, and support in their lives comes from. It comes from us—not to mention the things they really value: the VCR, scratch-and-sniff stickers, the car keys!

Children don't readily grasp the concept of discipline motivated by love. Only with maturity—and maybe a few kids of their own—will they fully understand our feelings. Nevertheless, loving disciplinarians know that consistency in discipline refers to more than following our words with action. It also means consistently letting the kids know of the love which drives our actions.

From Sioux Falls, South Dakota, Karol adds a qualifier to her concept of parental love. "You want to have the right kind of love in that you don't endlessly give the kids things or allow them to do things that are not healthy for them in the long run. Buy them too much or give in to their every demand, and you raise self-centered people who have a hard time living in this world." Karol stressed that limitless love does not mean limitless freedom or material pleasures. It means a limitless willingness to wipe the slate clean after each episode of discipline.

If there is an unwanted side effect to love without limits, it's that the kids try their ugliest behavior on the safest people. In part, this does explain why we might hear things like, "Your son is just the nicest young man. I wish I had a whole classroomful of him." And after picking ourselves up from the floor, we mutter something like, 'No, my name is Miller. His name is Billy, Billy Miller. Am I at the right school?' "

Julie, mother to Kara (ten) and Andy (six), says, "Sometimes we see the worst of Kara and Andy because I think they feel secure enough to try out new techniques and tricks with us that they won't try with the baby-sitter or when they are at school. They feel safe enough with us to spread their wings, knowing we will still love them." While Julie does discipline Kara and Andy's at-home stunts, she gets satisfaction from their sense of family security. Then again, if misbehavior were the only gauge of how much some kids feel loved, their parents must be the most loving people in the universe!

Sensitive disciplinarians rewarm the home atmosphere as soon as possible after disciplining—if the kids allow them to. For example, many parents require a child to spend time quietly occupying a chair, a corner, or his room as the price for his misconduct. After the discipline is over, these parents follow up with a hug, kiss, or some verbal sign of acceptance. In so many words, they are stating: "This discipline is not personal. We don't love you any less because we had to punish you."

Routinely, parents complimented their youngsters for reacting calmly to discipline. For example, preschoolers were told "Thank you" or "You acted very nice" after they served their time in the "quiet chair." One mother laughed, "Many times I had to make him sit, standing over him the whole time, but when he finally settled down, I told him how much I appreciated him acting so grown-up." Savvy parents compliment a child for his nice behavior even when that behavior was forced upon him.

One father followed this homemade love and discipline formula: two parts love for every one part discipline. Meaning, after each discipline incident with his sons, dad made sure to say at least two positive things about them to them. He did add wryly that every so often the boys' bouts of misbehavior came in such rapid succession that it was hard squeezing his compliments in before the next round of trouble began.

A term frequently mentioned side by side with unconditional love was *positive reinforcement.* Positive reinforcement is a psychological phrase which refers to any reward for a desirable behavior. In assessing her discipline style, Nancy, a parent of three teenagers, noted that when the children were younger, "Positive reinforcement and verbal praise seemed to eliminate much of the need for discipline."

The most defiant two-year-old, or tantrum-prone three-year-old, or rowdy five-year-old behaves appropriately most of the time. If you were to time your youngster's bouts of misbehavior with a stopwatch—clicking it on as soon as trouble starts and off when calm returns—you would find, believe it or not, that over ninety percent of his waking moments he is *not* misbehaving. It may seem as if he's constantly acting up, but this perception arises because bouts of unruliness are far more memorable than quiet or even-keeled times. Good disciplinarians are skilled at minimizing their discipline by maximizing their positive comments. If Rocky has just asked his little sister to play with him—a first in his four years on this earth—immediately compliment him for his cooperation. If normally whirlwind-paced Melody has just spent nine minutes absorbed in a puzzle, don't let her concentration pass without comment. If Carlisle, without a word from you, has cleaned up his toy litter, make a fuss over his initiative. It is far easier to be ever-ready to reward the good than to punish the bad. Preschoolers especially are parent pleasers. They can't get enough praise from us. Every day is filled with behavior that can be nurtured by a few well-timed, positive words.

Lois from Minnesota, in disciplining Michael and Kristen, stressed the need to "Accentuate the positive. I put that phrase on my refrigerator when the kids were little because it seemed so easy for me to focus on the one area to be corrected rather than on the ten that are positive. We also have a special dinner plate that we use for the special person of the day—special because of an achievement, birthday, or just because a lift is needed."

Doug, a superintendent of schools in Wyoming, uses a "slot-machine" approach to lengthen his children's spells of nice behavior. Every so often, without notice, just like a slot machine, he gives Sasha, Shiloh, and Shoshone (aged seven to fifteen) a special treat—for instance, an extension of bedtime, a trip for ice cream, fifteen minutes' extra phone time. This is one of dad's more fun ways to say, "Great job, guys." Betting on when and how their father might surprise them next helps keep the kids walking with their better foot forward. Should you choose to implement a similar system, expect some letdown in behavior immediately after the bonus reward. Kids can only be good so long. Call it the fatigue factor.

The last words on unconditional love come from fourteen-year-old Nolan, son of Rita and Jerry. Nolan's idea for fostering strong positive feelings, not only between parent and child, but between child and child, is the foundation of effective discipline. "If you ever see something nice about someone in your family, let them know."

GUIDELINE #2:

THE EARLIER, THE EASIER

"It is so important to start disciplining almost from infancy," said Betty from Missouri. "No parent can expect to suddenly tell a sixteen-year-old what he can or can't do if, for the past fifteen years, the child has never had rules enforced." All parents agreed with Betty: The earlier, the easier. As children get older, they get bigger, smarter, more independent, and overall more bent on doing things their way. No matter how much effort it takes to teach limits to a two-year-old for the first time, it will take far more effort to teach them to a seven-year-old for the first time. In the words of one father, "Discipline now. Be consistent now. It is not going to get any simpler."

If we define *discipline* in a narrow sense—to place some consequence on a child's behavior—discipline options in dealing with toddlers are pretty limited. If we define it in a broad sense—to teach—then we can begin disciplining children very young by implementing the three S's: supervise, sidetrack, and stop.

SUPERVISE. Toddlers are the closest thing to perpetual motion ever created. What's more, they move faster than the speed of light. One second, Brewster is clinging to your legs, whining for more Kool-Aid. The next second, you sneeze, and by the time you open your eyes, he's downstairs eating the salt cubes in the water softener. Toddlers require the absolute peak of parental supervision. "The most energy you put into discipline with a young child is just keeping an eye on him," said a father of two. One eye usually isn't enough. Preferably, we use both eyes, ears, and one hand if possible.

While toddlers may fear strangers, they don't fear much else, so we have to provide the caution. Up to dozens of times a day we have to remove them from potentially hurtful places, or, more wisely, to remove potentially hurtful places from them. "That's why you can always tell houses where toddlers roam," said one mother. All electrical outlets are boarded over. Nothing made of anything more breakable than concrete is less than five feet off the ground. All tables are barren save fingerprints. Supervision is the indispensable ingredient in raising and disciplining a toddler. Several parents offered this reassurance: Even the most super supervisor will have kids with bumps, scrapes, and bruises, because if you miss toddler-proofing the most inaccessible spot, little Dudley will find it four seconds after his feet hit the floor.

SIDETRACK. Toddler's attention spans, if stretched, can reach a full six or seven seconds. There is so much they want to see, hear, smell, and mutilate that nothing captures their interest very long. Therefore, once your son begins to maul, say, the irresistibly dangling phone cord, sidetrack him onto something else more able to withstand his assault, like a brick wall.

Rita believes her best discipline with all seven of her children when they were toddlers was "distraction. If I saw them heading toward a table to climb,

I would try to divert their attention with a toy or some other activity. Sometimes, I'd take their hand and guide them in a different direction. I called it 'guide to the good.' I tried not to pull them backward, or in the opposite direction from where they were headed, but took them on more of an angle away from something." Skillful sidetracking leads to less contests of wills.

STOP. Let's say your little one decides to take a slap at your face while you're feeding him—maybe he's just getting downright tired of strained peas. Here you have a couple of options: One, move out of arm's reach; or two, gently hold his arms for several seconds, accompanied by a few firm no's. With either option, you effectively *stop* your son from hitting you or from continuing to hit you. Many parents used mild restraint as discipline with their toddlers. Young children do not like having their motion curtailed. Physically preventing them from going after the cat or throwing food can teach them very early that such behavior will not be allowed.

As their children move beyond the early toddler stage, strong parents begin disciplining with time-out. Time-out is psychological parlance meaning to remove a child from a problem situation and to place him in some boring or isolated spot—a chair, corner, bathtub, bedroom, or on the steps—for a certain length of time. Although with their seventeen-foot video screens and nine-line phones, some kids' bedrooms probably wouldn't qualify as either boring or isolated.

Childrearing specialists have long touted time-out as very effective discipline with younger children. Little ones quickly get bored when forced to alight in one place for even a few minutes. There is far too much they have to see and do. The more a child likes to move through his environment, the more he wants to avoid time-out.

The parents we interviewed typically began time-out when the kids were between the ages of eighteen months and two years. Misconduct most often earning time-out included aggressive behavior, temper tantrums, spitting, throwing things, and ignoring or defying a parent's request. Time-out generally lasted anywhere between a minute and several minutes, with timers often used to monitor a child's stay. Some parents ignored any nagging, whining, crying, even sleeping that took place in time-out. They felt that as long as a youngster stayed there, how he occupied his time-out was his choice. Other parents took a more active posture toward verbal resistance. "I never started the timer until they were quietly sitting, and many times I reset it because they started acting up before their time was over."

Children typically don't comprehend the reason for time-out initially. The logic "If A (I act up), then B (I sit down)," needs to be repeated to be absorbed. Children also aren't always willing to stay in one place just because we tell them to. Time-out is not fun, so they may not accept it standing still. Frequently, parents had to stand over a child, hold him, or swat his seat to make him remain in time-out. In other words, they had to enforce their time-out physically. As one mother put it, "No matter how much he resists me, he's still only two. And I'd rather get things under control now than battle about them years from now. It's not easy, but I can't see it getting any easier with time."

The opinion from all parents was the same. When begun early, discipline is at its most effective, its most durable, and, believe it or not, its easiest. *Terrible two's* is a relative term. Compared to a defiant ten-year-old, or a rebellious fifteen-year-old, a "terrible" two-year-old is a parenting dream.

GUIDELINE #3:
EXPECT CHILDISH BEHAVIOR

Stress can be defined as the difference between the way we would like things to be and the way they are. Put another way, stress is the gap between our expectations and reality. This definition aptly fits the stress parents often feel during discipline. "When are you going to learn?"; "How many times do I have to send you to your room?"; "You know better than to talk like that"— these are common signs of our frustration at the reality that Dexter is not acting as we've taught him or as we think he should.

The most competent disciplinarians have been forced—by their kids—to accept this parenting truth: Children will act impulsively, mischievously, thoughtlessly, defiantly, manipulatively, and almost every other way ending in "-ly," not because they're nasty creatures solely bent on driving parents to the emotional brink, but because they are immature, developing human beings who need years to grow up. "It is the nature of the child to misbehave," said Lucille, as she thought about the one common characteristic of her eleven children. According to Lucille, an alert parent expects misbehavior. In no way does she suggest we overlook it or allow it. On the contrary, we must deal with it. We will be calmer and more effective, however, if we never for one second forget that kids can behave counter to our best discipline solely because they're built that way.

Before moving further, one clarification needs to be made. *Expect* is not being used here as it was in chapter 12, that is, "to set a level of standards." Rather, what it means here is, "Know that it's coming."

"Because I'm two, that's why" is the catchphrase of Ted and Naomi, parents of three girls. It arose years ago when dad, in frustration toward two-year-old Sarat, cried, "Why do you act like that?" From another room, mom replied, "Because I'm two, that's why." Though the girls are now two, eight, and twelve, the phrase is still used. In essence, it's come to mean, "Because I'm a child, that's why." Naomi is quick to point out, like Lucille, that this is not an excuse for nasty or irresponsible behavior. It is a reason for it, and remembering that will help parents lengthen their emotional fuse.

When asked what insights she would include in a book about discipline, Sally from Hawaii said, "Accept the fact that with kids, there are joys and problems with each phase and that stages go on as long as one is alive. Parenting is a to-the-grave proposition." Sally can verify, after nearly twenty-four years of motherhood, that two-year-olds can bite, three-year-olds can battle eating and sleeping, six-year-olds can slap sisters, ten-year-olds can "forget" homework, and fourteen-year-olds can do all of these and more. A child's repertoire of main misbehaviors is ever-evolving, as new antics emerge and old ones fade. We parents observe the process, working to keep the list from becoming unmanageable, but certain problems will present themselves, no matter how conscientious our childrearing. We respond to them when they do, and realize that over time if we persevere, most stages pass, although sometimes they push us to the edge before they do.

Bob, a father of four children, knows that a child's physical development can give a parent false expectations. "Sometimes I made the mistake of thinking that because a child is a certain size, he should be acting like a child that age. But really, mentally and emotionally, he is not that big. There were times when I called on him to be more than he was." Bob acknowledged having to remind himself constantly that size is not a measure of maturity. A seven-year-old is a seven-year-old, whether he's forty-eight, or eighty-three, pounds.

In offering her basics of discipline, Sandy from Ohio said, "Above all, be a parent. Don't try to be a peer with your children. Teach them not to lie, cheat, or steal *early* in life." Pausing, she then added this piece of reality gained from the experience of disciplining nine children, "When—and most kids will try one or all of these things—they steal that gum from the store or cheat or lie to you, make them face up to their responsibility by taking them back to the store and returning the gum or at least 'fessing up' to whatever they did."

As Sandy's children have obviously taught her, even the best-behaved youngsters will have rowdy moments. The most truthful child can tell a lie. The calmest of teens will stomp and slam doors. The best students will muff an assignment through carelessness. Inconsistency is a defining characteristic of children. In fact, it's a defining characteristic of all humans. That is why competent parents stress: Expect the unexpected. Know that some misbehavior is inevitable.

As parents, our responsibility is not to ensure that our children will not act foolishly or irresponsibly. That is not possible. Our responsibility is to teach our children that when they do act hurtfully or irresponsibly, whether once every nine days or nine times a day, they will be held accountable for it.

A concluding thought on keeping our expectations close to reality comes from Mary in Des Moines. "Don't expect children to behave like adults in miniature. Their emotions, perspective, and intellect are less mature than that of their parents—some days the gap is less evident, I'm afraid." As a basic law of stress reduction says: When you know that something is certain to happen, you will be less upset when it does.

GUIDELINE #4:
THE BEST DISCIPLINE BEGINS WITH THE SELF

"Teaching by example is the strongest parenting tool," believes Stephen, a physician and father of two girls in West Virginia. Indeed, teaching by example is a concept that emerges everywhere in successful parenthood—instilling religious and moral values, communication, relationships, and discipline. Children learn more quickly and durably how to live well when a parent lives well. Since we've talked at length about the value of parenting through example, we won't retread ground we've covered earlier. What we will do is share a few more ideas on teaching or, more specifically, disciplining by example.

Connie, mother to a nationally known science scholar from Ohio, has distinct feelings on the effectiveness of discipline devoid of example:

• "Children learn by the example set before them. It is deeds far more than words which provide the example to children. Although parents may not always be equal to living up to the standards we present to our children, we must be constantly striving to live up to them. There should be no double standards of behavior. We need to be constantly looking within ourselves for any thoughts and qualities that are unlike the example we would like our children to follow. And this takes absolute honesty with ourselves."

Parents regularly identified self-discipline as a first ingredient for effective child discipline. Jane from Miami, Oklahoma, during her most frazzled moments, still made herself adhere to the no-name-calling rule that she demanded of her children. "I always said that I didn't care how mad I got at the children, I was *never* going to call them names, and I never have. I could be mad at them, and they could be making terrible mistakes, but it wasn't because they were 'stupid,' or any other names." Jane maintained that she'd better behave by the same standards she held up for her children, for a weak example can sometimes bring down the strongest discipline. Bill and Joanne from Mississippi agree that discipline makes a more permanent mark in the context of a parent's example. "It wasn't until we learned to say I'm sorry that the kids would say I'm sorry and really mean it."

Using "we" in place of "you" is how Rita and Jerry communicate to their youngsters and themselves that good discipline is a goal for the whole family, not just the child. "We try to make policies by stating, '*We* don't do that,' or 'That isn't the way *we* talk to each other.' In any discipline, to say 'we' includes the parents in the rule, and lets the child join the family instead of being singled out with a '*You* can't do that,' or '*You'd* better stop that!' "

To be a particularly courageous disciplinarian, you can take the route traveled by Sam and Margaret from Michigan. When asked, "What was your most creative discipline decision?" they responded that they discipline themselves for infractions as they would their children. In other words, if a youngster has to occupy his room for half an hour to cool down after an emotional explosion, should mom or dad erupt similarly, they too earn a half hour in their room. If a son has to define ten dictionary words (four syllables or more, not easy words) for flinging reckless language, mom also will profit from the dictionary if her mouth gets the best of her.

Living by the what's-good-for-the-kids-is-good-for-us discipline philosophy requires superior stamina, but if you attempt it, you'll be a rare parent. Further, you'll derive several benefits. One, you'll put substance behind the term self-discipline. If you don't meet the standards you expect of your kids, you'll meet the same consequences. Two, your children will perceive you as much more fair, even if a trifle confused. That is, if they had your authority, would they use it on themselves? And three, now and then the kids may even feel sorry for you. Said Margaret, "When I have put myself on 'punishment,' it usually hurts the kids to see me go through loss of privileges, no TV, outings, etc., right with them."

Certainly parents can't discipline themselves for each and every piece of misconduct they hold their children answerable for. From a logistics standpoint alone, you couldn't do that. How could you simmer in your room for thirty minutes after a screaming fit—even if you'd like to—when supper needs to be prepared, an errand is waiting, or there's a child to watch? For those behaviors, however, that you'd like to see controlled in you as much as in your children, Sam and Margaret's practice of real self-discipline is one option to consider.

Good parents offer this reassurance on the notion of self-discipline. No parent can live everything he tries to discipline his children to do or not do. Sometimes we discipline quickest for the very things we ourselves are most guilty of. And that's not completely bad. A good parent wants his children to become better persons than he is. To the extent, though, that we are willing to learn our own discipline lessons, they will soak in all the more solidly, for the kids and us.

GUIDELINE #5:
USE THE LITTLEST DISCIPLINE WORD—*NO*

Positive parents appreciate the value of the word *no.* They depend on the word often, as they base decisions on their youngster's welfare, and not on how much he nags, pleads, sulks, even threatens until he gets a *yes.* "Love your kids enough to say no when needed," affirms Betty, mother of Judy and Rick from Missouri. "Yes can sometimes be the coward's way out."

No is among the smallest of words, but it speaks one of life's biggest lessons: You can't always have what you want. And the younger a person is when she grasps that lesson, the smoother her life will be. That is why better parents aren't afraid to say no, be it in response to a two-year-old's climbing onto the table, a four-year-old's sobbing for more ice cream, or a fifteen-year-old's, "Can I go to the quadruple drive-in feature with Rocky tonight? I promise I'll be back in time to study for exams tomorrow."

Bob from Cleveland asserts that the word *no* must become a comfortable part of a parent's vocabulary. "The kids have to see that life is not a candy store with all the shelves open all the time. When I was growing up, my father put certain restrictions on me, and I really didn't enjoy them too much at the time. As I got older, though, I could understand why he was doing some of them. I've come to believe that telling kids no for certain things is natural."

Even if saying no comes naturally to parents, the kids generally aren't happy about hearing it. Can we really expect them to be? Self-denial is a quality that is developed from the outside in. That is, kids need parents to impose early limits on them, and only with many years will they more completely be able to self-regulate their desires. Even so, do any grown-ups exist who are able to deny themselves everything that is harmful to them? The most self-denying of us occasionally need to be told no by somebody else.

Despite their outward displeasure, kids do appreciate a firm stand. That's what Linda, mother to Kevin (sixteen), Heather (thirteen), and Megan (nine), thinks. "Children don't want carte blanche on anything they want to do. I believe they want that limit set. They want to push you, but they want to know that limit is there so they can test it. They want to respect you." Linda believes that children are more content when a parent draws a definite line and stands by it. Otherwise, they'll spend a lot of time relentlessly poking and prodding to see just where the boundaries are, making themselves and us agitated in the process.

For example, a three-year-old will relentlessly badger you to go outside if he thinks you'll weaken and ultimately let him go. He'll learn quickly to persist as long as necessary to get you to crack. Similarly, a two-year-old may not accept her first evening with a baby-sitter, or maybe her first ten evenings. The kindest way for you to say, "No, you can't go with us," is quietly to tell her once that you'll be back, kiss her, and then leave. Regardless how many times and how many ways you tell your daughter no, as long as you're still at home struggling vainly to convince her to enjoy the baby-sitter—who is probably thinking, 'This job is not worth two dollars an hour'—she will cling to the notion that no isn't really no yet.

Young children are born to resist no. Their world is a self-centered one, guided by impulse. The younger they learn that your no's are definite and not maybe's, the more content they, and you, will be.

Lucille, looking back over her eighteen children and forty-five years of motherhood, regretted that she required a few years, and a few kids, to understand the worth of no. "Our biggest failures as parents were when we were afraid to say no and make the kids unhappy. When we saw that there was no way to make them completely happy with our decisions, we began to stick with our discipline better. And the younger kids turned out happier because we did."

Other parents cite additional long-term benefits of a firm no. Dudley, father of three, observes, "The hardest times of parenting can also turn out to be the most rewarding. I'm referring specifically to those times when we did not allow our children to do something, much against their wishes—such as go to a party where we knew there would be alcohol—and perhaps ended up being key people in changing the whole party around by influencing other parents and their children. Then, too, after much arguing and bitterness, to have your child tell you that he thinks you did the right thing is a wonderful feeling." Dudley's counsel: Persevere in a prudent, however unpopular, decision. Others, your kids included, will often come around to the wisdom of your judgment.

Sometimes our wisdom is apparent to our children after only a few hours. Nancy from Cleveland tells this story. "About three weeks ago our seventh-grader was going to the zoo on a school trip. All week long he talked about how everyone was wearing jams [a colorful pair of shorts]. I kept saying we'll see what the weather's like. Zoo day came with forty-five degrees and rain. He insisted on wearing jams, but I said no jams. He said if he couldn't wear jams, he wouldn't go. I said, 'Fine, don't go.' He even called a friend who said he was wearing jams. Finally he went to the zoo in jeans and was happy he did. The first thing he said getting off the bus was, 'Thanks, Mom, for making me wear jeans.' " Parents don't always have to wait years for our no's to be appreciated.

Betty from St. Louis asserts that a parent's no can be a youngster's earliest tool for resisting peer pressure. "I tried not to let myself be blackmailed into the everyone-has-one or everyone-is-going type of argument. Saying no when I felt uneasy about something or knew it was not a good thing for our children helped me to teach them at an early age that one doesn't always need to go along with the group. I felt it helped build the strength that was needed later to stand up to peer pressure." Other parents reinforced Betty's words. They said to their kids, in essence, "If your friends or anybody else is pushing you to do something you don't want to do, tell them that your mother [father] said no. Blame us. Tell them we'll ground you for six months if we ever found out what you did." To competent parents, no can work to the good even when it is never actually spoken.

Many young parents today have been made unduly nervous by experts who somberly warn: "Never tell your toddler no. It stifles his natural curiosity." Strong parents, especially the older ones, vehemently disagree with such simplistic advice. First of all, it's not easy to dampen the built-in inquisitiveness of little children, especially not with a mere no, which to most toddlers is a bothersome verbal mosquito and nothing more. Secondly, as we've said, no is part of the real world. It's a statement of existence kids must learn to accept. And the sooner they learn this, the easier life will be for them.

Should you present your reasons underlying your no? Once, or maybe even twice, if you suspect you truly weren't heard or understood the first time through. Any more than that is just asking for an argument, as no triggers a reflex in kids to ask "Why?" and "Why?" is only the forerunner of more "Why?" 's. To shut down these verbal merry-go-rounds, you might try a response favored by one father: "I gave you my reasons. You didn't like them." And then cease the discussion. Walk away. Or, give the kids the same dumb look they give you whenever you ask them why they did something. If these fail, you could try the words of a popular poster, "What part of no didn't you understand?"

No will elegantly speak for itself if it isn't buried beneath a mound of rationales and justifications that typically only spur more arguing and further convince your kids that "You say no just to say no." We know that's not true. Someday so will they.

GUIDELINE #6:
RESPECT THE POWER OF TEMPERAMENT

No two children are alike—physically, intellectually, or temperamentally. This truth every parent encounters firsthand the instant her second child enters the world. Because of his nature, or inborn "wiring," each child will react uniquely to life and to his parents' efforts to teach him about life. With Chastity, raise your voice three decibels, and she'll immediately quit pushing her little sister, apologize fourteen times to you, her, and the neighbor lady who saw her do it, and won't touch her sister for the next six weeks. Spike, on the other hand, has to stand in the corner 212 times—once for every attack on his older brother this week—just to limit his punching to only one hand. Oxford will make his bed three weeks straight to earn a single sticker of Spider Man. Spikette can be fined twenty-five cents per unmade bed, and after three weeks will be hocking her toys to pay off her five-dollar debt. Respect for the tremendous temperamental differences among children is something most every one of these parents has gained over years of disciplining:

- "Our major parenting change came with our second child. The first child responded to a no by stopping completely in his tracks. No made the second child simply try harder to continue the undesirable behavior. Our entire house changed with our second child. All vases and knickknacks were put away. All doors and drawers had childproof latches. None of this had been necessary with our first child."
- "With Nick [aged ten], the best thing for us to do when he's done wrong, and he knows it, is to put him in his room to just sit and calm down. That drives him batty. He is very active. With Brittany [aged eight], we don't send her to her room because that is where she goes to play. We make her remedy what she has done wrong, usually making her say she is sorry. We approach her more emotionally. With Zachary [aged six], we have to get him to realize he's done wrong. That takes a lot. Just getting him to realize he's done wrong is the battle."

In assessing her discipline style, one mother said, "Every child is truly an individual, and what works with one doesn't necessarily work with another. I had to learn that early and not be afraid of it." Smiling, her husband added his opinion, "Some children need a lot of praise, and some need an occasional kick in the butt."

Perhaps the most colorful testament to inborn individuality comes from fourteen-year-old Sarah. When she was asked to describe her relationship with her twelve-year-old sister, Emily, she pulled no punches.

- "When asked one time if we were alike, we looked at each other. She said, 'Alike.' I said, 'Different.' Emily is a mental giant, but a social leper and very immature. I love new wave, pop, and heavy metal. She's really into show tunes. I'm fashionable and have strange tastes—daring. She's classic. I'd rather party. She would rather read. The few times I've drank and done naughty stuff were this year. She probably never will. I probably will more."

No question, Emily and Sarah will pose disparate discipline dilemmas for their mother and father. And although many parents may not encounter such distinct polar opposites in their offspring, it is a law of parenting that discipline does not demand equal effort from every parent. Consistency, patience, perseverance, stamina—all factors involved in any discipline vary immensely from child to child. You and your sister both might have eleven-year-olds who've been shirking homework for the past nine weeks. In handling the problem, you both could use the same words, the same consequences, the same tone of voice, with the same consistency—in short, identical discipline. She'll witness a reversal in her son's behavior in three days. You'll need three months just to be able to declare, "Things are somewhat better." In no way does this indicate anything is wrong with your discipline, or that your sister is the more skillful parent. Your approach may be first-rate. But you are dealing with your youngster and his unique style of interacting with the world, and he's just not the kind to yield quickly to any mere parent trying to teach him something.

Every day retell yourself, "No two are alike"—tape it in bold letters on your refrigerator or maybe on your son or daughter's forehead—and you will greatly reduce discipline frustration and impatience. Also, you will be less likely to blame yourself if your youngster is making an agonizingly slow trip toward self-control or maturity. Realize that there are no shortcuts or easy solutions to managing some children. You downright just have to persevere, and love and discipline with all your might.

There's a bright side to raising a temperamental tempest. Looking back now from a safe distance, many successful parents are appreciative that they were pushed to the maximum of their childrearing mettle. They've seen that high-spirited children who are taught some self-control can channel their enormous inborn energy into becoming vibrant and achieving young adults, even if they do leave some frazzled parents strewn in their wake.

GUIDELINE #7:

THE CALMER, THE BETTER

Excellent parents are not paragons of patience. Not one mother or father in these families claims to attain complete calm every discipline instant. Each is acutely aware that as long as children are the objects of our discipline and not something easy, like untamed circus tigers, parents will get emotional.

Nonetheless, strong parents strive for composure, particularly during discipline when everyone's emotions are at peak.

Norman from Florida believes that calm is a key to good discipline. "I would strongly recommend that parents work hard on the ability to be dispassionate in discipline and in working through problems. I don't mean to never have any emotions, but to try and reduce them to a minimum." Norman understands that parents aren't robots—it was he who couldn't tolerate his daughter's "turkey" boyfriend. Still, Norman works hard "to be dispassionate in discipline" because he, like most parents, has had his worst childrearing moments during an excess of discipline passion.

When we can remain controlled, the whole family benefits. Our blood pressure doesn't reach headache levels. Heated words and hasty actions are less likely. Discipline focuses on what a youngster *did* wrong, not what's wrong with him. And, not least important, calm discipline works more quickly. If we are enraged as we banish Elmo to his room for an hour for misbehaving, he may think, "Sure, Dad, I'll go to my room. Look at how you're acting. I ruined the rest of your day." By getting so angry, we allow Elmo to control our emotions. He acts bad and we get mad. That's a lot of power for a child, and the temptation to use it can be overwhelming.

Keeping composed is especially hard during that initial realization that our youngster has just acted counter to everything we've tried to instill in him since birth. "Acting out of anger is somewhat of a reflex reaction. I need to decide ahead of time not to react when angry, if possible," says Carroll from North Carolina, who also admits, "I sometimes burn slowly inside, causing the pain to last longer."

The calmer parents don't try to choke back swelling anger through sheer force of will. Instead, they use a number of strategies to soothe their emotions before deciding on discipline.

TIME-OUT. A preferred approach for quieting down all parties is time-out. Several pages ago we introduced time-out as one of the first forms of discipline strong parents use with their children. Time-out works by making a child take a break from his misbehavior or from the scene of the problem. Effective parents have discovered that time-out is not just a break for the child. It is also a break for them. "We get out of each other's faces" is how one father appraised the cooling power of time-out. When a parent and child are separated by a room or several walls, they can't aim their emotions directly at each other. Ross, father to four, aged four through thirteen, says, "The best discipline decision we ever made was to use time-out. It does two things. It gives the kids a chance to think and give us a chance to think, so we don't react so emotionally." Mary Jo from Kentucky gets a similar tranquilizing shot from time-out. "I tell the kids to go to their rooms and give me time to cool off. I tell them that the roof is coming off and mom is turning green, and they know that they'd better clear out or change something quickly because I'm at my boiling point." Separation is great medicine for bringing temperatures down.

DELAY YOUR DECISION. Nearly as reliable as time-out for soothing ragged nerves is the delay-your-decision decision. "Few problems require an instantaneous solution," believed one mother. Many parents agreed, so when possible, they postponed tackling trouble until they felt settled enough to untangle it logically. Susie from Wyoming recalls, "One evening our eldest son, Kip [now nineteen], was out with his girlfriend until the early morning hours. Rather than react in anger that night when he came home, I simmered down all the next day and by early evening was over my anger. I was then able to visit with him and his girlfriend, telling them what I expected, and they haven't been late since."

A delayed response carries added benefits. The kids are forced to wonder for several hours or more what we're concocting as punishment. This in itself can be potent discipline. We also allot ourselves ample time to devise an appropriate consequence, one that fits the misdeed and is enforceable. In letting time temper the tone of our talk, we're less likely to fire off a dictum like, "As long as you live in my house, young man, you are never again permitted to even look at a girl."

To be sure, a parent doesn't always have the luxury of delayed action. Response sometimes must be immediate, as in the instance of a child running into the street, or an all-out brawl between siblings. Then, too, with younger children, the closer the discipline is to the infraction, generally the better the connection is made between "cause" (i.e., name-calling) and "effect" (i.e., apologizing). Aware of these realities, even-tempered parents are saying: If a problem doesn't need quick intervention, restrain yourself until you're in a better emotional state to confront it.

SELF-TALK. Some parents practice talking themselves calm. Frank from Pennsylvania, father to twins, Rachel and Jessica (thirteen), and Caitlin (seven), takes a parenting lesson from the actor John Wayne, who, when once asked the secret of his success, replied, "Talk low, talk slow." When encountering some discipline turbulence, Frank says, "My volume goes down, and I am a little slower to react." From experience, Frank knows that if at first you don't feel composed, sometimes you can bring about the feeling by acting composed. Besides, if you're a good actor, the kids can't tell how close to the emotional edge you really are, and kids are less willing to challenge a picture of composure. Carrying Frank's technique to its limit, every so often you might try whispering your discipline. Besides wondering what's wrong with you, the kids could be shocked into attention.

Sue, a mother of four, guides her discipline with one main question. "Is this action for the child's best interest, or am I venting my anger, expressing what is in my best interest? It's so important to question one's own motives before making decisions on behalf of each child." Sue says that assessing her motives helps her focus on the purpose of her discipline and not on how upset the kids are making her. She stressed that all discipline is teaching and that children take a long time to learn. That's why childrearing takes a couple of decades to complete.

Naomi, a parent of three girls, keeps calm in the face of misbehavior by repeating to herself, "Don't take this behavior personally. It is not intended just to upset me." In other words, Candy is not taking forever to eat just to make my life miserable. She's not being obnoxious in the store to make me look like an incompetent parent in front of the whole world. She is being difficult because she's a child who is upset, or frustrated, or trying to get away with something. If you accept that misbehavior most often is nothing more than misbehavior, and not an insult to you or a childish comment upon your childrearing, you will get less frustrated by it. "Once I realized that kids misbehave just because they're kids, and not to drive parents crazy," said one father, "I disciplined better, or at least less emotionally."

PICK YOUR BATTLES. This phrase and others like it—choose your struggles, pick your discipline—arose often when parents spoke of calm discipline. Marilyn, a mother from Oregon, says, "Three of our four children sucked their thumb. Our daughter picked it up when her older brother told her, 'Try this, you'll like it.' She did. We tried everything trying to get them to stop—constant reminding, rewarding them with candy, taking pennies away from them each time we saw their thumbs in their mouths. Finally, we decided it just wasn't worth fighting about, and eventually they all stopped on their own. Our attention was just adding to the strength of the habit." Ed, Marilyn's husband, adds this reassurance, "Thumb-sucking takes a lot longer to cause problems with teeth than parents think." Ed should know, he's a dentist.

"Is this hurting anyone or anything, or is it mainly an irritation to me?" This is the question a number of parents used to determine whether to intervene and discipline a behavior, or to ignore it and let it pass. Hair-twirling, nail-biting, nose-picking, squirming in chairs, clinging to security blankets and toys are examples of behaviors that, while potentially able to drive parents to the brink of patience, are not discipline-worthy in the eyes of good disciplinarians. If Holmes asks Grandpa sixty questions per minute, and Grandpa doesn't mind, should we? If Lena sings herself to sleep every night, as long as she sings in bed, is there a problem? Such conduct is "kid stuff," as one dad tagged it, and is probably best handled by being removed from our discipline to-do list. It doesn't deserve our effort.

Our task as responsible parents is to discipline behavior that hurts others or infringes upon their rights. If we try to keep pace with all the kid stuff that children display and discard while growing up, we won't just frazzle ourselves. We'll effectively give benign behavior equal status to real misconduct. "Don't fuss over the little things," advised one parent. "Save the fussing until it's really needed."

One mother, in finally deciding to quit fussing over her four-year-old son's constant vice-grip on his favorite stuffed animal, said, "I was talking and nagging at him in vain. Then a little friend said, 'Why do you carry that with you all the time?' and that had more effect than all my words."

The less we have to discipline, the easier it is to stay calm. And we'll discipline much less when we wisely select what's worth our effort. Marilyn concluded, "The better you pick your battles, the more you'll win."

REVERSE ROLE-PLAYING. Dudley, a New Hampshire physician and father to Heidi, Mary, and David (aged seventeen to twenty-three), used this creative strategy to make a quiet point when the kids were younger. "For lesser offenses, I have done some role-playing—getting the kids to play my part as dad, and I would play their part, acting as they were acting. This had a humorous side, but it would also get my side of the situation understood a little better." By mirroring each other's behavior and reactions, Dudley and his children could see themselves by watching someone else. The kids could personally experience, say, dad's exasperation over their antics at dinner, and dad could take a close-up look at his dinner discipline style, with a few laughs exchanged along the way. And laughter alone is among the best sedatives for a case of emotional fits.

Whatever strategies you use, keeping a steady frame of mind will raise your credibility. Let's assume that Wyatt has just sprayed the neighbor's cat in the ear with his squirt gun for the seventeenth time this week. If we're infuriated as we inform him we're junking his favorite toy, he may not believe us, figuring that once our frenzy is past, we'll reconsider, especially if that's our pattern. If we tie our tongue until we can coolly present our discipline, Wyatt will have fewer doubts about our resolve.

A father from Atlanta talked of one of his most vivid recollections of childhood. "My father took me and my brother for a drive. He began to calmly explain why he did what he did as far as we kids were concerned. Although the conversation lasted for only fifteen or twenty miles of road, I'll never forget it."

Betty from St. Louis found a calm demeanor to be especially helpful in handling delicate situations. "Our son went through a looking-through-catalogs-in-the-underwear-section-and-giggling stage. I didn't scold, but in a matter-of-fact way said that I happened to be needing someone to fold the family's underwear. Folding underwear for two weeks was a practical way for our son to learn that underwear is just another article of clothing that needs folding like any other piece of clothing. The catalogs were always there, but folding all that laundry seemed to satisfy his curiosity once and for all." Betty recognizes that had she overreacted to her son's blossoming interest in the opposite sex, she might have added more appeal to this perceived forbidden fruit. An unruffled parent takes some of the fun out of mischief or misbehavior.

No matter how well timed our time-outs, how well delayed our discipline, or how well intended our self-talk, inevitably we parents at times will "lose a grip," as the teens call it, and lash out at the nearest juvenile. Good parents misplace their composure, too. That is why, after the dust of discipline clears, they apologize for any outbursts. "I think it is very important to be able to admit to your child that you made a mistake. If you have disciplined your child and blown your top, when you cool down or realize you were wrong, go back to him or her and say, 'I was wrong. I understand that, and I am sorry.' " Good parents don't apologize for disciplining. They apologize for cluttering up their discipline with unnecessary verbal attacks or ill will. An apology is not a sign that our discipline resolve is weakening. It's a sign that we are secure enough in our discipline to admit when we overdid it.

GUIDELINE #8:
PERSEVERE TOWARD CONSISTENCY

The key elements of discipline for strong parents can be summarized by the three C's—calm, consistency, and consequences. Having heard these parents' opinions on keeping calm, let's turn our attention to consistency.

Listen to any childrearing specialist talk about discipline, and within a sentence or two, you'll probably hear the word *consistency.* Experts can't say enough about the importance of a parent's willingness to follow through with discipline consequences. These expert parents agree fully. To Brad from California, the main ingredient in any discipline is, "Consistency. If something is bad, it is always bad. If it is no big deal, then act that way."

For Eetha, mother of three, consistency means, "We did not make promises we didn't keep. If the children did something they were forbidden to do, they knew they would be punished."

Connie from Ohio also believed that consistency and consequences, while not always easy to implement, were the backbone of discipline. "It's so important to set standards, to teach children to accept responsibility, and to teach them that if they choose to act wrongly, they must be willing to accept the consequences. I would also like to emphasize the importance of consistency in parenting. Sometimes it's very difficult to be consistent or to follow through. Frequently, the easiest path is inconsistency and lack of follow-through, but these deprive the child of the opportunity to learn important lessons."

Joanna, whose four sons all are currently in their twenties, was pressured into consistency as a young mother, not just by her boys, but by her need for sanity. "With the boys close together in age, especially when they were between the ages of two and four, it was a war, and I was going to win! I wanted the boys to know that I meant what I said, and I would not keep saying over and over, 'If you don't stop, I'll . . .' Once that was established, life was much easier, on them and on me."

No parent is one-hundred-percent consistent. Even the best are not close. Parents are not computers. We get tired, we forget, sometimes we surrender. Excellent parents accept that they cannot achieve perfect consistency, so they don't demand it of themselves. Complete consistency is an ideal to reach for; what's practical is to consistently strive to be consistent.

A word often paired with consistency was *perseverance.* At times, parents have no option other than to persevere and discipline as long as necessary to change or redirect a behavior. If Oral has to visit the chair one hundred times for spitting, eventually, even if weeks from now, he will conclude: "I spit, I sit." Perseverance means doing whatever it takes to make discipline stick, especially in the face of intense resistance. None of these parents, for instance, upon first sending their children to a chair or their rooms to settle down, met with, "Oh goodness, Mother, I didn't realize I'd upset you. Please, tell me how long you'd like my discipline to last, and I'll double it." Initially at least, many had to take extra measures to enforce their discipline. Some children had to be physically escorted to their time-out. Some had to be carried there. Some had to hear, "If you leave your room, you cannot play outside for the rest of the day." And a few spitfires had to be incarcerated temporarily.

- "When Stewart was younger, he would get hysterically angry at times, and I could not do anything with him, so he went to his room. But he wouldn't stay there. So, what I did was hold the door. I was on the outside crying, and he was on the inside screaming. I would say, 'When you let go of the door and back up, I will let go of the handle out here. I am not locking it, but you *are not* coming out until you settle down.' "

Stewart taught his mother early in her motherhood that she'd better persevere while he's four feet three and 61 pounds, because someday he'll be five ten and 168 pounds, and much too strong for her to hold the door shut.

Other parents added resolve to their discipline with a one-time expenditure of effort designed to head off repeated future clashes. "Our twin boys would never stay in bed for their afternoon nap. They shared a bedroom with us and would climb out of their cribs, take the sheets and blankets off our bed, and pile them on the floor. They thought it was great sport to empty the dresser drawers. Finally, my husband made a top for their beds out of chicken wire, and they were forced to stay in bed. We thought that was better than scolding or spanking. This way, mom had more peace and quiet, and the boys got their afternoon nap." To good disciplinarians, consistency means more than initial follow-through. It means the willingness to put forth whatever energy is needed to ensure that fair discipline is carried out regardless of how much a youngster resists it.

Several parents emphasized that consistency is not rigidity. It is not stubbornly clinging to some overkill consequence blurted out in a discipline frenzy. "I have had it up to my eyeballs with you, young man. This is the third time today I've stumbled over your tennis shoes. You're grounded one month for each trip." Occasionally, as wise parents know, discipline needs to be logically reassessed, either to make it better suit the misdeed, or if a lesson has been learned.

Bob from Cleveland says, "There are times when I've gone back and modified my discipline. Sometimes I was confident the kids got my main message, or I saw that what I originally had imposed on them may have been too much, so I changed it."

In other words, getting back to the tennis shoes, instead of sticking to the three-month grounding—remember you'll have to live with Jordan underfoot for the duration—a one-dollar fine per incident might be levied. This is not backtracking on discipline. It's a genuine attempt to rectify an overreaction, and the firmest of disciplinarians are open to doing so. The basic discipline sticks; the particulars are adjusted.

GUIDELINE #9:

DISCIPLINE IS ACTION, NOT WORDS

Excellent parents are good listeners and skillful talkers. When it's time to discipline, they are doers. They know that words alone are not effective discipline. No parent, no matter how eloquent or persuasive, can talk a child into behaving with any regular success. She must back up her words with consequences—the third C of effective discipline.

To paraphrase an adage: One consequence is worth one thousand words. Holding a child accountable for his behavior will teach him far more than will dozens of lectures, naggings, or threats. In teaching through consequences, strong parents operate by three words: *preparation, separation,* and *reparation.*

PREPARATION "I don't think it's a good idea to surprise children with your consequences after they have committed the act," says a father of three from Kentucky. "They need to know the consequences beforehand, so the choice is theirs. Sometimes there are things that the kids don't think are any big deal, but parents have a stiff penalty for them. Let the kids understand the results of their actions before they do them. Then how they act is their decision."

A mother of four from Wyoming concurs. "The best discipline strategies we've ever tried involved talking to our children—laying out the choices before them and the outcomes as we could see them—and allowing them to choose which road to take, thus determining what kind of circumstances they wanted. We also expressed our approval or disapproval of each option and our measured response if the wrong one were chosen."

Several parents coined the same term for their practice of informing kids ahead of time of the consequences of their actions—preventive discipline. Let's say that your telephone's ringing is a signal for your daughter, Belle, to begin acting up just beyond the phone cord's reach. Preventive discipline involves establishing a rule: The first time Belle rudely interrupts or disrupts while you're on the phone, she will spend the duration of your call in her room. Rather than periodically disciplining her after the fact, that is, in a slamming-down-the-phone, OK-just-for-that fashion, you have put your new rule in place as notice. Effective disciplinarians make generous use of a basic law of discipline: Rules with consequences clearly stated are powerful deterrents to problem behavior.

Preventive discipline is a concept we will talk about further in chapter 15. For now, here are a few examples of preventive discipline that saved a lot of time and trouble:

- "The kids always acted their worst at the grocery store or at restaurants. They were about three or four at the time we decided on a strategy. We made little cardboard tickets, and we would give them one each time they acted up. Each ticket meant five minutes' sitting when they got home. If they got more than three tickets per outing, and we had to leave a place prematurely, they also earned an early bedtime. Sometimes we had to just pull out the tickets and say, 'You earned one,' because they'd either lose them, fold them, or whatever if we gave them to them. We gave out a lot of tickets at first."

- "I was always fussing at the boys about picking up their things, making beds, etc., to no avail. It seemed like I was always telling them to do this or to do that, but nothing was working. After working all day, I was tired and didn't want the house in a total mess. So, I started charging them a dollar for each thing I picked up. We sat down and talked about this rule before I started it, and they knew exactly what would be expected of them. There would be no arguing. Why one dollar instead of a quarter or dime? The boys work hard for their money, and I wanted an amount that would hurt their pocketbook. Things are much neater, and mom is easier to get along with."

- "We put Elizabeth on a clothing allowance about the time she entered eighth grade. Rather than have her pleading for a new piece of clothing every other day, I decided to work out a plan. About three times a year, we go through her wardrobe, weeding out clothes that no longer fit, are worn out, and so forth. Then we figure out what gaps are in her wardrobe, what she needs, what she desires. We budget for the various categories, put down a dollar amount that will cover a four- or five-month period. She is free to buy what she wants, keeping the needed items in mind. When the allowance is used up, she is done, or else needs to supplement with her own money. We don't hassle her. After two years, we are both pleased with the process."
- "When the time came to think about buying a third car for the boys to use, my husband and I were concerned about it and doubted the necessity of it. After much talk and weighing of the issues with the kids, we wrote up a contract between us and them, outlining their responsibilities—things like gas, general maintenance, their contribution toward car insurance. It laid out the guidelines and responsibilities for the privilege of having a car to use."

An added thought on preventive discipline: Make sure your consequence is enforceable. "You get out of bed one more time, and you'll sleep in the garage" may scare a youngster back into bed a few times, but on the whole, kids either disregard or get more feisty at the sound of a far-out threat. And some will even dare you to abide by your overheated words. Pat, from Georgia, who has run a family restaurant while raising Gianna, Patrick, Carolyn, and Christine (aged eighteen to twenty-five), recalls, "Once I was so frustrated at our daughter's procrastinating on cleaning her room that I told her to either clean it or leave. She cleaned it and left, going to a friend's house in Atlanta, about ninety miles from here. Even though we knew where she was and that she was okay, we were devastated that she would literally do what I said. I learned to be very careful about future ultimatums." As we noted early in this book, excellent parents are neither paragons of patience nor all raising docile children.

Undefined consequences are similarly troublesome. "You leave her alone, or you'll be sorry"; "I'm warning you, stop that right now"; "Come straight home after the game, or you'll wish you'd never gone." Open-ended warnings like these may evoke some compliance, usually out of a child's apprehension of the unknown, but again, the better disciplinarians state: The clearer your plan, the more effective it will be. Carole, a parent of three teens from Colorado Springs, was grateful that, as preschoolers, her children never challenged one of her more loose discipline techniques. "When the kids were younger, we counted to ten if they didn't listen to us. We never got to ten, which was good because we had *no* idea what would happen if we got there." Carole was fortunate. Nine out of ten kids will eventually take a count to its limit to discover what lies at the end of those numbers. Maybe Carole's success had something to do with her relying on a ten count, a much more tolerant version of the common three count.

SEPARATION Time-out is not discipline only for preschoolers. Skilled parents use this technique with all age ranges, from two-year-olds through teenagers, sometimes even spouses! The rationale underlying time-out, or separation, as a discipline consequence is simple: Conduct yourself well, or you will temporarily lose the privilege of being in the mainstream of things. Mary Patricia, a mother of three natural and three adopted children, said, "We started disciplining very early by just removing the child from the family center when they were rude, fighting, or whatever. We told them, 'You can come back when you are ready to act nice.' As teenagers, I sent them to their room where there was no telephone and no television." Her husband, Don, agrees that removing the kids from the scene of the problem was their most basic discipline. "We would send them to their room, leaving the door ajar, and tell them they could come out when they could behave."

Mary, mother to Jason and Meisha, also favored a time-out chair. "We had a certain chair in a certain place and a timer. From the chair you could see the timer and hear it. The kids sat according to the crime. They could read books on the chair. It was one of our best disciplines." Some parents prefer to let the kids determine when to call time-in and rejoin the family. Other parents set time limits themselves. The choice often depended on the child. Some youngsters, if the option is theirs, after two seconds will forsake time-out, promising, "I'm ready to be good now." Other youngsters, as we said earlier, have to be placed in time-out, or stood over, or held there, with the understanding that "Time doesn't begin until you're quiet." Typically, the time-out area—variously targeted as a chair, corner, couch, steps, floor—was in a parent's line of sight. Corners were popular for this reason; several are available in each room.

Allowing a youngster to occupy an unsupervised time-out spot can cause complications, as Sandy from Washington, mother to Tammy, Teri, and

Tracy, explains. "We had them sit in chairs for a certain amount of time, but when we left the room, they made a game out of switching chairs. The joke was on us." Sandy found out quickly that few kids take discipline lying down, or sitting down, and that even with a consequence as straightforward as time-out, parents have to be prepared to supervise.

Time-out is particularly appealing because it's simple. Given the speed and creativity with which kids can misbehave, parents can't be expected to always respond with "new-and-improved" discipline. They regularly need something fast, firm, and fair. Time-out answers all three requirements. Emphasizing the value of keeping discipline simple, one father said, "Children see their parents as powerful, as mighty. We have such control. Sometimes when discipline is needed, I, as a parent, am ready to give it all I've got. Whereas, maybe the situation needs only minor correcting, if at all." Time-out, or separation—a great form of minor correction.

REPARATION Excellent parents adhere to this elegantly straightforward philosophy of discipline: If you do something wrong, you accept the consequences, and whenever possible, you make it right. This covers all behavior. If you call someone a name, you apologize, verbally or in a letter. If you break someone's toy, you replace it, pay for it, or give him one of yours. If you use your bike foolishly, you lose it temporarily. If you disrupt a game, you don't play. Nothing fancy, just commonsense accountability.

The first step toward reparation is a good old-fashioned apology. A child who has acted poorly toward others is expected to admit so in words. He may not feel sorry, but saying "I'm sorry" is a forerunner to the feeling. A father of three from Hanover, New Hampshire, said, "Much of our discipline had to do with insisting on apology when one was due—to Joan, myself, or others. When I told the story of "Goldilocks and the Three Bears," the story always ended with Goldilocks and her mother going to the house of the three bears and apologizing. The three bears would then invite Goldilocks and her mother in for cookies and milk. I also remember once when our son skipped school. We made him apologize to each of his teachers and then checked with them to make sure he had done so. If he didn't, he was going to lose some major privileges."

A second principle of reparation is captured by the acronym KISS, meaning *keep it short and simple*. These parents prefer consequences that allow for a swift return to routine after the "sentence" has been served. The consensus was that any privilege—bicycle, phone, television, car, dessert—is best removed for a specific, preferably short, time period. Long or indefinite discipline denials can lead a youngster to an attitude of, "Well, it's gone now. I'll just get used to living without it." A child will work harder to get a privilege back if he sees he can regain it sometime soon.

To Bob from Iowa, keeping discipline simple means handling problems individually. "I used to get angry at the children for several different things all at once. It was an overload. They cried, and I felt bad. They didn't know what to do. I've been trying to keep my discipline simpler. I deal with one situation at a time." To illustrate, Carlisle has just stumbled in forty minutes late, tracking mud into the house, while telling you to "Get off my back" in a less-than-diplomatic tone. Bob would respond to each behavior rather than unloading indiscriminately on the whole irritating display. The curfew violation might earn a day's grounding. The floor will need to be cleaned, possibly vacuumed. And a one hundred-word essay on "Respect for others" may be assigned. Keep it short and simple. We'll make discipline easier for us and more memorable for the kids.

Perhaps the award for the best KISS discipline should go to eight-year-old Adam's parents, Sam and Marge. They're the parents who disciplined themselves with the same consequences they levied on the kids. When we asked Adam, "How do your parents discipline you?" he answered candidly, "They yell 'Hey!' and then we usually stop." You can't get much more basic than that. Whatever works.

"Fit the crime" is another phrase that defined reparation for these mothers and fathers. "Whenever possible in discipline, fit the crime," said Al from Ohio. "For example, child #1 keeps bothering child #2 while child #2 is trying to clean the kitchen. If child #1 persists after the warning, child #1 ends up cleaning the kitchen." In essence, make the consequences relate to the infraction, if possible. Examples of this concept are:

- "If the kids are showing ungrateful or selfish and complaining attitudes, we make them go into a room and sit down and write five to ten sincere things that they have to be thankful for and need to change their attitude about. Then, they have to tell these things to us, and we talk about them."
- "When David was eleven or twelve, we put him on a bus to visit his grandmother in Wisconsin. He had clear instructions to call us when he got there. He forgot, and after waiting several hours, we called. When he returned home, he found that the television in his room had been replaced with a toy telephone."

- "If a child is too sick for school or church, he or she spends the day in bed, with no activities in the evenings until all makeup work is completed or until the next 'well' day."
- "I was tired of the boys letting their bath towels lay all over the floor after their baths. They always 'forgot' to pick them up. So, each time it happened, they helped with the laundry. They helped me separate the clothes, wash, dry, fold, and put away."
- "Merritt took a small sixty-nine-cent toy animal from a store in Berkeley, California, as we traveled through. I didn't discover what happened until about four hours down the road. Our discussion started with, 'What happens when someone takes things from a store?'; 'I believe you are trustworthy, but how can someone else know this if you take their things?'; and, 'What would you do if your kid did this?' Merritt then had to write a letter to the store, explaining that she had not really given much thought to the consequences of shoplifting. She also enclosed both the money and the animal."

Kurt and Joann from Augusta, South Carolina, showed their young son what it felt like to be on the receiving end of his rowdy behavior. "When our son backed the dog into a corner and squirted him with the garden hose, we reversed the situation. We stood our son in the corner and squirted him with the garden hose. He never squirted the dog again." Sometimes kids learn best when they themselves are put in the shoes—in this case, paws—of their target.

One category of privileges that these parents were reluctant to target as consequences were school- or community-related interests or events. Seldom were choir practice, boy scouts, a school club meeting, even sports practices and games used to discipline irresponsible behavior. When they were, it was because they were judged to be interfering with academic performance. On the whole, these parents grounded ("In our house, that meant no phone, no friends, no music"), assigned extra chores, reduced allowances, or tried nearly everything else before tampering with those activities they considered healthy to their child's social development.

NATURAL REPARATION The will to discipline includes the will to let life discipline. That is, sometimes a child's behavior elicits consequences from the world around him that are more natural and beneficial than anything his parents could do. Lois, a mother for twenty-two years, wishes she would have realized so at the beginning of her parenthood. Of course, if parents knew everything at the start, childrearing wouldn't be nearly as exciting. "Dan and I tried to make everything too right for the kids, especially when they were young. We tried to make their lives very smooth. Well, life's not like that. The children have the right to make mistakes, experience some failure, and learn from it. Certainly parents want to protect their children from big, life-changing events, like serious car accidents, drug addiction, eating disorders. But maybe it's okay to learn from experience that if you don't fill the car with gas, you may run out in some very inappropriate locations. It's better to learn these lessons while at home, where children have the help and support of parents to cushion the mistakes and failures."

Natural reparation means not replacing a toy rusted from two nights' abandonment in the rain. It means clearing the table when it's time, even though Cookie has refused to eat a bite, and not making food available until the next meal. It means not digging into your pocket for three dollars so Wheeler can still go roller skating, even after he zapped all of his allowance on video games. Feeling the realistic outcome of shortsighted or irresponsible behavior is often discipline enough for kids. Mom and dad don't need to add anything more.

Sometimes the hardest thing for responsible parents to do is nothing, as they watch a child encounter the unanticipated effects of her decision. "Prior to our daughter's senior year in high school, we moved from Michigan to Florida. Dawn wanted to graduate with her friends in Michigan and wanted to stay there. We let her make the decision, but stressed that once it was made, she had to live with it. She decided to stay in Michigan with some friends from the church. During Christmas break, Dawn came to Florida, and when it came time for her to return to Michigan, she didn't want to go. We reminded her that she had made her decision and she had to live with it. A sad girl returned north." Mom added this epilogue, though. "After graduation, Dawn came to Pensacola to attend college and be with the family."

A parent's strongest instinct is to protect, but to be a strong parent one has to overcome that instinct at times, obviously within safe parameters. We don't permit a two-year-old to pet a chained-up watchdog to teach her the potential dangers of such behavior. Whenever possible, though, conscientious parents allow a child to feel the reactions of her actions, for her own long-term well-being. "Parents have a natural tendency to protect their children from disappointment and failure," observes Julie from Wisconsin. "Don't do it. It's important early in life that children experience both success and failure. These must be experienced before adulthood so they know how to handle them, especially failure."

CONSULT A CHILD Experienced parents suggest one more option for fine-tuning discipline: Ask the kids. Children are capable of some incredibly inventive mischief and misconduct. Therefore, why not find out if they know how to rectify their actions? When Susie from Wyoming was asked how much input her children have into their own discipline, she answered simply, "A lot, since they choose their behavior."

Bob from Cleveland says, "The kids have some input. Sometimes I will tell them that if they can come up with something appropriate, then we can make a deal. Sometimes, I won't agree with their ideas based on a given situation. There are other times when I'll tell them what they have done is really wrong, and I want them to come up with their own punishment or give me ideas."

Kids give the ideas; parents make the final selection. "Discipline for us is usually taking something away for a while, but the end goals are defined. We say, 'This will be restored to you if you do such and so.' The kids have a right to an opinion. They tell us what they think would be appropriate goals, and someplace in between our two goals we find a compromise. But if they fall below the criterion, there is no more discussion."

Asking children to concoct their own consequences—one adolescent referred to this as "picking your poison"—has several advantages. First, kids are generally more openly cooperative with their own personal discipline. Since he publicly picked the outcome, it's likely Armstrong will quietly shovel the snow alone as his price for smacking his brother in the head with an iceball.

Second, offering ideas for reparation gives children the opportunity to mull over their behavior. Kim likes to ask Nicholas, Brittany, and Zachary (aged seven to eleven), " 'Do you know what you did wrong?' 'What do you think we should do about it?' I think this makes them realize more fully what they did. And if I let them have some input into their discipline, more often than not they won't do it again."

Of course, most kids would think, "What do you mean, 'What should *we* do?' " You aren't going to make *you* pay for the broken lamp. You aren't going to deny *you* your allowance!" Nevertheless, our "we" implies this particular discipline can be a cooperative venture.

A third benefit of consequence consulting is that the kids may give us some good ideas, after we get past their initial "I don't know." Did you ever notice how much kids don't know when it concerns them? "I think I should pay to replace the piece of aluminum siding where I carved my initials, and I shouldn't have any TV until it's paid for." This youngster is likely to become a financier. Even as a child he knows to put a time limit with leverage on a remunerative agreement.

Then, again, not all children are so self-moderating. At one extreme is Spike: "I still say I didn't do it. But if it'll make you happy, I'll write 'I'm sorry' twice. You got any carbon paper?" At the other extreme is Justice: "I think I should write one million times, 'I am very, very, very, very sorry for totally destroying our house and making it the ugliest place anybody could ever live in.' Then I should pay for the siding by mowing the lawn at a penny an acre . . . with the weed-eater." After sorting through all suggestions, the parent determines what's fair.

Many children are like Justice. They will think up much heavier penalties than we ever would. Jerry, father to four sons in Oregon, feels that the boys, in choosing their own consequences, lend him a chance to show his merciful side. "We have had the children help decide what their discipline should be. Often they are harder on themselves than we would be, and then we can lessen their chosen discipline to show parental fairness." Jerry knows that a standard hazard of parenthood is hearing, "That's unfair." By tempering his sons' self-discipline, he enjoys the opportunity to be thought of as equitable. And that's an opportunity parents don't regularly get when disciplining.

Some parents, even though not initially seeking their children's input, decided to later on. Carroll from South Carolina was one such parent. "After things returned to normal, I would ask our children what they thought about the discipline. I need to be able to take constructive criticism from the kids." For Carroll, even if three times out of four the kids' feedback is childishly unreasonable, when they do have a legitimate point, however sharp, she'd best consider it for the future.

————

Calm, consistency, and *consequences*—the three C's of discipline for strong parents. *Preparation, separation,* and *reparation*—the guiding words in enforcing consequences, the basic tools of discipline.

Discipline is indispensable to a successful family life. It cannot, indeed must not, be neglected. As long as children need parents and other adults to teach them skills for living the rest of their lives, they will need discipline. The will to discipline, therefore, is among the most loving, durable gifts a parent can give a child. How parents choose to exercise that will is much a matter of personality and style, as we will see in SPANKING: SPARE OR SPOIL?

Chapter 14

Spanking:
Spare or Spoil?

"My master's degree has a cognate in counseling, and I must admit that when my oldest son turned two and started asserting himself, I burned my books and got out my wooden spoon. Contrary to many popular theories, we spanked when necessary."

Mother, Bozeman, Montana

No discipline is more controversial than spanking. What was once considered acceptable, even healthy, parenting practice has in the past few decades come under increasing assault from childrearing specialists. The case against spanking covers a range of indictments:

- Spanking is not effective discipline.
- Spanking teaches children to solve problems through force.
- Spanking conveys a double message about the appropriateness of hitting others.
- Spanking breeds aggressive children.
- And most ominous, spanking is a form of child abuse.

With so many harsh accusations swirling around a once-appropriate discipline, parents are understandably confused. No form of discipline arouses more questions, mixed feelings, and anxieties. Does a mere swat on the seat really breed aggressive children? Should you *never* spank, even to teach a child to avoid physical danger, like running onto the road? If you spank, do you spank when you're angry or not angry?

Who, then, can pass judgment on spanking? Despite the number of experts who vote nay on spanking, probably a similar number still vote yea. Is spanking really guilty of causing so much psychological damage to children and families? Or is this an expert-driven phenomenon born of permissiveness and overreaction?

We asked these expert parents their opinions on spanking. Their answers may be a bit surprising but nonetheless reassuring, especially to those of us who still believe that a well-timed and well-placed swat can save much more trouble than it creates.

To begin, do excellent parents spank? In a word, yes. Seventy percent of these mothers and fathers acknowledge having employed some type of physical discipline with their children. Reliance on spanking varied greatly, with some parents regularly turning to it and others only rarely, as a very last resort.

Ellease, mother to eight children, aged ten to twenty-three, has long been at ease with spanking. "To discipline, I usually give them a spanking, and it is not child abuse. It is something that they need if they do something wrong. I also do not think it is wrong to spank an older child. But now, where they used to cry, they laugh." Ellease is slowly abandoning spanking, not because she fears any psychological repercussions, but because of practicalities. It doesn't impress the kids anymore.

Dan from Louisiana, father to Tammy and Butch, concurred with Ellease, "Some people say you don't have to spank a child. I think there are some children—I don't know if it is inherited or not—that you can talk to forever and they still will listen. Other children have to have a little bit of fear put into them." Dan discovered one potent factor in a parent's choice to spank—a child's temperament.

At the spank-when-all-else-fails end of the spectrum were parents like Rita and Jerry from New Hampshire:

- "When we talk about spanking, we are talking about maybe five per child per life. It would be for a very serious situation, and it is always a controlled spanking. It is not when we are just angry, and it is mostly with our hands. It is almost like a ceremony. The few times I have spanked the children aren't as serious as when Jerry spanks them. I think the emotion of it being daddy who spanks is half the punishment. I also think that you have to let children know you are not tickled to punish them, that the spanking is something you have to do to serve justice."

Of those parents who do or have spanked, most began when their youngsters were toddlers, between the ages of about eighteen months and two years. At that time, spanking meant a brief swat on the fingers or leg at the instant of infraction. Further, spanking was generally considered to be one tool in a parent's discipline repertoire. It was neither a main method nor a last-ditch intervention. It was a response used when judged appropriate.

Even as the children got older, spanking remained a swat or two. Rosemary from Florida said, "I don't think I've ever given them more than a good, swift swat with my hand, although it was a pretty hard swat sometimes. And when I do spank, within five minutes, I go back to the kids and talk to them. I don't think there has ever been a time that I have spanked that afterward I didn't say, 'I love you.' "

Sherry from California added, "We never spared a swift smack across the rear end. I have always followed the advice of my mother, though, and that is never to spank when I was furious. One is much stronger when angry and what is intended as a spanking could become a beating. So, when I felt really angry, I would send them to their room to think about what they did while I collected myself."

Carol, quoted at the beginning of this chapter, like a number of parents, entered parenthood with no intent to spank. Within a few years, her preconceived notions were forced aside by some developmental demands of child-rearing. As she implied, no matter how smart you become in the ways of talking to kids, sometimes you just have to grab their attention first. A spank here and there spoke more eloquently for Carol than all the words she could muster.

The main spanking instrument was the hand. The main target was the backside, leg, or fingers. A few parents, like Carol, did occasionally resort to a wooden spoon or small paddle, but these were mostly placed in highly visible places for a deterrent effect. "We have a wooden paddle affectionately named Betsy. It's not used often, but it's there as a reminder." I don't think the kids find anything affectionate about Betsy.

Though willing to spank, some mothers and fathers wrestled with ambivalence. While outwardly resolute, inwardly there were some internal struggles. "Physically punishing the boys with my hand or the wooden spoon were my worst times as a parent," admits a Montana mother of two. "My husband only used his hand, but he agreed that it was the hardest thing for him to do, too. Because we loved them so much, it seemed a paradox to have to punish them physically, and yet we both felt it was our responsibility to do so. They needed limits as well as love." An Albuquerque father of two daughters recalled, "The worst discipline we used was spanking. We always ended up more disturbed than they were."

A touching example of spanking-induced guilt comes from a Rhode Island family of eight. Tom, the father, has been blind since prior to marriage, but as all his children affirmed, dad's lack of eyesight in no way made him a less determined disciplinarian. Beatrice, his wife, tells a story in which Tom spanked their son, Tommy, for being unruly toward a baby-sitting, older sister. After pouting a while, Tommy approached his father and asked for a dollar, which he was given. When Beatrice saw the dollar, she asked, "Where did you get that?"

Tommy replied, "From daddy. I asked him for it."

Confronting her husband, Beatrice said, "What did you give Tommy a dollar for?"

Tom replied sheepishly, "He asked for it."

Beatrice said, "Tom, under any other circumstances, he'd have to tell you his life story to get a dollar. You paid him for spanking him." To this day, Tom denies that, but Beatrice believes, "He felt guilty and sorry, and that was his way of saying, 'You know, Tommy, I love you.'"

When do spankers spank? There are three main occasions:

1. When teaching a child to avoid potentially dangerous situations.
2. When punishing for outright disobedience.
3. When punishing for showing disrespect.

In the first instance, parents spank to put across a quick, forceful message: Don't *ever* do that again. A toddler can't comprehend the life-threatening risks involved in biting a lit Christmas-tree bulb, but he can comprehend the hurt of a spanking. These parents' attitude is: When a child's safety is involved, forget finesse. The need is for action, fast and memorable.

A second reason for spanking was deliberate defiance. Vallie, mother to Kimberly and Chip, said, "The only reason they ever got a spanking was for disobeying. So we first had to run their behavior through our filter to make sure they had actually disobeyed instead of just doing something we didn't like. We also never spanked in front of other people." For instance, Chip's thoughtlessly slamming shut a car door is something Vallie might not like, but it isn't a conscious act of unruliness. On the other hand, refusing to remain in time-out is willful defiance, and Vallie believes that a sure and firm spank here can head off similar refusals and resulting conflict in the future. In other words, if Conan accepts our first-line discipline—a visit to the corner—he won't bring upon himself second-line discipline, such as a spanking.

Showing disrespect, the third occasion for spanking, like flagrant disobedience, is a challenge to a parent's authority. All children act unruly, but disrespect and disobedience are a step above common misbehavior. Many parents reserved their more serious discipline for more serious misconduct. "I had a little paint stick on top of the refrigerator and a wooden spoon in the car," said Mary from Phoenix. "We only spanked for real disrespect or maybe something nasty against another child."

Few parents spanked for accidents, childish behavior, or impulsiveness. They preferred to employ other consequences. The first time Art draws on the wall in preference to his brand-new, 640-page coloring book, he would not incur a spanking, but would instead be made to scrub until his arms drooped. The second time, though, he might earn a discipline of a different color.

Jan, mother to Sean and Christy, regrets her one misdirected use of spanking.

- "When the kids were young, the neighborhood was full of a lot of young kids. Several of us mothers were sitting together visiting, and our three four-year-old girls came and asked, 'Which way is the Atlantic Ocean?' We pointed and off they went to play. Being the responsible mothers we were, we sat around and talked a while longer. When we went to look for our children, we couldn't find them anywhere. We panicked, and everyone took off in different directions. The kids had gone to find the Atlantic Ocean. Being a reactionary, I spanked Christy when I found her. Then I realized, what she did was perfectly logical in her mind. That was the only time I spanked her."

At what age does spanking begin to yield to other forms of discipline? As their children's early elementary school years approached, that is, at ages four through six, most parents slowly phased out spanking. Margaret, a Michigan mother, said, "Early on, our discipline was often mild spankings, usually an open hand on the rear end. After about the age of four and a half, it was talk, talk, explain, explain, deprive, deprive, or whatever worked short of physical discipline."

Jerry's parental judgment told him when spanking would no longer be a discipline measure. "As the children get older, there are obviously no more spankings. There is a time when, as a parent, you can feel that. You have a sense that you could paddle them with a two by four, and it would not make any difference. The time has come for other things."

One mother was shown a definite sign that her days of spanking were well past. "In total frustration I attempted to use the wooden spoon on my son once when he was fourteen. He was three inches taller than me and had a second degree black belt in karate. I held the wooden spoon and walked toward him. He very firmly, but gently took hold of my wrist and said, 'Mom, we are way past this. I didn't realize you were so upset, and I'll do what you asked.' I asked myself, 'Who is the child and who is the adult here?' We both had a good laugh."

While the majority of parents regarded spanking as one useful means of discipline, about one third of them either never spanked or quickly became personally dissatisfied with spanking.

Some parents felt no emotional misgivings but abandoned spanking for practical reasons. That is, they considered it largely ineffective. Bob and Nancy, parents of four, aged four through fourteen, asserted, "We tended to get away from spanking because when the kids were young and their attention spans were real short, any discipline had to be constantly reinforced to work. Spanking is a quick attention grabber, and we feel that is all that it is meant to do. It doesn't teach them anything."

Eetha, a mother in North Carolina, endorsed this view. "We both believed that denial of something was more effective in the long run than a spanking. Spanking is a quick punishment, but denial can last." Did the kids have a choice of discipline? "They usually wanted a spanking, but we never gave in to that." For Bob, Nancy, and Eetha, spanking didn't move children to think as long or deeply about their behavior as did other, more protracted consequences.

Some parents were quite uncomfortable with physical discipline. Naomi from Vermont said, "We have never spanked our girls. We feel hitting someone else is not appropriate under any circumstances." Other parents regarded spanking as a contradiction, as an action which sent a two-sided message to their youngsters. "When my son was two or so and started to hit me, I said, 'Mommies are not for hitting.' He said, 'Oh, children are for hitting, not mommies.' That was the beginning of the end of any spankings."

Similarly, Marge from Virginia, in answering questions about her discipline, replied, "Now I generally send them [Justin, fifteen; David, thirteen; Adam, eight] to their rooms. When Justin and David were younger, I would spank them. I found myself telling the kids, 'Don't hit anyone!' but I was hitting them. When I realized that, I didn't hit anymore and found other ways to discipline."

Dave from Idaho discussed his change of mind toward spanking. "When the boys were little, I used to spank. I wouldn't spank a child now. Children look to their parents as being the persons to protect them. I can't see myself physically hurting somebody who is looking to me for protection."

Because a parent was unwilling to spank did not mean she necessarily shunned all forms of physical discipline. Lois from Minnesota, a high-school counselor and mother of two, offered, "I think holding a young child firmly, looking him in the eye, and telling him no is much more effective than spanking."

Dave replaced his spankings with "dual-benefit" discipline. Not only did he intend for his sons and daughter to learn something, he opted for some physical fitness at the same time. "Instead of spanking, they did a lot of push-ups. That usually worked pretty well." You'd recognize Dave's kids in a crowd. They're the ones with big arms.

Ten-year-old Molly from Wisconsin wishes she'd get more spankings. She isn't amused by her parents' substitute. "Sometimes they tickle us instead. That is punishment to us."

What conclusions can we draw from these parents' opinions about spanking? First and foremost, a majority of excellent parents are willing to spank. They consider it a healthy discipline option, particularly for teaching lessons about physical danger, defiance, and flagrant disrespect. Second, spanking is *not* child abuse. Spanking and abuse are distinctly different phenomena. Not one of these parents is a child abuser. They were selected for this project because of their intense commitment to their families. Third, spanking does not in and of itself lead a child to be aggressive or to approach problems with a might-makes-right mentality. Consistently, the youngsters in these families were identified by their teachers as morally mature and sensitive. They were judged as anything but aggressive and violent. Certainly, if a parent routinely swings first and asks questions later, he risks raising similarly disposed children. But these excellent families prove that spanking, when done in the context of a loving home life, neither causes psychological damage nor sends confusing messages.

Finally, one need not spank to be a good parent. A significant minority of mothers and fathers chose not to spank, for personal and practical reasons. They neither viewed spanking as the psychological dark side of discipline, nor as an outmoded, even brutal technique. Rather, they agree with those parents who spank in concluding that spanking must be judged as all discipline is judged: How well is this working—in your home, with your child, your value system, and your level of comfort?

Ignoring the dire warnings of some childbearing experts, many extremely competent parents spank, with long-term results that can't be challenged. They don't like having to spank, but they will spank when they judge it wise. Wisdom is something that kids collectively force on parents, as we shall see next in SIBLINGS: THE BENDABLE BOND.

Chapter 15

Siblings: The Bendable Bond

*"Sometimes I can be good to her. Other times I try to
beat her up. Sometimes she pulls my hair. Other times
I like to play with her."*

Son (aged nine), New London, Connecticut

*E*very family in this book has at least two children. Three fourths have
three or more. How the kids interact with one another can affect the family's
balance as much or more than how they interact with their parents. While
cohesive is the best single word to describe these sibling relationships, it
doesn't imply bonds that don't bend or even crack now and again. In well-
adjusted families with well-adjusted kids, siblings still squabble, wrangle, and
on occasion all-out brawl. That's how they get along.

Sixteen-year-old Jacob from Arkansas used an apt analogy to explain his
relationship with his sisters, Becky (twelve) and Abby (seven). "Have you ever
ridden a roller coaster? You're on top of a hill, but all of a sudden you are
taken to a deep valley, only to find yourself once again heading for another
mountain peak. This is the best way to describe our relationship. We are the
best of friends, though we have our scuffles. Even though the roller coaster

goes up and down, when you step off, you can't wait to go again. But sometimes you end up getting sick!"

Now-grown Mike, looking back on living with three brothers, focused on the developmental nature of their fraternal confrontations:

• "Arguments among my brothers and me went through different stages. In the first stages, it was generally a free-for-all with a lot of hitting involved. This was also known as the might-makes-right stage. Whoever was the biggest and the strongest generally got his way when my parents weren't looking. If you got caught or finked on, you fell victim to the same kind of policy. Regardless who was biggest and strongest among the boys, though, my father was bigger and stronger than any of us. My parents spanked us for those battles when we deserved it. In addition, the two or three or four of us who had been fighting were cruelly forced to sit next to one another and hold hands for a while. As we got older, spankings were replaced with lectures that seemed to hurt as bad as the spankings used to. After one of us had been lectured, we often said something to the effect that we wished they would just spank us instead of talking to us that way."

As is true with much of family life, it is the younger ones who most simply reveal the essence of siblings. Eight-year-old Adam said of himself and his brothers, Justin (fifteen) and David (thirteen), "We kinda do get along, and we kinda don't get along. We are in between."

When asked how she got along with her brother and sister, perky seven-year-old Emily from Louisiana replied in her sharpest southern accent, "Ah don't even like 'em. And you can take 'em back on the plane with you!" Emily's parents, Jimmy and Marlene, sheepishly asked if they should withdraw from this project.

Perhaps the best commentary on the slip-knot nature of sibling ties comes from eleven-year-old James and fourteen-year-old Christopher from Washington. Interviewed separately, and unaware of what the other said, they spoke with one voice. James on Christopher: "Sometimes my brother is okay, but sometimes he can be a real jerk." Christopher on James: "He can be okay at times, and he can be a real jerk." Guys, you don't realize how much alike you are.

Similarities between siblings may indeed be a source of some intense rivalry. Just ask ten-year-old Merritt and fifteen-year-old Amanda. Both share an affinity for the piano. Amanda is very good. Merritt is among the best in the world, recently placing fourth in her age group at international competition. The piano was scene to their most off-key moments. Big sister felt upstaged by little sister, and her resentment culminated one day during practice. Stumbling repeatedly over a tricky passage, Amanda was already strung tight. Little wonder she slammed down the piano cover refusing to practice anymore after Merritt, in her most disgusted six-year-old prodigy voice, yelled from the kitchen, "It's a B *flat!*" What could thereafter have escalated into open antagonism didn't for two reasons.

A wise mother helped Amanda understand her and her sister's individuality. "Amanda, we're lucky. Merritt does the work. We get to listen. Obligations come with talent, and Merritt has to practice three hours a day, focusing on one area. You can focus on many areas of talent."

Too, Amanda quit fighting reality. Within the year, she accepted that Merritt was in fact incredibly gifted and not a threat to her self-esteem. Initially, she appreciated Merritt's talent only because it enabled the family to travel to far-off recitals. Since then, she has grown immensely proud of her sister, especially when she sits and listens to her practice. The last note on this once turbulent relationship comes from Merritt, "We don't even fight anymore."

What are all these children really saying to us parents? Essentially this: Some sibling discord is normal, even healthy. As long as kids share a roof with others near their age (*near* is defined as "in the same generation"), they will find common ground for disagreement. This is not a sign of disorder in the household. Nor is it an indication of parental incompetency. It is a fact of family life.

More reassuring is that, like Amanda and Merritt, most of the children felt their ties with their siblings strengthen with age. A roller-coaster ride, as Jacob said, may well portray the early years, but over time the peaks and valleys are replaced by gentler landscape. Michael, aged twenty-two, has a new appreciation for his sister Kristen, aged eighteen.

- "As youngsters, my sister and I teased and quarreled quite a bit, probably more than is normal. Even through high school, our antagonistic relationship continued. As a younger sibling, my sister, I think, felt that she was in some way being measured by the standards I set, which was *not* the case. Also, as an older brother, I had the tendency to dictate what my sister should and shouldn't do, and gave her advice she neither needed nor wanted.

"When I went off to college, our relationship took a change for the better. When I came home during the holidays and summers, we got along well. We really took an interest in what the other had to say. My sister and I have always overall had a loving relationship, but it wasn't until we were older that we openly expressed our affection and made a point of being close as brother and sister."

A little distance, in space or time, often stretches and tightens formerly slack bonds. Then, too, sometimes the maturation of one sibling is more than enough to improve the whole relationship. Nineteen-year-old Garret now sees his siblings in a warmer light.

- "My relationship with my brothers and sisters has not all been competitive, however. I believe the admiration they sometimes show me spurs me more than praise from my parents or teachers. It's when my youngest brother rushes home from his third-grade gym class to tell me of the three soccer goals he's scored, stressing the moves I taught him, that I am motivated to become the player he believes me to be. It's when another brother asks for help with a bug in his computer program or my oldest sister wants help with trigonometry, each saying thanks with a 'you're awesome,' that I have the most pride in my accomplishments."

A strong family life forges strong sibling ties, after allowing for natural personality differences. But even the most stable bonds can creak and groan under the weight of children growing up. Excellent parents have learned to expect this, although as we will immediately see, they're not always sure how to shore up those bonds or at least how to keep them from cracking temporarily.

SETTLING SIBLING QUIBBLING

Because sibling quibbling is nearly automatic doesn't mean parents should idly watch as the skirmishes escalate into all-out warfare or simmer into an unsteady truce. Sometimes we must intervene, because the behavior displayed—such as name-calling, hitting, insults, and selfishness—is not something we want from our children.

Competent parents are not ashamed to admit that sibling quibbling can baffle them. Barbara, writer and mother of four children from New York, when asked about sibling rivalry, said, "Yup, we've got plenty. When I was young and innocent, I thought I could convince the kids that an accomplishment of one was a positive reflection on all, and we could all 'party' together. I was foolish! The books I've been driven to read say that some amount of sibling rivalry is healthy and a good preparation for life. I hope they're right!"

Bob and Joan, raising Elizabeth (nine), Bente (twelve), and Dawn (eighteen), confessed, "Sibling rivalry—or just plain fighting with one another— seems to be the most frustrating problem we face. We would like to deal with it in a positive way; the trouble is that this often involves trying to figure out who is at fault, and that is often not possible. On the other hand, we try not to take sides, a delicate balancing act. If anyone has answers to this one, we'll be glad to hear them!"

Kathleen may not be quite sure how to ride through her five children's fussing and feuding, but she does seem to have a grasp on how the kids see themselves and each other.

• "Sibling rivalry is natural, but I find it hard to discipline. We all talk about it, and my husband and I try to stress to each child that God gave them all talents, he made them all different, and each is loved as much as the others. But, please, don't ask the oldest. He's sure he's been overprotected and has had to sacrifice more and more as each of his four siblings arrived. Then again, don't ask our second son. He knows for sure that our oldest is definitely spoiled and that we are prouder of him than we are of our second born. Our daughter will tell you that even though she's the only girl, no way is she spoiled. The boys get everything. Sibling #4 will say he is overlooked, while all the rest say that he is the most spoiled. Last, but not least, our youngest says he's 'scrubbed the most.' By this, he means that when all the others are taken care of, then we worry about taking care of him. When the chips are down or an emergency occurs, though, they do seem to forget all this and pull together to help each other."

Kathleen has obviously encountered a common cause—and effect—of sibling turbulence: perceived inequity. Regardless how hard parents work to be fair, regardless how scrupulously measured our actions, children—as do all humans—look at life through subjective glasses. Occasionally they will interpret our behavior as leaning toward their siblings. If pushed, most likely they would admit that on the whole we are fair. On a daily, hourly, or minutely basis, they're not unwilling to charge us with playing favorites. The good news is that they tend to outgrow this narrow view as they mature. The bad news is that in the meantime we may have to weather some unfair accusations, despite our true evenhandedness.

Sibling quibbling, not surprisingly, is the most recurrent discipline issue for these good parents. While being a source of uncertainty and exasperation, it is also a source of some very resourceful discipline. Chronic frustration can be a parent's springboard to creativity.

Sibling competition can begin while one child is still in the womb. To alleviate this, these parents advise preparing a child for a new sibling before the baby is born. Talk about the birth, discuss the reasons for the new crib, explain mommy's changing appearance, let a child feel the baby move in the womb. In essence, reduce the uncertainty over what this new person might mean to a child's established status in the family. As one mother remarked, "Young children fantasize a lot about what a new baby will do to their relationship with mom and dad. They need to hear that it will make not only their relationship better, but the whole family's." A natural time to begin explaining and preparing a sibling for a new family member is when mom begins to show her pregnancy.

"A good way to reduce competition once the baby has arrived is to involve the older children in its care," says Rita, a mother of seven. "Let them do as much as their age allows." A two-year-old can bring diapers, talk to the baby, wipe its mouth. A three-year-old can hold the baby with close supervision, entertain her with toys. A four-year-old can help dress a baby, tell it a story, even hold its bottle with parents nearby. To the extent that a child feels helpful and appreciated in the care of a new sibling, he will see her less as an intruder and more as a fun addition to the family.

You can reduce rivalry by emphasizing the specialness of becoming a big brother or sister, making a child feel important in his or her new role in the family. A father said, "A child may not be the sole center of attention anymore once a brother or sister arrives, but he can still feel unique if you make sure to give him status as big brother." Little children love being referred to as big. If this new arrival makes them feel a little bigger in our eyes, they may decide he's not such a threat after all.

Cooperation eases competition among siblings as they grow. Parents from Ohio encouraged older siblings to read stories to younger siblings. Mom or dad listened and gave hefty doses of attention to both the reader and the readee. Another mother frequently asked her older son to build something out of blocks or to draw something for his younger brother. She said big brother gobbled up her compliments over his creativity while little brother felt more special to big brother.

John and Barbara from New Jersey illustrate other ways to enhance cooperation. "Tom and Rob used to have bouts of rivalry as they competed for our attention. So, we purposely arranged games for them to play together, and if that failed to help, we came up with a project they had to work on together. We tried to set up situations where they were alone and had to depend on each other for company and activities. Also, we'd give them a joint Christmas gift which forced them to cooperate."

When, despite our best efforts, siblings refuse to cooperate, experienced parents offer this first-line defense: Stay neutral. If at all possible, don't try to ferret out who started what with whom when. You'll be assaulted with stereophonic discord and pulled into a verbal, bottomless quagmire.

ROCKY: Mom, tell him to quit looking at me.
BRUNO: I'm not. Why would I want to look at your puke face.
ROCKY: See! He's calling me names just because I wanted my truck back.
BRUNO: That's not your truck. Grandma gave it to both of us.
ROCKY: No, sir. She gave it to me on *my* birthday. Besides, you weren't even playing with it.
BRUNO: I was too. I just set it there to go to the bathroom.
BUTCH: *(entering the scene)* Has anybody seen my truck?

Smart parents don't even begin to search for the origin of such convoluted conflicts. They favor standing at a safe distance, ignoring minor battles and allowing the kids to restore order. At times, though, the fray gets too loud or rowdy to ignore. Assuming we still don't know where the root of fault lies, the suggested intervention is identical consequences for all parties.

At the unwitting insistence of her sons, Carlene from Illinois established this procedure for brotherly bickering. "Billy and Tommy both would accuse us of favoring the other. I told them I didn't realize that was happening; so, from now on if one accused the other of doing something wrong, both would get punished, just to make sure we weren't disciplining one more than the other. They called a truce within days. They still complain from time to time, but we just remind them of our remedy."

Equal but separate is a preferred policy for sibling quibbling—all contenders to separate corners, chairs, rooms, counties—for a set period of time. The consequences are alike for everyone, and no parceling of blame is attempted.

A number of parents, however, reverse this policy. Linda's tack with her eight-, twelve-, and fifteen-year-old is risky, but thus far has quieted things. "When they are fighting, I make them sit in the same room and get to know each other. They can sit there all day long until they make peace."

Mary, a mother of four, aged four through thirteen, adds to Linda's idea. "When one child hurts another's feelings, both are to go privately into a room and talk and set things right between them. If one wrongs another verbally or physically, he is to go to a quiet place alone for a set time, depending upon age and offense, and think of three to five things he really likes about that other person. Then he tells me and that person those three to five things. This changes the focus from hurt to love."

Putting children in sight of each other who are likely to tangle when they are in sight of each other is a calculated gamble. But like all discipline speculations, if it pays off, you're ahead. So are the kids.

An extreme example of forced contact comes from Kerwin and Marilyn, parents to Aaron (eight), Alan (fourteen), and William (seventeen). Kerwin recalled, "I came home one day and found two of the boys hugging each other on the sidewalk. They had been fighting, and Marilyn made them go outside and hug each other for ten minutes." Kerwin thought he had the wrong house. Marilyn's rationale? "Before they learn to hate each other, they will learn to love each other." Though born of Marilyn's frustration, like many serendipitous childrearing discoveries, this response proved powerfully effective. The boys avoided arguments for fear they'd have to make up.

From Kentucky, Mary Jo places no time limits on her children's (aged seven, ten, twelve) post-fight cool down. Instead, she leaves it to them. "When there is a conflict, I usually let them work it out. Sometimes I put them in chairs at the table and say they must sit until they give each other permission to get up." Mary Jo is shifty. Not only does she extricate herself from any timekeeping, she designs the situation to make the kids show mercy to their antagonist, or they'll all sit until bedtime. In case she needs her table, Mary Jo has a backup. "If arguments are not resolved in a reasonable time period, the children must give each other a hug. If they hesitate, it's a hug *and* a kiss." Aw, Mom, that's gross. I'd rather kiss dirt.

A few parents reason that a child spending the effort to squabble is asking for help in redirecting his excess energy. When Clay (ten) and Cole (seven) clash, Retha says, "I separate them and give them chores to do." Likewise, Betty shares, "When the kids physically fought they were told, 'With so much energy, you can both do dishes.' One, this made them work together, and two, I became their adviser in the dishes, which made us a team." Dual-benefit discipline is clever discipline. Not only do Betty and Retha's children learn the futility of conflicts, they learn the value of cooperation. Of course, given the amount that kids can bicker, some parents would never have to touch a household chore again.

Should you have an overwhelming urge to track down the truth in a sibling contest of wills, you might try Norman's judicious approach. "As Kimberly and Chip got a little older, I used to hold court. Sometimes I would put a dishrag on my head and say, 'I am the judge.' I would then call court to order. We had witnesses, and no one could talk while another person was talking. Usually I knew how things would end up. There would be fault found on both sides. I would pass judgment and give suggestions about what the kids could do if a similar situation came up. Court bothered them because it took time and because one would have to shut up while the other talked. I think they got to the point where they dreaded court more than the discipline."

When you know who provoked the trouble—in a kid's eyes this means you watched it start, recorded it on videotape, and have twelve independent eyewitnesses—you can use Bob's strategy. "If the two older boys (aged ten and thirteen) are arguing, I make them write fifteen things good about their brother. First of all, it really kills them to have to admit there are good things about their brother. Then, I go over the list and, if there are any spelling mistakes, they correct them and write that line again. I would like to think that the list makes them more aware of their brother's good qualities and helps them give each other a little more space."

Bob's wife, Nancy, employs a spin-off of this idea. "Sometimes, for example, the boys will tease Gabrielle [aged seven]. They then have to do five things for her, no matter what she asks, within reason of course. If they keep teasing, I build it up. Once, Christian worked it up to fifteen things."

Over a period of twenty-seven years, Sandy and Ron have used a range of methods with their nine children. Says Sandy, "Fighting between children is a way of life. We had to be inventive. Once we bought boxing gloves for two of our boys and let them go at it in our basement, with supervision. Another time, we bought one of those four-foot clowns with sand in the bottom and let them punch him instead of each other when they were upset." What is your most creative solution? "If they are fighting, we don't allow them to talk to each other for a specific time. This results in just the reverse.

They think I'm the ridiculous one, and you couldn't ask for better relations between them, at least for a while." Sandy has discovered a core characteristic of kids: If they think we don't want them to do what they don't want to do—that is, cooperate—they want to do it. Maybe we should not want them to paint the house together.

Answering haggling with humor was a technique proposed by Dennis, a father of four. "We have the child who feels aggrieved by a sibling propose the punishment for the perceived transgressor and the child called the transgressor proposes a punishment for the aggrieved child for instigating the matter. Each in turn suggests more horrible punishments until the whole matter is reduced to absurdity. It's complex, but it allows for humor by exaggeration." Can you tell that Dennis is a lawyer?

When siblings are quibbling over having to share something, such as food, some parents set up a divide-and-choose situation. For instance, one child divides the cookie and the other chooses his part first. It's straightforward and fair, but don't expect kids to accept it for those reasons. Robin, mother to Merritt and Amanda, the young pianists we met earlier, gives this example of a sibling's concept of fair:

- "Sometimes our best plans for discipline didn't quite work. For example, when Ryan was about six and a half and Amanda was five, they were in a horrible bickering stage when each one was just sure that the other was getting more, taking more, and was favored more. There was only one can of pop in the refrigerator, and they were arguing about who got there first to get it when I walked in. Having reached the end of my patience quota for the moment, I used what seemed to be a great solution. I told both of them that one could divide the pop into two glasses and the other could choose which glass. That stopped the bickering. They decided Ryan would be the pourer and Amanda the chooser, so I left the room. Many minutes later I returned only to find that Ryan was still hard at work pouring the precious drink—pouring a little in one glass, hunkering down to check at eye level and then pouring just a little more. This was serious business. After much deliberation, he finally put the can down, turned to Amanda, and defiantly announced that she could make her choice. That also took quite a while. A tough decision, as the levels were close as close could be. She made her selection and walked out of the room. Ryan, not knowing I was observing, picked up the can, poured the rest into his glass, and left."

Let's close with a story from Norman in Florida. Humorous and touching, it illustrates both the exasperation and quick solutions that dueling siblings can evoke from parents.

- "I recall an incident when my dad was driving a bus. We lived on the busiest street in town. My brother was just beating me to a pulp one day—I was about four and he was about six—and my dad was driving by our house and saw us out of the side of his eye. He stopped the bus with a jerk, jumped off, and ran over and grabbed my brother. He just appeared out of nowhere. He paddled him and said a few words to him and sat him back down. I was afraid I was going to be next. He got back on the bus and somebody said, 'Do you know those kids?' and he said, 'I never saw them before in my life.' He never cracked a smile, he just started driving again."

If the saying "You only hurt the ones you love" is true, then the mutual affection of some siblings knows no bounds. Few attachments are more durable than that between siblings. Few can take such self-inflicted assault and emerge stronger. Parents watch the relationship unfold—in awe, frustration, admiration. Sometimes we discipline, sometimes we do nothing, but always we should know that some sibling rivalry is to be expected, even welcomed. In this light, we need not abandon a basic desire—the desire for peace. That desire will be nurtured next, in RULES OF THE HOUSE.

Chapter 16

Rules of the House

*"With four boys, three of whom are now teenagers,
peace and quiet are rare in our house. Chaos is nothing
compared to pandemonium, but anarchy is unacceptable. Some rules are necessary for peace."*

Father, Lake Oswego, Oregon

smooth-running household is a fundamental pursuit of most parents. In some way, each chapter of this book speaks to that end. The stronger
a family, the better the day-to-day cooperation among members. Even the
strongest families don't rely totally on cohesiveness to create harmony, however. Whenever two or more people share one roof, conflicts of interest
inevitably will arise. In order to promote the common good and to ensure
domestic tranquillity, successful parents establish basic operating policies, or
rules of the house.

The better parents lean toward fewer rules with firmer enforcement. They
have found mutual respect and cooperation to rise greatly with only a handful
of well-chosen rules. This chapter is a gathering of those rules. Some are
shared by many families; others are followed by only a few. All are presented
for your consideration based upon your value system and parenting style.

RULES OF RESPECT

NO BACK TALK. If any rule can be considered universal among these families, it is this one. No parents condoned back talk, and most took an unbudging stand against it. *Back talk* here is not defined as respectful disagreement or questioning. Neither is it a whiney, complaining commentary—"When I'm a parent, I'm going to let my kids wear their socks as long as they want"; "I'm nothing but a slave around here"; "How'd you run the house before I was born?" Such comebacks are best described as grumble talk, which parents typically ignored or acknowledged with a silent stare. On the other hand, back talk is distinctly unpleasant. It is nasty, or abusive, or disrespectful in tone. It prompts a fast and firm reaction.

Pat from New Jersey, mother to five natural and dozens of foster children, states adamantly, "We did not tolerate back talk. When it occurred, we ceased dealing with any issue other than the rudeness. Later, we discussed the problem that provoked the back talk."

Carol, mother of two sons, said wryly, "Our children value their lives, and therefore we don't have too much of this problem."

The standard response to back talk is to cut it off abruptly, and if necessary remove the offender from the scene—to his room, a chair, a couch. Time-out not only is quick, it keeps smoldering emotions from bursting into flame. With parent and child beyond eye-range, and preferably ear-range, back talk loses momentum. Sometimes kids still grouse more faintly while turning their backs and walking away. Veteran parents will recognize this as the "mumble grumble."

Sandy, a mother of nine youngsters—some more openly opinionated than others—preferred brief time-out early on, but added length and weight to her discipline as the kids grew. "Back talk was never tolerated by my husband or me. We have always told the children in no uncertain terms that they were being out of line and disrespectful. When they were smaller, they were sent to their rooms immediately to sit and think about what they did. As teens, they are grounded for a specific time or have other privileges taken away."

Gary and Marge, parents of two teens in Fort Collins, Colorado, say, "Back talk, when it does sneak into the conversation, is pointed out as showing a lack of respect, and if not stopped at once, consequences such as not driving the car or going out for the evening are used. Usually, when the kids realize the potential consequences, the tone of the conversation changes." Older kids more closely regulate their self-control if the car keys, curfew, or telephone are linked to it.

Dale and Bev give Christopher (fourteen) and James (eleven) a warning, "Excuse me, do I talk to you like that?" Most of the time this is enough to shift the direction of the interchange; if not, action follows.

Debra from Oregon uses dual-benefit discipline. Back talk automatically earns a child an unpleasant task or chore. The conflict settles and the garage gets swept.

It's not uncommon for parents to be unsure occasionally about where respect ends and disrespect begins. Jerry, a father of four boys from Oregon, admits, "There is a difference between disrespectful back talk and respectful discussion, usually apparent in the tone of voice and attitude. Sometimes it's a thin line, and I don't always guess right." Jerry is the father quoted at the beginning of this chapter. Raising four boys, three of whom are now teenagers, no wonder he doesn't always guess right!

Solid families are founded upon mutual respect. Back talk can breed mutual disrespect. It's not easy for parents to keep cool in response to a testy child. Therefore, strong parents urge: Stop back talk the instant it occurs and clamp consequences on it. Back talk is like any habit. The best way to overcome it is never to let it take root.

NO NAME-CALLING. Back talk most often is aimed at parents. Name-calling most often is targeted toward siblings. The rationale underlying this common rule is: Act with respect toward others, even when it's forced. With time, respect will feel natural. Consequences for name-calling include a verbal or written apology to the ill-named party, being her servant for an hour or day, writing five nice things about her, staying away from her, giving her the toy that provoked the fight that provoked the name. Bob and Joan let their three children substitute more benign labels—like turkey lips, moldy, bean-head—for nasty names. They feel these allowed the kids to blow off steam without exploding.

NO FOUL LANGUAGE. This rule is related to the last one. When first experimenting with language almost every child will gather a few colorful words from the environment. Most parents felt it was wise initially to draw no attention to such language. Young children are attracted to certain words for their shock effect on others, particularly parents. Show no reaction and the words lose appeal. "I acted as if I didn't hear my daughter when she first used some nasty words. To my surprise, they just disappeared," said one mother.

Other parents quickly gave the children substitutes, for example, "What in the world," "Rats," "Doggone." Essentially any word or phrase can serve as a good replacement, especially if the kids think it's as titillating as the original.

Out of desperation, Naomi from Vermont stumbled upon a tactic that purified her four-year-old daughter's language. "On the way home from town, a drive that probably takes about twenty minutes, my daughter started saying a particularly coarse word. Like a machine gun, she rattled off the word for twenty straight minutes. I don't think she really understood what she was saying. She seemed to be experimenting. I tried not to overreact, and by time we got close to home, I said, 'Sarat, you don't want to waste all those words because you might need them someday and then won't have them.' That appeared to make sense to her, and I never heard the word again. You just never know what's going to work."

Possible consequences for older children are copying and defining vocabulary words, listing ten benefits of clean language, or writing an essay on the worth of proper English. One father used a technique psychologists call overcorrection, making his son write the offensive word five hundred times. By word four hundred or so, not only was his son's hand worn out, but the spicy word had lost some of its flavor. Anything repeated five hundred times in less than an hour is bound to lose luster. With similar intent, Mary Jo allows coarse words to be aired only behind a locked bathroom door and only softly enough to be heard inside the bathroom. She's found this ruins the fun of fiery language. Every so often the kids head for the bathroom to use "potty words," but the times between are getting longer and the times within shorter.

PLEASE AND THANK YOU REQUIRED. Of all rules, this is among the easiest to live by, especially when begun young. Any request—be it for a cookie, a bedtime extension, a designer box lunch—must be prefaced with a "please" in order to be considered. Likewise, any favor received must be accompanied by a "thank you." In short, you need a please to get it and a thank you to keep it. As Norman from Florida observed a few chapters ago, teaching manners is so elementary, yet it produces incredible dividends for a child's self-respect and for others' respect of her.

WAIT TO TALK. To open up communication, but to keep a lid on verbal chaos, several families invoked a no-interrupting policy. When someone is speaking, everyone else must let her finish before talking, even if she's not telling the "real truth." Should a youngster force his words over another's, a "stop" gesture with one hand or a sport's time-out signal can remind him to be polite. A child's impulses run naturally counter to this rule, but as he too benefits from free speech, he should learn to curb his instincts.

NO PUT-DOWNS. In other words, no one is permitted to make fun of another person's looks, dress, behavior, disabilities—in short, everything that is him. Betty from Missouri abruptly shut off any such talk from Rick and Judy while they were growing up. She adhered to the guiding philosophy behind most rules of respect: Don't vent every negative urge, and you will eventually feel fewer negative urges.

An offshoot of the no-put-down rule is one from Stan in Omaha. "No one can say, 'This is boring.' " Kids get bored quickly. They begin life with an attention span measured in seconds and only with years do they lengthen it to minutes or an hour. Consequently, parents become bored with hearing about kids' boredom. Stan does something about it. His kids still got bored, but he and their mother don't have to share the experience anymore. What are consequences for "This is boring"? For younger children, temporarily having to sit and watch the boring activity from a distance should be even more tiresome than the activity itself. It sometimes makes them grateful to return and participate. Older children could write, "This is boring" one hundred times for each time they've complained. Now that's boring.

Sandy, a mother of three girls in Washington, decreed that no one can retort with "So?" or "So what?" when another expresses herself on anything. Certainly she can disagree, but she can't minimize anyone's feelings or opinions. "So?" too easily provokes words meant to up the ante until the indifferent party is sufficiently incensed to cease "so"-ing.

RULES FOR RESPECTING THE HOUSE

A house has no feelings or ego, nonetheless it can be hurt or bruised. If a child carelessly damages or destroys something in the house, he is responsible for paying for it, working off the debt, or making payments for items too costly to cover in one sum. This is "basic civilization," as one mother called it, and it is a basic expectation in these homes.

Certainly, very young children can't legitimately work off a debt. Still they can learn a lesson about reparation. One parent told of her response to her preschooler after he carelessly broke a lamp. To allow him to "pay" for the lamp, mom created "make-work." For instance, she gave him a bag and told him to fill it by picking up leaves from the yard. Later, she handed him a broom and had him sweep the sidewalk several times, telling him he'd earn a dollar for his effort, which she would use toward a new lamp. A few make-work sessions won't buy much of a lamp, but they will buy a solid lesson about responsibility.

Additional rules for house respect are:

ENTER WITH CLEAN SHOES. A minor courtesy, it prolongs carpet life and spares undue cleaning. Sharon and Doug from Wyoming say: Any room touched by mud or dirt must be completely vacuumed, even the clean parts.

NO DOOR SLAMMING. Susan, mother to Emily (eleven) and Sarah (thirteen), instituted her soft-shut policy when the girls were very young after fingers were bruised by a slammed door. Susan believes that a youngster can express her anger in less loud and potentially hurtful ways. Response to a flung door? How about the time-proven, open-and-close-it-quietly method one hundred times?

NO GYMNASTICS, HIDE-AND-SEEK, OR BALL-PLAYING IN THE HOUSE. Barbara and Steven from New York see too much risk of hurt bodies and broken furniture with this type of roughhousing. Julie from Omaha concurs and implements a broader policy: No running when there is a roof over your head. Predominantly for her children's safety, this rule also keeps vases and other breakables in one piece for a longer time.

NO FOOD OR DRINK IN BEDROOMS. Martha from Connecticut says, "If I find the kids disregarding this, I don't buy their favorite things for a period of time." Eating boundaries are customary in households with younger children. Chrissy narrows her three kids' eating rooms to one. "No eating outside the kitchen." It is the nature of kids to spill; what's more, it is a law of nature that within seconds most spills are stepped on and ground inseparably into the carpet. Knowing this three times over, Chrissy makes eating more palatable for all by confining messes to the kitchen. She doesn't nervously nag, "Be careful." The kids aren't nervous about being careful. And the carpets keep their original color and texture.

RULES OF SUPERVISION

A developmental clash between parents and children centers on supervision. Virtually every step of the way, from toddlerhood to teenhood, kids want more freedom than parents are willing to give them. Toddlers rush to sneak outdoors unattended almost every time they spot an open door. Nine-year-olds play outside until the last twinkle of twilight is left, righteously proclaiming upon entering the house, "It's not totally dark yet." Adolescents bend and mutilate curfew rules to fit sudden "unexpected" circumstances and changes in plans. Good parents allow children enough rope to feel some independence but not so much that they tangle themselves into hazardous situations.

No parent can know where his children are every minute, and the minutes stretch into hours as the years mount. Responsible parents, however, are not comfortable with ignorance. Realizing the limits of their supervision, still they strive to keep pace with their youngster's movements. A range of rules helps them.

STAY IN THE BACKYARD. Used mostly with preschoolers, this rule is meant to put clear-cut, safe, geographical boundaries on a youngster's freedom to roam. It distinctly lays out a parent's expectations, leaving no room for error. Abusing this rule results in an automatic "one day inside." If a day inside would be more restrictive for parent than child, an option is: No leaving the patio, or porch, or some portion of the yard. Essentially, if outdoor geographic boundaries are ignored, they are narrowed for a time.

PLAY WITHIN SIGHT OF A WINDOW. Any well-placed window can serve as the observation point from which children can be monitored periodically. The window rule allows for freer movement in an outward direction from the home, but puts limits on a child's side-to-side meanderings. Changing the observation window can also result in wider play boundaries as a youngster matures.

PLAY WITHIN YELLING DISTANCE FROM THE HOUSE. Craig and Julie require Kara (ten) and Andy (six) to play by this rule. They are to remain within a parent's voice range at all times, for two reasons. One, with a word they can be called home—for lunch, for chores, for emergencies. Two, if they are doing something wrong, mom or dad can usually grab their attention.

As children get older, not only don't they stay within earshot of parents, sometimes they don't even want to be in the same area code. More complex rules of supervision apply to them.

ANSWER THREE QUESTIONS BEFORE LEAVING THE HOUSE: WHO? WHERE? WHEN? Anytime a youngster has plans away from home, he must give his parents the particulars of those plans. Said Barbara, a mother of four, "No one disappears from the house without leaving a note or telling someone where they're going and when they will be back." Sandy was more hard-line. "We always want to know where you're going, with whom, and when you'll be back. Not knowing can result in someone coming and looking for you and grounding for several weeks." Kurt and Joann, parents of three in South Carolina, say, "If plans change, call."

WAKE US UP WHEN YOU GET HOME. You'd recognize the parents who lay down this policy. They're the ones with the bloodshot eyes. A wake-up call lets parents return to sleep more soundly and establishes exactly when a youngster comes home. Without a check-in, the assumption is that Knight bent curfew. And that's faced in the morning, when the folks are alert.

ALL SLEEPOVERS MUST BE DISCUSSED. A child is not allowed to ask another child to sleep over, nor can she agree to sleep at her house, without first asking parents. This is the core sleepover rule. There are several corollaries: We must know the parents of the child, whether he sleeps here or you sleep there; We need the child's address and phone number and a written note from her parents; Permission may not be sought in front of that child. Doing so results in an automatic no. Kids are crafty. By putting us on the spot, they hope to provoke permission by pressure.

Carol and Bill from Montana want all the details, whether sleeping overnight is involved or not. "If the boys are invited to a private party, we call to discuss the rules and supervision with the host family. The boys don't like this rule, but the fact is that they can't go unless we call." Larry and Nancy, parents to Susan (fifteen), David (thirteen), and Julie (twelve), enforce a broad social guideline. "No friends at the house if a parent isn't home. No going to a friend's house if at least one parent isn't there."

COME STRAIGHT HOME AFTER SCHOOL UNLESS PREARRANGED. Any after-school plans or diversions must be cleared at least one day in advance. Parents want time to consider requests. Kids prefer we don't have it. They believe the less we can ponder their plans, the more likely we are to allow them.

NO DATING UNTIL AGE SIXTEEN. As a group, good parents are conservative compared to their peers regarding dating. Sixteen is a common minimum dating age. These parents receive some intense pressure to relax this rule, directly from their children and indirectly from parents who allow dating at younger ages. A cardinal rule of rules: The less others live by it, the harder it is to live by. Even when her three children reach sixteen, Susan from Wisconsin is adamant: "There will be no dates on motorcycles." As another mother said, "I'd rather have my children alive and angry at me than pleased with me but hurt somewhere."

RULES FOR TECHNOLOGY

Technology provides convenience, safer living, instant communication—in essence, an easier life-style—but it doesn't make parenting easier. Technology means more to monitor and screen. It means information that often runs counter to a parent's goals. Television can dump a completely foreign set of values into a family's living room. Telephones can put a child in contact with nearly anyone, good influence or bad. Radio can air programs and music that assault good taste and decency. Technology is integral to a society's development. To be a successful parent we needn't return to simpler times, but we do need to moderate the influence of technology on our children's morals.

In the average American household, the television is talking over six hours a day. Although our interviews didn't specifically explore the TV habits of strong homes, a good picture did come into focus. On the whole, these families fall far below the national viewing norm. One reason is their preference for activity, as individuals and families. Another is the limitations that most of these parents place on television. For instance, some homes refuse to subscribe to cable movie service, because it can steal time from the family and because of some of its content. David from Kentucky says, "We had cable television, and we took it out. It wasn't good for the kids (aged twelve, ten, seven), and we also saved money. We shared some of the savings with them."

Jerry and Susan, parents of four adolescent sons from Oregon, represent the strict end of the spectrum. "No school-night television." They add a rider to this policy. "No more than thirty minutes per day on computer games." Technology increases the ways to have fun; it also increases the need to parcel time responsibly.

Typically, parents don't exclude television from weekday routine, but limit it. Chico and Crissy tell Shawn (fourteen), Tara (twelve), and Brittany (five), "No television or radio after dinner."

Jan and Scott from Idaho, whose children are now twenty-one and nineteen, permitted television one hour per day. A family from Ohio watched television only as a family. Overall, these families view television as beneficial when controlled and not allowed to stifle or crowd out other interests.

Limited television is also easier to screen. Conscientious parents are vigilant to prevent graphic violence, crude language, or obscenity from accosting their children via the airwaves. The attitude is that we *all* don't watch things offensive to our value system. A Christian family assesses all material with the question, "Is this consistent with the beliefs we profess?"

A large family from Georgia worked out an arrangement for more peaceful TV time. "No seat-saving. If you leave your seat, you lose it." This terminated haggling over who left the room for what reason and for how long. Mother did comment that the scene of the hassles then moved toward the bathroom between shows.

Along with television, the telephone is a child's vital link to the world, at least that's how he sees it. Consequently, he and his folks are often at odds over how much link is vital. Here are some phone rules to eliminate repeated bad connections between you and your youngsters:

- Calls are limited to fifteen minutes.
- No accepting calls once in bed.
- No phone calls after 10:00 P.M.
- The phone is off the hook during meals.
- No phone calls during homework time.

From Omaha, Stan and Sharon take an uncommon approach to phone control with Julie (nineteen) and Hans (fifteen). "We have always had only one phone. It's in the kitchen. This promotes courtesy, because no one can monopolize the phone. It promotes honesty and openness—there's no hiding in one's bedroom telling secrets on the phone. As parents we've always had an ear on what's going on because we can hear the phone conversations."

RULES OF POSSESSION

NO ONE BORROWS ANYTHING WITHOUT ASKING FIRST. Bob and Joan from Michigan hold that if a borrower ignores this courtesy, the "borrowee" can borrow back whatever she wants, no questions asked. They uphold a companion rule. "Except in very unusual circumstances, if someone asks nicely to borrow something, you will loan it." Their rationale? "You too may want to borrow something someday." Parents from North Dakota take a nonnegotiable position on possession swapping. "If borrowed, it needs to be returned in the same condition, replaced, or paid for. Otherwise, it is considered stolen."

TOYS MUST BE PUT AWAY. Once play is over, toys are to be returned to their resting place. Julie and Ross swept up toy litter quickly and quietly. "We have a gunny bag. It can swallow toys anytime. If something is not put away, it goes into the gunny bag. The kids then have to buy it back at ten cents an item. Two times in the gunny bag, and it goes to the Salvation Army." Darwin and Debra, parents of six (aged two to twelve), use a similar collection policy. Any toy gathered up by mom or dad goes into a bag. To pull it out costs one chore. With six kids and their toys, the question is, Can Darwin and Debra think up enough chores?

IF YOU WORE IT, HANG IT UP. If it's found lying around, you help with the laundry this week.

CLOTHES ARE LAID OUT AT NIGHT FOR SCHOOL THE NEXT MORNING. Lucille found that this drastically curtailed morning wardrobe wars. Anything selected the previous evening was dress for the following day—discussion closed.

IF YOU BUY CANDY OR TREATS, NO EATING IN FRONT OF YOUR SIBLINGS. You can, but you must share. Olene and Oscar, who made all seven of their children eat by this standard, routinely discovered candy wrappers under beds where a child sequestered himself to eat in solitude.

ALLOW YOUR BROTHER AND SISTER TO JOIN IN A GAME, OR PUT THE GAME AWAY. Nancy from Cleveland felt this kept the kids from excluding a sibling or forming unfair alliances. Once past the initial begrudging "Okay, you can play," cooperation usually followed.

THE PERSON PRACTICING A MOVABLE MUSICAL INSTRUMENT MUST MOVE ELSEWHERE IF SOMEBODY IS PRACTICING A NONMOVABLE INSTRUMENT. In other words, practice your drums downstairs if your sister is practicing her piano in the living room. To which Buddy is likely to counter, "A piano is movable." Of course, if you have drums and a piano in the same house, maybe you'd better move to the garage.

ALL ROOMS MUST BE IN GOOD CONDITION BEFORE BEDTIME. Thirteen-year-old Sarah and eleven-year-old Emily from West Virginia are on the receiving end of this one. If it's nearly bedtime and the rooms aren't nearly straightened, they start cleaning them earlier tomorrow night. Kim and Chip from Florida pick up their rooms while their mother sits and supervises.

THE VALUE OF RULES

The presence of rules is not a sign of disorder. It is a sign of a parent's foresight and a family's consistency. Rules define expectations. They enhance cooperation in a household by minimizing recurrent haggling over the same trouble spots.

Strong families derive some of their stability from house rules. The content of the rules changes as the family evolves, but their purpose remains constant: to promote mutual respect, responsibility, and a more pleasant environment for everyone. Even as children mature toward independence, house rules offer a sense of continuity. "When our children left for college, I made one condition," said Betty, mother to Rick and Judy from St. Louis. "I would respect the fact that they were adults and no longer had to live by every guideline I set up. However, when they came home, home would not be changed. It would remain as it was when they left. There were certain rules regarding language and conduct that they had to accept. So far, our home is the same, and in a way I think our children have been glad."

Rules benefit the whole family, and as such many parents allow the kids input into their formulation. In the end, though, it is the parents who decide how to run the house and raise the kids. Susan from West Virginia reflects the sentiment of most parents in telling her daughters, "Parents have the final word on rules. If you don't like it, you can change the rules when you're a parent someday—and that better not happen too soon!"

Many of these house rules are generic. Solid families live by some version of them as their children move from preschool to adolescence to young adulthood. Some rules may appeal to you, others not. Every observation or bit of advice in this chapter—indeed, in this book—is for you to ponder, practice, or pass by as you judge its value to you and your family. To complete our look at successful family life, let's review the basics in PULLING IT TOGETHER.

Chapter 17

Pulling It Together

"A successful family is a ninety/ten proposition. Parent and child each give ninety percent. I can't expect my children to do as much for me as I do for them, but they do, and a great deal more."

Father, Columbus, Ohio

One hundred excellent families have spoken in this book. They've opened their homes and their hearts to tell us what makes family life succeed. They've shared their victories and failures, their hopes and hurts. Some of what they've said may have been surprising, since it runs counter to prevailing childrearing theories. Some may have confirmed what you already believed. All is intended, in one way or another, to help you be an exceptional parent.

The diversity of families selected for this project demonstrates that a strong home life does not depend upon a parent's education, creed, occupation, or social status. Neither is it limited to biological parents, two-parent homes, or a low-stress existence. Excellence is not the product of external causes. It is born internally. It evolves from commitment, from the determination to build upon your family's strengths, regardless of what factors may be pulling against you.

Successful parents are not all products of successful childhoods. While many knew upbringings filled with positive examples from which to anchor their own parenting, others have lived through childhoods best described as cold, abusive, even traumatic. Their parenting role models were reverse images of what they have become as mothers and fathers. Parents who have risen far above their childhoods are living proof that, contrary to some experts' opinions, the quality of your past does not put a ceiling on the quality of your present, as a parent or as a person.

Excellent parents are models to observe and learn from. They are not perfect or even close. They wrestle with the worries, insecurities, and guilts all parents feel. They don't have all the answers, endless patience, or perfect children. Their lives reveal that skillful parenting is not inborn. It is developed over time, along with a healthy acceptance of one's imperfections. Better parenting results from recognizing our limits and working to overcome them or live with them.

Good parents love to parent. They've experienced the challenges and fears inherent to childrearing and remain grateful for the opportunity to be parents. "Childbearing is not an expensive burden, but a privilege," believes Mary, mother of four from Iowa. Life-styles and priorities can change radically with the decision to raise children. Responsible parents accept this reality, even welcome it. "Our children must be one of our most important accomplishments in life," asserts Sharon from Wyoming.

Common sense and good judgment form the foundation for sound parenting decisions. Having discovered that no one right way exists for handling any situation, effective parents strive for self-confidence. It leads to more decisive parenting and more secure children. Childrearing is a never-ending process. It is drawing upon the knowledge and experience of others—children, parents, and experts. The willingness to learn from others is indispensable to better parenting, but ultimately you must judge for yourself what will work for your family, based upon your value system and unique circumstances.

A parent's personality has far more influence on her childrearing than being aware of all the latest childrearing trends. "Preparation for raising a child begins before his conception in the way you live—your thoughts, attitudes, even eating habits," says John from Maryland, father of four children. Work to become a better person and your parenting will automatically improve.

Wise parents are open to guidance from the youngest child psychologists— children. Children are natural teachers of childrearing. They know us well— in many ways, better than anyone else does. Since they are with us every day, they are ready and able to give us feedback on our technique. Living mirrors, they reflect back at us who we are, what we act like, what we sound like. Lessons most basic to successful parenting are taught by children:

- Show your love.
- Teach through example.
- Listen before you talk.
- Look through a child's eyes.

Brian, a teenager in Minnesota, maintains, "You don't have to go very far in life to learn about yourself. Your family will teach you."

A relaxed parent is a better parent. Veteran parents have discovered that a more easygoing attitude comes with experience. Their advice for more enjoyable parenthood includes:

- Don't try to be a perfect parent. Undeserved anxiety and guilt will follow.
- Don't fear mistakes. They are necessary for maturation. Good parents become better through mistakes.
- Parent in the present. Second-guessing yourself or dwelling on the uncertain future will erode your confidence and ability to give your best to your children today.
- Expect that your children will misunderstand and dislike you at times. That is a reality of responsible parenthood.
- Laugh whenever and however you can during childrearing. Humor helps maintain perspective and eases anxiety. "Childrearing is too short not to laugh during it," says Cloraida from New Mexico.

Much of parenting is on-the-job training, learning through experimentation and misjudgments. Lucille, speaking philosophically to her eleven children, says, "You know, kids, we could be better parents if we had a second time around." Accept your humanness, and you will be a better parent the first time around.

Spiritual beliefs are a dominant presence in cohesive families. Faith in a Creator and in living by His guidelines provide values which nurture each member's personal growth and thereby the family's. Spirituality fosters parenting through example, the most durable parenting. It is a source of comfort and strength, enabling parents to call upon a supreme authority for wisdom and direction. "Children are on loan to us from God to raise as best we can for him," believes Mary Jo from Kentucky. Most successful parents agree.

There are no shortcuts to an excellent family life. A parent must invest time. "It's not possible to underestimate the sense of dedication needed for parenting," observes Norman, father to two in Florida. Excellent parents assert that dedication means a willingness to give quantity time, which is necessary for quality time. Norman continues, "We need to invest enough time to let things happen spontaneously."

Time provides the framework for all elements of family success—communication, discipline, values. Making family a priority fosters a child's self-esteem and sense of belonging. Nothing is more precious to a child than the presence of a parent. "Children are in our homes such a short while. It is worth it to sacrifice to be there for them," says Sue from Wisconsin. On the value of time to a family's well-being, Don from Connecticut concludes, "The single most important thing I'd write in a parenting book—chapter one, page one, first paragraph, first sentence—is that you get back what you put in."

Competent parents concentrate on mastering the basics of communication. A few good-sense principles guide them:

- Talk less at children, and listen more to them. Attentive silence is the simplest way to evoke a child's feelings.
- As important as how you communicate is when you communicate. Become sensitive to a child's prime times to talk. Arrange them or be present when they occur. They are windows to his thoughts.
- Affection is continuous communication. It is love without words. Strong families know the binding power of affection.
- Whenever possible, allow children a voice in family decisions. While in most cases, parents retain the final say, merely being consulted makes a child feel an integral part of the family.

"Children are well equipped. Expect their most, their best, and nothing less," says Annetta from North Dakota. Responsible parents expect much of their children and of themselves. Their attitude is, "Success is not measured against others but against yourself. Striving for your personal best is success." Excellent parents counsel:

- Insist on your children's full effort in academics. It is their future.
- The family home is everyone's home, so make it everyone's responsibility, down to the youngest members.
- Judge a child's capabilities—social, emotional, personal—and expect him to live up to them. Don't allow him to live down to the norm.

John has always told his four children, "The only failure you will ever have is to not try to succeed."

Strong parents believe in strong discipline begun young. They are willing to exert whatever effort is necessary to discipline their children today so life won't discipline them tomorrow. The firmest parent, if loving, is a more gentle teacher than the world. For a child's sake, parents need the will to discipline.

"When your children are acting their worst, that is when they need your love the most," asserts Connie from Delaware. The best discipline is motivated by unconditional love, love that is unaffected by a child's misbehavior. Good disciplinarians focus most on what kids do right not wrong. They emphasize the positive. Not only does this make for less discipline, it enhances a child's self-image. Rita from New Hampshire observes, "When you tell your children the good you see in them, they are a little less afraid to test it on others."

"Be a parent first, friendship will follow," advises Joann from South Carolina. By their nature, children test limits and want more than is healthy for them. Loving parents are not afraid to say no. They draw clear boundaries within which a child is free to operate.

The mechanics of effective discipline are summarized by the three C's: calm, consistency, and consequences. Calm discipline works more quickly and leads to less regrettable behavior from everyone. Consistency is predictability. It enables a child to understand and accept the results of his actions. Consequences are indispensable for teaching personal responsibility. Consequences, not words, are the basic tools of discipline.

Spanking is a discipline option in the healthiest homes. It is used most often with preschoolers and in response to physical danger and willful disobedience. In the context of love, spanking neither breeds aggressive children nor causes psychological damage. Some very good parents choose not to spank; they are not comfortable with it. In any family, spanking must be judged as all discipline is judged: How well is this working, for us and our children?

In the happiest of families, siblings will compete, bicker, and sometimes battle. This is a fact of family life. It is not a sign of disorder or rifts in the family's cohesiveness. The sibling bond is pliable, bending as each child matures. Competent parents allow siblings to test the strength of that bond, but not to assault it recklessly. At times, parents have to intervene to teach respect and cooperation. In solid families, the sibling bond becomes more durable with time.

Excellent families rely on simple, clear-cut house rules enforced by consequences. Established according to a family's needs and goals, rules make for a more content household.

Refined to its most basic elements, successful parenting is unconditional love, commitment, teaching by example, and the will to discipline. Family excellence is a high-sounding phrase. The prime lesson of this book is that it is a reassuringly attainable reality. Build upon the essentials, and no level of family success is beyond your reach.

Epilogue: Your Turn

*I*f special means exclusive, we're not. Everyone has something special to offer as a family." These words typify the reaction of these families upon first learning of their being selected for this project. While flattered, most were simultaneously surprised. The prevailing attitude was one of, "Why us? Many families are like ours."

Though these families are special, they are not exclusive, as they are the first to point out. Strong families are everywhere, quietly raising tomorrow's excellence. It is to you we now turn. You have heard how one hundred exceptional families love, communicate, discipline—in short, live. We would like to hear how your family does the same.

The following questions are similar to those asked of the parents in this book. We're interested in your answers—to all, one, several—at whatever length you'd like. We believe that an inexhaustible wealth of parenting wisdom lies untapped in the millions of responsible mothers and fathers who make childrearing a life's priority. Our hope is to be able to gather together more of the best from good parents throughout the country. So select a question or two or three. Give us your wisdom, your story, your memories, that we might continue to paint a positive portrait of the American family.

- What do you see as your most enduring contribution to your child(ren) or family?
- When and how have your children taught you to be a better parent?
- What is the best discipline approach you've ever tried or heard about?
- What do you believe are the most important principles for good communication? What are your family's do's and don't's?
- What is your most recurrent discipline problem? How have you responded to this challenge?
- How do you motivate your child(ren)—spiritually, academically, athletically, socially, and artistically?
- What are your most rewarding ways to spend time with your child? With your family?
- What do you consider your main parenting shortcomings? How have you worked to overcome these?
- What is the single best piece of advice you could offer today's parents?
- If you were to write a parenting book, what would you include as your main points?

On a final note, if your child(ren) would like their turn at any of these questions, we most certainly welcome their perspective. And if they let you read their answers, you might have to rethink a few of your own. We look forward to meeting your family.

Please mail your replies to:

David Paul Eich

c/o In The Company of **kids**(sm)

Children's Hospital
281 Locust Street
Akron, OH 44308

Please include your name, address, and phone number for possible further contact.

ABOUT THE AUTHOR

DR. RAY GUARENDI is a clinical psychologist who specializes in parenting and family issues. He has consulted for numerous school districts, head-start programs, mental-health centers, and juvenile courts. Nationally known as a speaker and syndicated parenting columnist, he is also the author of *You're a Better Parent Than You Think!* (Prentice-Hall/Simon and Schuster, 1985).

ABOUT IN THE COMPANY OF KIDS (SM)

This book is a result of a project originated by the Akron Children's Hospital. In the Company of Kids (SM) was formed as an effort to meet the needs and concerns of the American family through advocacy partnerships with health, business, education, and community leadership. The primary vision for these partnerships is to provide greater parental education and empowerment in the nurturing of children and their futures, with books like *Back to the Family* and seminars on parenting and advocacy issues and initiatives. The company and its partners will endeavor to make a difference in America's future by guaranteeing the future of America's children.